Twisted Triangle

Twisted Triangle

A Famous Crime Writer,
a Lesbian Love Affair,
and the FBI Husband's Violent Revenge

Caitlin Rother

with John Hess

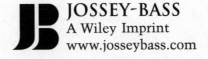

JOSSEY-BASS
A Wiley Imprint
www.josseybass.com

Published by Jossey-Bass
A Wiley Imprint
989 Market Street, San Francisco, CA 94103-1741—www.josseybass.com

Jossey-Bass books and products are available through most bookstores. To contact Jossey-Bass directly call our Customer Care Department within the U.S. at 800-956-7739, outside the U.S. at 317-572-3986 or fax 317-572-4002.

Jossey-Bass also publishes its books in a variety of electronic formats. Some content that appears in print may not be available in electronic books.

Library of Congress Cataloging-in-Publication Data

Rother, Caitlin.
    Twisted triangle : a famous crime writer, a lesbian love affair, and the FBI husband's violent revenge / Caitlin Rother with John Hess.—1st ed.
        p. cm.
    Includes index.
    ISBN-13: 978-0-7879-9585-0 (cloth)
    ISBN-13: 978-0-470-44251-7 (paperback)
    1. Women—Crimes against—Virginia—Case studies. 2. Bennett, Marguerite, date. 3. Attempted murder—Virginia—Case studies. 4. Bennett, Eugene Allen. 5. Criminals—Virginia—Case studies. I. Hess, John E., date. II. Title.
    HV6250.W65R68 2008
    364.152'3092—dc22

                                                                                2007044998

Printed in the United States of America
FIRST EDITION
PB Printing   10 9 8 7 6 5 4 3 2 1

Contents

*To Margo,
for her spirit,
courage, and strength*

Preface

The story of Margo and Gene Bennett has fascinated me ever since I read about it in *Vanity Fair* and the *Washington Post* in the late 1990s. I was working on my first crime novel at the time and was an avid reader of Patricia Cornwell's forensic thrillers. Also, as a newspaper reporter who covered sometimes dry government and politics, I enjoyed reading in-depth true crime stories.

This one had so many sexy components: two married FBI agents involved in a love triangle with a best-selling crime novelist who wrote about FBI agents and the serial killers they profiled. And then to find out that Cornwell's affair was with the female agent—now *that* was intriguing.

As a budding novelist myself, I appreciated the ironic parallels between Cornwell's fictional and personal lives: her female protagonist, Dr. Kay Scarpetta, was having an affair with a married FBI agent, and Scarpetta's niece was a lesbian. I still wonder whether Cornwell's real-life affair preceded the fictional one.

Fast-forward to 2005. *Poisoned Love*, my first book, about the Kristin Rossum murder case, had just been published. Soon afterward, my agent called and asked if I'd be interested in writing a book about the Bennett case; Margo had never told her story to a reporter before. Of course I jumped at the chance.

Like Cornwell, I was seeing my own worlds intersecting. While I was covering the Rossum case for *The San Diego Union-Tribune*, Rossum, a forensic toxicologist, testified that she, too, was a fan of Cornwell's, a fact I included in my first book.

The universe truly does work in strange and wonderful ways. As Margo would say, there was a reason I held on to that yellowed *Washington Post* article all those years. This was meant to be.

Now I'd like to explain my research methodology and how I put this book together.

At the start of this project, Margo shipped me four boxes of documents, including her FBI personnel paperwork, her divorce records, and personal papers about her family's health, finances, and property transactions. She also sent me piles of official documents from Gene's two court cases, the letters he'd written to his daughters over the years, and her sizable collection of news stories.

Over the next two years, Margo continued to send me extremely sensitive information, such as her and her daughters' psychological evaluations and the diary she'd kept during her first pregnancy. She also made sure I had access to her Cornwell novels, which included personal inscriptions, and to many of the people I interviewed who might not have talked to me otherwise. To my knowledge, Margo held nothing back because she wanted the story to be told properly.

Before I came along, former FBI agent and Quantico instructor John Hess spent a few years putting together his version of this story, interviewing his close friend Margo for many hours along the way. When he couldn't get his manuscript published, his agent approached my agent, and I took it from there.

What this meant for Margo was that she had to go over the entire story again with a stranger and in even more excruciating detail. Initially, she told me that talking about it gave her nightmares. I often heard the strain in her voice during our marathon series of phone and face-to-face interviews. Sometimes I felt awkward having to ask so many personal questions, but I pressed on. Eventually I stopped being a stranger, and Margo opened up to me more and more. It was personally fulfilling when I heard her tell a friend of mine that she felt as if I were inside her head and often could articulate what she was thinking and feeling.

Much of the dialogue in this book was reconstructed or approximated based on Margo's surprisingly good memory, as are many of the events that I describe. Testimony in the courtroom scenes was edited down for story-telling purposes, however, no scene or piece of dialogue was invented or embellished in any way. I was amazed at how many times the people I interviewed said that Margo had a better memory of a particular conversation or event than they did, and that they trusted her recollections. That said, no one's memory is perfect, so I cross-checked Margo's recollections whenever possible with those of other people involved in those conversations or events and also with official sources, including published news reports, court transcripts, depositions, FBI-generated interview reports, memos, and letters.

Sometimes cross-checking was not possible, as in the case of the conversations or events involving Cornwell, who refused independent requests by me, Margo, and John to be interviewed for this book. Nonetheless, Margo and I agreed that we should portray her interactions with Cornwell as sensitively and respectfully as possible.

Gene, too, refused to do an interview with John and later declined my repeated offers as well. Nor would he allow his attorney, Reid Weingarten, to speak on his behalf. I tracked down Gene's sister, Linda, who didn't want to cooperate either. Gene had written many of his family members (including his daughters), some of his former colleagues, and his psychiatrist, asking them not to talk to me. Thankfully, some of the key players ignored his request.

As I interviewed them, I uncovered things that even Margo was hearing for the first time, and vice versa, apparently sparking some interesting and healing conversations among her family members and close friends.

Although this story is largely told from Margo's point of view, I felt it was important to show Gene's unique perspective on all of this, drawing from memos and letters he'd drafted, official reports detailing interviews with him, and his written and verbal statements during the divorce.

With twenty years of experience as an investigative reporter who has covered local, state, and federal government and politics, I also made sure to ask Margo tough questions so that I could tell this story as fairly and accurately as possible. To that end, I went over each chapter with her to catch any factual errors.

Despite Margo's understandably negative feelings about Gene, she answered my questions as truthfully as I think she could manage, so that he would be a three-dimensional character, just as she is. During Gene's trial in 1997, his attorney said Gene was not a monster. Like him, I believe Gene truly loves his daughters very much, just as I believe he loved Margo at one time.

To protect the privacy of a few women with whom Margo was intimately involved or knew to be lesbians, I used a handful of pseudonyms, which, along with the name of Allison's boyfriend in Chapter Fifteen, are marked with asterisks so that you can distinguish them from the others. Any errors in this book are completely unintentional.

I hope, as Margo does, that this story proves inspirational for people everywhere who are living in denial about their sexuality or are tangled up with abusive and manipulative partners and, until reading this book, may have felt unmotivated or helpless to change their lives.

Acknowledgments

This book would not have been possible without Margo Bennett's willingness to tell this story after so many years of wanting to lay low and remain quiet about it. As I told her many times, she's a very brave woman, for it takes courage to talk about such traumatic events, not to mention one's own flaws and mistakes, the way she has. But, as I've also told her, she has a story of survival and triumph to tell that could help and inspire other people. I believe it was this need to help others that kept her going. For all of this, she deserves my utmost thanks and gratitude, and John Hess's as well.

I also convey my appreciation to John for persuading Margo to share her story, for laying the groundwork, and then for allowing me to take this project to the next level so that we could get it published.

Margo's daughter Allison deserves my thanks and admiration for being so open about her feelings and experiences, as does Margo's younger daughter, Lindsey.

Although this book is mostly told from Margo's perspective, I interviewed her friends, former coworkers, and family members to flesh out the details and cross-check everyone's memory. For this, I am grateful to Margo's sisters, Letta Akers and Jackie Standridge; her aunt Martha Coats; her former FBI colleagues George Murray, Caroll Toohey, Tony Daniels, Ed Tully, and Ed Sulzbach; her good friend Dianna Beals; and her divorce attorneys, Betty Thompson and Kathy Farrell.

Thanks also go to others I interviewed for this story, including prosecutors Paul Ebert and Jim Willett, police officials Ron Mc-Clelland and Debra Twomey, the Reverend Edwin Clever, Judge Richard Potter, and Mary Ann Khalifeh.

I send appreciation to those who helped me gather my research materials, including Phil Edney, John Fox, and Dan DeSimone from the FBI; former agents Joe Pistone and Steve Band; psychologist Michel Girodo; Bob Marsh and his assistant Michelle Jones from the courthouse in Manassas; Julie Linkins from Quantico; Rosemary Raeske from the Urbana Free Library; Dian Strutz, librarian for the *Champaign News-Gazette*; and Terry Gosa and Martha Marshall from Guin, Alabama, where Margo was born.

Many thanks to the staff at Jossey-Bass/John Wiley & Sons, Inc., including Seth Schwartz, Carol Hartland, Paul Foster, and Jennifer Wenzel; to Vince Cosgrove; Michele Jones; and to Alan Rinzler for editing this book and helping me develop my narrative nonfiction writing skills.

John and I are grateful to our literary agents Rick Broadhead for his tireless efforts to sell this book and to Stephany Evans for bringing this fascinating story to me.

Thanks also to John McCutchen for his photography advice and general support; Robert Rother for his IT efforts; Jon Sidener for his Web site and computer help; Carole Scott for her emotional support and writing advice; Anne Dierickx for her legal advice; and Bob Koven, Samuel Autman, Kathy Glass, and Susan White for their help in keeping me sane during the tough months.

Caitlin Rother
San Diego, California

Foreword

Why now? Why tell this story now, after so much time has passed?

Some years ago, my good friend John Hess expended great effort documenting the events of my chaotic life with Gene Bennett. It was a story that he often said "needed to be told" if for no reason other than to give my children a factual account of events. I agreed and gave my approval.

With John's manuscript as initial background, Caitlin Rother stepped forward to research and write this book. I was not eager to pierce through the comfort created by the passage of time, but I continue to believe that this is a story that needs to be told.

My life has been blessed with amazing events—good and not so good—and I believe they connect to something far beyond me. For that reason, I opened myself up to Caitlin so that she could tell the whole story, my flaws and all. As she rummaged through my family's life, peeling back the layers of emotional skin that had healed over our wounds, I felt that raw pain all over again. But in the end, I think she has been able to tell a story that will reach those who need to hear that such pain can be endured and such terror can be overcome, that survival and even triumph over adversity are entirely possible.

A lifetime ago, I was musing through one of Dear Abby's columns in the newspaper. As I read through the heartache and pain of others' lives, I was taken by a quotation by Harry Emerson Fosdick: "To laugh often and much, to win the respect of intelligent people and the affection of children, . . . to endure the betrayal of false friends; to leave the world a bit better, whether by a healthy child, a garden patch or a redeemed social condition; to know that even one life has breathed easier because you lived. This is to have succeeded."

I ripped out the clipping and carried it in my wallet for years, taped it up when it tore, then finally placed it in my desk, where it gave me comfort every time I reached for a paper clip. Ultimately, the coveted scrap of newsprint got lost in a move, but the words came back to me as Caitlin led me through my life's most difficult memories and compelling moments.

I have two wonderful children who love me, solid friends who have been rocks for me, and loyal family members who have carried me through some challenging times. If telling my story allows even one person to breathe easier, then the pain, the terror, and the struggle to survive will all have been worth it.

Margo Bennett
Berkeley, California

Twisted Triangle

Chapter One

Fighting Back

Margo Bennett was barely one step inside the lobby at the Prince of Peace United Methodist Church when the door to the sanctuary burst open to her right. A man, dressed in black and a stocking cap with eye holes, leapt in front of her. He was holding a gun.

"Margo, don't fight me on this," he commanded.

She recognized the voice instantly. It was her estranged husband, Gene, a former FBI agent, just like her.

Margo reacted instinctively, raising her hand and shooting a stream of pepper spray toward his head. As she saw him stagger backwards, she knew that she'd hit him, she hoped in the face. She also knew she had only a split second to run for cover before he'd come after her.

Racing into the office of her minister, the Reverend Edwin Clever, she dove for his desk in the corner. She landed on her hands and knees, scrambled behind the short end, and turned her body toward the doorway.

Still holding the pepper spray in one hand, she dug frantically in her purse for her gun. Gene, looking for an advantage, poked his head around the door frame several times. Each time he did, she sprayed him—once, twice, three more times.

By the fifth spray, she noticed that the stream had significantly less force. She was scared that Gene had noticed, too. But by then she'd gotten her finger curled around the trigger of her .38.

"You're not going to kill me, Gene," she said. "I am not going to let this happen."

Gene stuck his head around the doorway again. "I don't want to kill you, I just want to talk to you," he said, as if he were trying to sound sincere. "If I'd wanted to kill you, I could have had you any time."

"If you wanted to talk to me," she snapped, "you could have called me on the phone. I'm not coming out. You are not going to do this."

Crouched behind the desk, Margo pointed her gun at the spot where she'd last seen Gene's head. A stack of letter trays was partially obstructing her view, so she knocked them onto the floor with one swipe.

"What do you want to do, get into a shootout?" Gene asked. The feigned sincerity had evolved into irritation that his ploy wasn't working. "We can get in a shootout and see who's the best shot."

"I don't care Gene, I am not coming out there."

"Edwin has got explosives around his waist. I'll kill us all. Come on, let's talk, or we'll all die," he said, the frustration in his voice rising. "Do you want to die?"

"You want to blow us up, blow us up," she said. "But I'm not coming out there."

She could see her minister in his secretary's office, sitting in a green leather chair with a beige cloth bag over his head, his hands cuffed behind him, shackles around his ankles, and a bulging fanny pack around his waist.

"Edwin, are you all right?"

"I think so," he replied, his voice quiet and shaky.

Margo's adrenaline was high, and her fear had been overtaken by a clear focus and the drive to survive. Her choices would not be clouded as they were when Gene had attacked and abducted her three years earlier, in 1993. He could kill her as far as she was concerned, but she wasn't going to let him break her like he had the last time. She'd rather die than let him touch her again.

"You know I'm going to leave here and go and get the kids," he said. "You know I'm going to have to go through Letta. Is that what you want?"

Gene had already shown that he would use their two daughters to get to her during the last attack. That's what had made her cave in. But she didn't believe that he'd hurt her sister, Letta. The risk was too great that he'd get caught.

Even so, she didn't want to call his bluff. If she could keep him yelling and screaming, she figured he wouldn't have time to think. If she could keep him off guard, she and Edwin would have a chance to make it out alive. She was determined not to let Gene violate her or her girls again.

"Gene, just do what you have to do," she said, stalling for time. "Get out of here. Just leave. I'm not coming out."

Truth be told, she saw no way out. Gene was blocking the only door out of the office. And there were no windows. She knew he wasn't going to leave, no matter what he said.

"Edwin, are you ready to die?" she shouted. " 'Cause I don't know how we're going to get out of this."

Edwin sighed. "I was afraid of that," he said.

"Are you praying?"

"I've been praying," Edwin said.

"Pray for me too," she said. "I'm a little busy right now."

Gene poked his head and his gun around the doorframe once more. Margo wondered why he didn't pull the trigger. He'd have such an easy shot at her. Her only choice, she decided, was to fire first. With any luck, she would hit the sliver of pale forehead he kept showing her like a target.

And that, she hoped, would be that.

Chapter Two

Till Death Do Us Part

Margo Akers had just finished her sixteen weeks of FBI training and started working as an agent when she met Gene Bennett at the Atlanta field office in February 1982. He was a big man—six feet two inches and two hundred pounds—with steely light-blue eyes, a full head of brown hair, and a confident swagger. She was a slender five feet six inches, with blond hair and hazel eyes, and spoke with a soft voice.

"Stay away from him," her training agent, Pat Johnson, warned her. "He'll try to get into your pants."

The scuttlebutt around the office was that Gene had been with the bureau for only ten months, and at twenty-seven he was already considered a boy wonder, working his first undercover case.

A few days later, Gene called Margo at home, and despite her initial refusal, he persuaded her to go out with him. She'd already had her share of self-destructive sexual flings with both male and female coworkers at the campus police department where she'd worked during college and graduate school. She wasn't looking for another one.

But Pat was right. She and Gene went out for lunch and to a movie, then spent the night at his house on Lake Lanier, having the best sex she'd ever had.

When Margo was transferred to the Kansas City office, she and Gene continued to date long-distance. In October 1983, she wrote him a letter proposing marriage, not just because they loved each other, but also so that they could work in the same city again.

"I want to be your wife and I want you for my husband and the father of my children," she wrote. "The very thought of getting orders for the West Coast makes me have nightmares about what it could do to our relationship. . . . This way we stand a better chance of getting as close together as possible."

Even though she'd had her first sexual experience and a year-long relationship with a female student named Donna Thompson* in college, Margo had convinced herself that it didn't define her sexuality; she had just been exploring and experimenting. Dismissing the connection with Donna as purely situational, she had no second thoughts about committing herself to a heterosexual relationship. Being gay wasn't something people really talked about when she was growing up in Alabama and Georgia. It was a secretive type of lifestyle. And if it was a secret, then it couldn't be good.

Besides, her Methodist upbringing had taught her that the only sexual union of which God approved was between a man and his wife. And Margo believed that she and Gene would live happily ever after, till death do us part.

"He was very in charge, charming, full of life, and had ambition in what he wanted to achieve personally, in the sense that he wasn't satisfied with life getting stale," she said later. "When you look at my family's life of constantly moving, ongoing financial instability and never knowing if success was ever going to be achieved, Gene had control of his life and calmed those stressors that I grew up with."

Margo and Gene were married in a Methodist church in Atlanta in February 1984. About half of their two hundred guests were friends from the bureau, who wore the telltale sunglasses, dark suits, and short hair, and who got very drunk. The rest were family and friends from Alabama, Kentucky, and Illinois. Gene even invited the father of his first wife, Karen, the high school sweetheart whom he'd divorced after only a few years, soon after he finished his six-year enlistment in the Army.

As Margo waited with her own father just outside the sanctuary, he pointed to a door to their right, smiled, and said, "You could leave now. It's not too late."

Margo appreciated his attempt at levity, but she said, "No, we're doing this."

Looking back later, she said, "It was almost prophetic."

In September 1986, Margo was eight months pregnant. For the moment, she and Gene were both working in Atlanta, waiting for their unwanted yet unavoidable transfer orders to come through. They hoped they wouldn't be sent to the huge office in New York City, known as the black hole, but rather to the one in Washington DC, where they could afford to buy a home and raise a family.

Margo had her eye on a teaching job at Quantico, the FBI academy, where there were only a few female instructors. When Margo had joined the bureau in 1981, she was one of about 350 female agents—less than 5 percent of the total number. All of these women had been hired after Director J. Edgar Hoover died in 1972.

One night, Gene took a call from Jerry York in the kitchen of their house in Marietta, which was unusual because he typically talked to Jerry in his office upstairs. Margo later realized that Gene had done this on purpose so that she could overhear their conversation. It didn't matter, though, because she hadn't been listening.

Jerry had started out as Gene's informant in his first undercover gig, Operation Forscore, which began with a stolen truckload of Oscar Mayer meat. Over the years, they'd become friends, and together they'd come up with a money-making scheme that involved jewelry, completely independent of any undercover operation. Gene started bringing home little black velvet bags of diamonds, but all he'd tell Margo was that he and Jerry were trying to build a business with a jewelry dealer in Atlanta.

Margo never liked this arrangement. The bureau had strict rules prohibiting outside employment because of the potential conflict of interest. She thought it was an unusual and risky way to invest their money. She was also concerned about the ramifications such a pursuit would have on his FBI job.

When Gene got off the phone, he told her that Jerry had recently bought a cheap house on Lake Capri Drive in Lithonia, a suburb of Atlanta, and had put some cosmetic work into it.

"Jerry had this crazy idea of having us use the Lake Capri house as our primary residence in the Home Relocation Program," Gene said.

"What?" Margo asked, confused.

Essentially, Gene was saying that Jerry had come up with a way for them all to make some easy money off his new house by having Gene and Margo use it to apply to an FBI program designed to help agents who needed to sell their homes because they were being transferred.

The FBI had recently instituted this program in response to the depressed real estate market, providing an immediate equity payout rather than making agents wait to collect that money in a sale that could take months. The FBI had agents' homes appraised at fair market value, then issued payments equal to the difference between that value and the outstanding balance on their mortgages.

"Yeah, he put some money into fixing the house up, and there should be some immediate equity in the house," Gene said. "If we claim it as our primary residence, it would be a quick turnover of profit."

Gene didn't mention this to Margo at the time, but he and Jerry had figured they could make a $100,000 profit from this scheme, which they would then split.

What Gene was proposing was clearly not the purpose of the program. What he was proposing was fraud. Gene and Margo did not own the Lake Capri house, nor had they ever lived in it, so they would have to submit a false claim, supported by phony documentation that Jerry had sold the house to them.

"That's crazy," Margo said. "No way."

"Yeah, Jerry's crazy."

Later, Margo figured that Gene had posed the scenario to feel out her reaction. Despite her refusal, Gene continued to work on the idea with his informant friend.

"Jerry wanted to get instant gratification, too," Margo said later.

This new scheme notwithstanding, life with Gene had been growing increasingly stressful over the past year. He'd been attempting to do what he'd previously done to set up his first two undercover operations, Forscore and Nickelride, and obtain funding for them—he was taking criminal leads from a previous operation and trying to use them to launch a new one, a practice known in the bureau as spinning. Only this time the bureau wasn't biting, and he was frustrated.

Margo was concerned about Gene's state of mind and the unease his undercover work had been causing at home.

"I saw him needing that constant high, focusing more and more on using an undercover operation to make himself feel good," she said later. "Gene was developing a sense of entitlement to working undercover operations, which I felt was unhealthy and inappropriate."

One day, Margo broached the idea of going to see a marriage counselor.

"You and I are not communicating well, and I'd like to go see someone who can help us," she said. But Gene didn't want any part of it.

"If you need somebody to talk to, you go right ahead, but I'm not going," he said.

Margo wasn't surprised by his response, but she felt that going alone wouldn't do much good, so she didn't bring up the subject again.

The Bennetts' transfer orders came on October 6, three days before their baby was born. They were both relieved to learn they were being sent to Washington.

As Margo's frustrations with Gene and their marriage grew, she clung to his softer side and their common goal of starting a family. When it came time to go to the hospital, Gene brought a video camera to capture every moment of the birth for posterity. At one point, Gene, dressed in scrubs, pointed the camera at the mirrored wall of the delivery room, peeking out from behind the lens and waving.

Because Margo had some medical complications, she stayed in the hospital for five days. Every night, Gene slept in a cot next to her bed.

Margo kept a diary of the birth so that their child could later read a blow-by-blow description. In the little blue hardback book, she explained that Daddy Gene was very attentive. "He kept rubbing my forehead as if I needed comforting," Margo wrote. "I really think it did more to comfort him." After the delivery, she wrote, "They finally gave you to him and he began strutting around the delivery room like a proud papa. . . . Dad leaned you over to me and I kissed your cheek. . . . Dad sat down next to me, held you out and asked me what I thought of the name Allison for our little girl. I thought it was beautiful, just like you, and he named you Allison Akers Bennett there in the delivery room."

After Allison's first bowel movement, Margo wrote, "We called the nurse to show your dad how to clean you up and change your diapers. From that point on, your dad became an expert in taking care of you. He wouldn't hardly let me have you. I remember waking up and seeing him in the chair, holding you, and just looking at you like you were the miracle that we believe you to be."

One evening in mid-November, Gene pitched the home relocation fraud scheme to Margo for the second time while she was preparing dinner, with Allison sitting in her carrier on the countertop. Gene explained once again what he and Jerry wanted to do, only this time he wasn't backing down. He told her he was moving on with his plan, whether she liked it or not.

"This isn't right," Margo said. "This is not what we are supposed to be doing."

"I'm sick of your holier-than-thou attitude," Gene said.

He looked at Allison and then back at Margo, his voice dripping with contempt.

"Do you want to raise her by yourself? Because if you do, don't let the door hit you in the ass on the way out."

By this point, Margo felt that she had no choice but to give in. She wasn't ready to give up everything she'd worked for all these years, and she didn't feel she could raise a baby on her own. Gene had also worn her down over the years with his head games, embarrassing and humiliating her in front of their friends and colleagues, constantly exerting his very strong will. All of this had eaten away at Margo's already fragile self-esteem, so she let Gene persuade her to bend the rules, a decision she would regret for the rest of her life.

Gene must have seen from her expression that he had won. He nodded, and it was a done deal.

The deeper they got into the scheme in the coming months, the worse Margo felt about it. But Gene was driving this train, and she didn't know how to get off.

"I felt I had sold my soul to the devil, and I couldn't get out of this," she said later.

When things got bad with Gene, Margo often looked back and thought to herself, "If my mom could put up with her life with Dad, then I, too, can do this."

Margo came into the world as Marguerite Elizabeth Akers on November 16, 1953, in the tiny rural town of Guin in northwestern Alabama. Later nicknamed Margo by her older sister, Letta, she was the third of four children born to Ed and Gerthaldean "Dean" Akers.

Margo, her brother, and two sisters were raised in an atmosphere of denial, perpetuated by her mother, who reinforced the principle that "we don't talk about things." Ed, who liked his Jim Beam and Cokes, ruled the roost with his dominant personality, leaving Dean beaten down and unwilling or unable to stand up for herself. With this dynamic as a model, Margo learned early on to accept that keeping the peace in an unhappy marriage, even amid verbal abuse, was the right thing to do.

One adolescent experience in particular left Margo emotionally scarred for years and sent long-lasting ripples of confusion through her sexual development.

When she was thirteen, Margo and her father were lying in bed, reading the Sunday paper together, when he reached around without warning, stuck his hand up her pajama top, and squeezed her budding breast.

"It feels like you might be growing a little bit," he said.

Margo was stunned, ashamed, and embarrassed that he had violated her this way, then mocked her to boot.

"Where are you going?" he asked, surprised, when she started to crawl out of bed.

"I have to go to the bathroom," she lied.

She never went back to that bed and, following the tradition set by her mother, never said a word to anyone about that morning until both her parents were dead.

Years later, Margo learned that he had touched her younger sister, Jackie, the same way. Margo didn't know until she asked Jackie about it in an e-mail after their father had died.

"Oh, that," Jackie wrote dismissively, explaining that she'd been able to shake off the episode long ago.

But this was not the case for Margo. The experience marked a dramatic shift in the way she perceived her own body, making her feel inadequate, that she was lacking somehow. It also made her feel self-conscious, that her body wasn't developing the way it should. Before that fateful morning, she'd never even considered how her body looked or that her breasts were small. She'd always seen herself as just a regular girl who liked to play kickball or ride bikes with the neighborhood kids.

Growing up with an abusive father primed Margo to be drawn to a domineering and manipulative man like Gene Bennett and caused her to stay far too long in their tumultuous marriage. Years later, she told herself that if only Gene had been a decent man, her feelings of attraction for other women probably would've remained on the shelf where she'd put them long ago.

Chapter Three

Diamonds and Denial

In early December 1986, Margo, Gene, and their new baby went out to explore northern Virginia for a place to live. They were hoping to find a house somewhere near Quantico and within easy driving distance to DC, so they targeted Prince William County, which was just north of the academy and west of DC.

"We felt that if it was looking like I was going to Quantico, it made more sense for me to be closer to home because of child-care issues," Margo recalled.

On a bureau business trip later that month, Gene did some house hunting and found about thirty acres of open space in the city of Manassas, which he bought over the phone from a realtor. Gene negotiated an unusual purchase arrangement for the $90,000 property: $60,000 down and annual payments of $7,000 until it was paid off.

Margo knew they didn't have that much in savings, and she was concerned that Gene was spending the cash they would need to buy a house.

"We don't have the money," Margo said.

"I haven't told you this, but I have some cash that my dad gave me before he died," he said. "I promised I wouldn't use it until I was thirty-five."

Gene claimed that his father had given him $60,000, which he'd kept in a suitcase in his mother's attic ever since. He said that his father had told him not to put it in the bank, so Margo figured his father had never reported it to the IRS, and this was his way of protecting Gene, who said he would take the old bills to the bank and exchange them for new ones so that no one would question any transaction or track the income.

At the time, Margo took Gene at his word.

Over the course of the next year, Gene and Jerry were busy working on the home relocation scam. Gene drafted a phony document to show that he and Margo had bought the Lake Capri house from Jerry, using a $15,500 watch as a down payment. The watch Gene described was an Audemars Piguet he'd been wearing for his undercover operation but had since returned to the bureau's forfeited evidence collection.

But when the first appraisal came back, it was disappointingly low. Gene and Jerry would have only made $16,000, or a split of $8,000 each, so he asked the FBI to have one of its contracted relocation companies do a second appraisal. However, it came back just as low.

"Jerry decided that for that money it wasn't worth it," Margo said later.

So Gene and Jerry came up with another plan, which was to transfer the house to Jeanette Gilliam, the sister of Jerry's wife, Brenda. Again drafting phony documents, Gene had a former professor, John Sullivan, pose as his real estate agent in the "sale." He then claimed that he paid $17,430 to Sullivan in agent's fees. In November, Gene submitted a reimbursement claim to the FBI for $17,873 in expenses.

Margo had signed all the real estate documents and deeds, but not the paperwork Gene submitted to the bureau for reimbursement, which was handled as part of his transfer to the DC office. In February 1988, the FBI cut Gene a $17,177 check.

"Gene ruined his career for $17,000," Margo said later. "He was not one to leave money on the table. He liked to know he got what was coming to him. If he was eligible for [such perks], he wanted to collect them."

For their third wedding anniversary in February 1987, Gene took Margo out to dinner at a fancy steak house in Alexandria, leaving Allison with Caroll and Gail Toohey to baby-sit.

Caroll had been the assistant special agent in charge at the Atlanta office when Margo and Gene had first started working there. He was also the one who had approved Gene's first foray into undercover work with Operation Forscore. In 1986, he'd gone on to become a deputy assistant director of the Inspection Division at bureau headquarters in DC.

After dinner, the Tooheys had a chilled bottle of champagne waiting for Margo and Gene. Gene and Caroll walked into the living room from the kitchen, each carrying two glasses. Gene handed one to Margo, and the four of them toasted.

"Happy anniversary," Gene and Margo said to each other, clinking their glasses together.

As Margo took her first sip, she realized there was something in her flute.

"What's this?" she asked.

Gene feigned surprise. "Oh," he said innocently, "is there something in your glass?"

Margo hurriedly finished its contents and saw an enormous, gorgeous diamond ring sitting at the bottom. She pulled it out, and Gene put it on her finger.

"Oh, my God, it's huge," Margo exclaimed as she took a closer look at the stone.

She'd had a similar reaction when Gene surprised her with a one-carat diamond engagement ring just after Christmas in 1983.

"If we're going to do this," he'd said as he slipped it on her finger, "then you need a ring."

"It's beautiful," she said. "This is more than I ever wanted."

When they'd talked about an engagement ring, she'd said she would be fine with a simple wedding band. But Gene enjoyed buying expensive toys and gifts for himself and Margo, such as the pair of matching Rolex watches—gold with black onyx, diamond-studded faces—that he'd bought for them before Allison was born.

Gene, like Margo, had grown up in a family where money was always tight. This was especially true after his father, a garbage man, died of cancer when Gene was only sixteen. Gene had to quit the football team and work odd jobs to help support his mother and older sister, then immediately joined the Army. So neither he nor Margo, whose father started one failed business after another, had grown up with nice things.

Gail's jaw dropped open when she saw Gene's latest gift, which was three times the size of Margo's engagement ring.

"I'm sure they were thinking, 'Where did he get the money to buy that?'" Margo said later. "Crazy me. I never once thought those things. I never once said, 'How'd you buy this?' I just didn't. I guess I just assumed that we could afford it, that it was coming out of our savings and salary."

Before Caroll had asked Gail to marry him, Gene offered to get him a good deal on a diamond ring from a jeweler he knew in Atlanta. Gene brought over three or four loose stones to show him, one of which Caroll bought, had mounted, and gave to his future wife as an engagement ring.

Years later, Caroll said he had had no inkling that Gene had been running a side business selling diamonds with Jerry York.

"I don't know of anybody who was allowed to have a side business," he said.

But like Margo, he hadn't asked himself questions about Gene either.

"I found out later that he and Jerry were involved in a number of things," he said.

Margo and Gene drove into DC for their first day at the Washington Metropolitan Field Office, which was in the southeast quadrant of the district. The multistory building was in a rundown neighborhood, surrounded by dilapidated houses and rusty shells of cars.

"We talked about how the place looked like a ghetto," Margo recalled. "Parking was plentiful, but they encouraged you not to leave your cars there overnight."

They both worked in the same building but on different floors. Margo was assigned to the Department of Justice Applicant Squad, where she conducted background checks on candidates for the federal bench. Gene was assigned to the White House Applicant Squad, where he did similar checks on people applying to work for the president. Margo wasted no time in applying for a position at Quantico.

Within a month, Gene moved to the FBI Liaison Office, next door to the White House, where he had the same duties but also worked as a conduit between the administration, the FBI's headquarters, and its Washington field office. Margo stayed behind, biding her time until she could land the teaching job she wanted.

"I was willing to dig in and do what I needed to do," she said later.

Gene disliked his job, but he knew it would be a while before he could start lobbying to get back into undercover work.

"He thought it was beneath him," Margo recalled. "He felt he was wasting his time. It was clear he wanted to be working investigations where he was calling the shots."

Gene's new job was a far cry from running a complex undercover operation like Nickelride, which he'd launched in late 1983. During Nickelride, he and his partner, George Murray, had developed 242 indictable subjects and recovered $8.5 million in stolen goods and contraband. As he had in Forscore, Gene used Jerry as an informant.

Gene and George, who also went out on SWAT team calls together periodically, had uncovered corruption among some local government officials, including a Fulton County sheriff's lieutenant and captain, and the operation expanded from there.

Posing as diamond thieves who sold cocaine and ran a car theft ring, Gene and George dressed well, smoked cigars, and wore

PPKs, small guns that law-enforcement officers would never carry. They both came up with stories, known in the bureau as "legends," to explain why they didn't use the drugs they were selling. George's was that he was training for a marathon; Gene used a sob story that an old girlfriend had died of an overdose.

George always thought Gene had a talent for making up these stories. For Gene, thinking on his feet was almost an art form.

"He was very good, very glib, very enthusiastic," George said later. "You'd throw out the most ridiculous legend in the world and they'd buy it. He was fabulous at this stuff."

Later, Margo could see how all this storytelling could have affected Gene. "In an undercover operation you were given encouragement to step outside the box and be creative—not to break any laws but certainly to be imaginative."

And with someone like Gene, she said, "one step leads to another."

In the fall of 1984, Gene began planning a raid to lure the dozens of suspects he and George had identified over the past year to one place and have them arrested at one time.

Gene was clearly in his element—organizing and coordinating every last detail with precision—as he explained to Margo how he was putting the big finale together.

"It's going to go like clockwork," he told her, laughing in appreciation of his own cleverness, which, in this case, was duly lauded and rewarded several months later by bureau officials all the way up to FBI Director William Webster.

Margo felt proud of Gene as she listened to him on the phone, making arrangements. His plan was to rent out a nice Italian restaurant called Tony's for an all-night party, allegedly to celebrate his underworld successes with his boss, a Mafia kingpin, who was coming to town. Gene and George often had dinner at Tony's with their suspects, so it was familiar territory for everyone. Gene would tell them his boss wanted to meet them, and when they arrived at Tony's, they'd be taken one by one by limousine to the now defunct Lenox Inn. After being told that the kingpin was uncomfortable with armed men he didn't know, the suspects would hand over their guns at the back door of the hotel, then be immediately arrested by five SWAT team members in the parking lot.

"They're not going to know what hit them," Gene said. "By the time they start to figure out that people are missing from the party, we'll be ready to come in and finish it."

It did go like clockwork. After many of the suspects had been taken from Tony's and arrested at the hotel, Gene's colleagues from the Atlanta field office began to infiltrate the restaurant. Ultimately, more than twenty agents, including Margo, were involved in the raid that night, storming into Tony's with their guns drawn.

The next morning, Margo felt proud all over again as she read about her husband's triumph in the *Atlanta Journal*.

"It was an elaborate plan, far beyond the imagination of any other undercover operation that I had heard of," she said later.

The bureau made dozens of arrests that night on charges ranging from trafficking stolen goods to narcotics distribution and police corruption. Every defendant who went to trial was convicted, and all others pleaded guilty.

Gene received numerous commendation letters for his work on Nickelride as well as a $1,200 bonus, known in the bureau as an incentive award.

While Gene endured his boring new desk job in DC, he looked for a new house that offered some privacy, preferably out in the woods somewhere. He was very excited when he told Margo about his discovery.

"I found this great house in Nokesville," he said. "It's in really good shape, and it has close to three acres of land."

Nokesville was not an officially incorporated city, but when the Bennetts moved there in spring 1987, about seven thousand people considered themselves residents of the community. It was more of a town, really, settled originally in the late 1800s by members of the Brethren Church because of the cheap farmland.

The one-mile "downtown" strip had one stoplight, just after the giant "Welcome to Nokesville" sign that was painted on the side of an old kelly-green barn. The sign featured two large cartoon cows dancing upright on their hind legs, a tribute to the region's dairy farms, which had gradually been replaced with single-family homes.

The Bennetts' two-story brick home had four bedrooms, two and a half bathrooms, and a separate one-bedroom, one-bath apartment in a converted basement. The $158,000 price was right for their combined income of about $120,000, and the house was conveniently located seven miles north of Quantico and about twenty-five miles southwest of DC.

A heavy tree line provided a sound and sight buffer between their house and the closest neighbor's, which was about fifty yards away and could be seen only in the winter, after all the leaves had fallen. Another row of tall hardwood trees lined the lawn in the backyard, where snakes, rabbits, and deer would wander in at night. Gene bought a four-wheeler so that he could ride it around the lot and down to the creek bed at the back of the property.

Because they had only one car, Margo and Gene would often drive into DC together, dropping Allison at the baby-sitter's on the way.

In March 1987, Margo had a phone interview with Ed Tully, who was in charge of Quantico's Education and Communications Unit. She told him about her education—a bachelor's degree in sociology with a criminal justice emphasis and a master's degree in counseling and educational psychology—as well as her teaching experience at the state police academy in Atlanta.

"John Burke gave me your application, and it looks like you've got what we're looking for," Ed said.

John, who had been Margo's field counselor when she was a trainee, had been impressed by Margo's academic performance at Quantico, when she'd tied for second place in her class. Ironically, Margo had never even considered aiming for the bureau before a mentor at the police academy in Atlanta encouraged her to apply back in 1981. At the time, she thought the FBI took only the best of the best, and it seemed out of her reach. As it turned out, however, her entrance test scores ranked third among the FBI's nationwide pool of female applicants.

By 1987, John had been promoted to deputy assistant director at Quantico. He told Margo there weren't enough female instructors at the academy, so he was going to recommend her for a teaching job.

Later, Ed said that Margo's gender had given her a leg up in getting the position, but neither that nor help from higher up was the determining factor in her hiring.

"Margo got the job because she was good," he said.

Ed acknowledged that her six years of experience may have been less than that of the other instructors. However, he noted that there weren't many female agents at that time who would've had more experience. By the time Margo applied for the job in 1987, the bureau had 9,434 agents, including 700 women, who represented 7.4 percent of the total force. Ed's unit, however, had only one female instructor.

The general consensus among agents was that Hoover had thought women were ill equipped, both physically and emotionally, for the demanding job of an FBI agent. Although the agency hired a few women as agents or investigators in its early days, the last one had resigned in 1927, and none was hired until two months after Hoover died forty-five years later.

"The joke when I was coming through was that Hoover was spinning in his grave because women had been admitted," Margo said.

Despite widespread rumors that Hoover was gay, the bureau culture did not tolerate homosexuality either.

A week after her phone interview with John, Margo was excited to learn that she'd landed the position. Gene was excited too, because her getting promoted to special supervisory agent meant she'd be making more money. When their colleagues joked that she was now at a higher level than he was, he'd say, "I can spend her money just as easy as I can spend mine."

Margo reported to Quantico for her first day as an instructor on April 1.

The academy, which had opened its doors a few days after Hoover's death, was located at the southern end of a 385-acre Marine Corps base, also known as Quantico, just west of the town of the same name.

Today, the two-lane road leading to the base runs through a very green, wooded area and is marked with signs that say "Ammunition Supply Point" and "Ammo Dump." Motorists who open their car window may hear gunfire from members of the military, shooting clay pigeons for recreation at the Quantico Shooting Club, or from agents practicing on the bureau's firearms range.

The academy itself, which borders on Hoover Road, has a sturdy, if not formidable, presence that conveys the seriousness of the work and study being conducted within its walls.

That said, the interior of the series of multilevel buildings, connected by walkways that agents commonly refer to as "gerbil tubes," feels surprisingly intimate, small, and somewhat dated, almost like a private school or community college that was once state-of-the-art but now feels more historically significant. The air is filled with a positive, conservative energy as well as a sense of patriotism and pride.

On her first day as an instructor, Margo remembered how she'd only recently been through the sixteen grueling weeks of training herself.

John Burke, who was still a special agent at the time, had greeted her class of trainees by distributing copies of the book *Dress for Success*, telling them that looking the part of an FBI agent was half of getting the job done.

She remembered how she and her classmates had worked hard to excel physically as well as academically, walking tall and with purpose through the halls of the academy, where agents and trainees alike seemed to share the feeling that they were doing something important with their lives.

Trainees were tested at the end of each block of training and had to score a minimum of 85 percent to pass. The pressure was excruciating because those who failed more than two tests were dismissed from the academy.

The fast-paced classroom curriculum was challenging for Margo, but the blocks of defensive tactics, strength, endurance, and firearms training were even tougher, testing not only her physical fitness but her emotional fortitude as well.

Margo initially failed to do the requisite number of push-ups, which was twenty-one for women. She also struggled as she learned how to use a shotgun, her eyes welling up with tears of frustration.

"I wasn't seating it right on my shoulder, and as a result, the recoil was bumping up and hitting me in the cheek, bouncing down on my shoulder," she said later.

But Margo buckled down and did what needed to be done. She did not let herself cry, nor did she let any of the exams get the best of her. And after fulfilling all the training requirements, Margo vowed never to do another push-up again.

When Ed Tully met Margo in person for the first time, he noticed that she was slight in size, yet she carried herself with confidence.

"She was a little slip of a girl, but she had a certain quality I was very impressed with," he said later.

He was also impressed by the way she looked at him. "It was just a determination in her eyes," he said. "She was very clean, neat, and professional. . . . As it turned out, she was one of the best instructors I ever brought to Quantico. Everyone respected her, treated her like a lady. She was always one of my favorites."

Appearances aside, Margo could put on a hard edge when she needed to. While she was working at her first job at the West Georgia College's campus police department in 1975, Margo soon earned the name of the Blonde Bitch, the meter maid who wouldn't give anyone any slack. It was only in her personal relationships that she wasn't so good at standing up for herself.

When she'd entered college, Margo had intended to become a doctor, thinking that she could make a difference in the world by helping people and at the same time maintain some financial stability in her own life. She soon realized, however, that organic chemistry and, therefore, a career in medicine were beyond her abilities. After mastering a criminology course, she followed her girlfriend, Donna, to the campus department, where she went from parking enforcement officer to dispatcher and eventually to police officer. Margo found that walking with a gun on her hip made her feel strong, as if she were wearing armor, and helped counterbalance her low self-confidence.

As Margo continued her graduate studies in educational psychology, she saw a nexus between counseling and police work. Once she realized that she could also help people as a police officer, she decided on a career in law enforcement. That said, she knew she wanted more for herself than to drive a patrol car her entire life. Once she was accepted into the elite ranks of the FBI, she knew she'd made the right choice.

Even after she'd become a full-fledged agent, she still liked the feeling of carrying a weapon on the belt of her skirt.

The ten instructors in Margo's unit worked in an office that was divided into two rows of cubicles, dubbed the Prairie Dog Unit, because if someone yelled out a name, that person's head would pop up like a prairie dog, obediently answering the call. It was also known as the Ant Farm because the instructors felt as if they were working on top of each other, milling around like ants in the mazelike arrangement of desks.

Ed assigned Margo to pair up with John Hess, who taught Interviewing and Interrogation, a duty his colleagues considered akin to purgatory. Margo, however, took to it immediately, and John, in turn, took immediately to her.

"She was the first one who came and showed any interest," John said later.

For the next few weeks, Margo sat in on John's classes, taking copious notes. John knew the material so well that he was able to teach off the top of his head. When Margo learned they were going to work together as a team, she told him she couldn't do it without a lesson plan, so her detailed notes of his lectures became their organizational backbone.

Margo thought John seemed like a very quiet and serious sort of guy, with a soft voice and an intensity about him. At first, she felt intimidated by all his experience—twenty-eight years in the bureau, fifteen of it in the field.

"He had instant credibility with me," she said later. "I literally was soaking up his every word. He wanted to share what he knew with me. He wanted to make sure I did a good job."

In the coming months and years, the two developed a special friendship, becoming as close as brother and sister. They often joked that if one were to walk out of the classroom midsentence, the other could come in and pick up where the first left off. They were the perfect team.

"We couldn't have been more compatible," John recalled.

Ed Tully saw their relationship as even deeper than that. "They would die for each other," he said later. "John Hess thought she was a queen."

Margo started teaching her own Interviewing and Interrogation course about a month in. Despite her initial feelings of nervousness, insecurity, and inexperience, she got some of the best student evaluations Ed had ever seen for a new teacher since he'd joined the unit in the early 1970s.

"She had a depth of knowledge and experience," he said later. "She was believable, she liked her students, and understood nonverbal cues like maintaining good eye contact. She was well prepared and treated her students with respect."

Margo felt that she had reached nirvana.

"I loved being at Quantico," she recalled. "I loved the academic environment. Everybody who was there wanted to be there, so the dedication and commitment to be involved in training were very high."

At the time, the academy offered courses to new agent trainees; in-service seminars to special agents; and a prestigious eleven-week program to qualified law enforcement officials, called the National Academy. These courses ran the gamut from death investigations to white-collar crime, undercover operations, hostage negotiations, public corruption, interviewing, and profiling.

As many as fifty students could sit in one classroom, ascending in tiered, curved rows of desks that were arranged almost like theater seating.

An average day for Margo would start at eight in the morning and go until five, with an hour for lunch in the Board Room, which was a cafeteria by day and a bar by night. Her days would generally consist of teaching two to four hours, sometimes six; going over lesson plans; writing professional articles with a colleague; and developing new course material.

John and Margo's class became so popular that they eventually had to teach three sections in the National Academy. Margo and John each taught one and split the third.

One afternoon that fall, Margo was typing up some lesson plans. Her hands were sweaty, and one of her rings, which Gene had given her for Christmas in 1985, was slipping around on her finger. It was top-heavy, made out of a gold Mexican coin, and had about twenty tiny diamonds around the circumference, just enough to glitter. Gene told her he'd gotten it at an estate sale.

"To be honest, I didn't particularly like it," she said later. "It was too ostentatious."

As she often did when she was typing, Margo took it off and put it into a zipperless pouch in her purse.

When she got to work the next day, she felt in her purse for the ring, but it wasn't there. That night, she looked on her dresser, in the pockets of the suit she'd worn the day before, on the closet floor, and again in her purse.

"Gene," she said. "I can't find my ring. Have you seen it?"

"What ring are you talking about?"

"The coin ring."

"When did you last have it?"

Margo was hesitant to tell him because she was worried he was going to get mad and accuse her of being careless. But when she explained what had happened, he acted very caring about it. He even helped her look, but they still had no luck.

"Don't worry about it," he said. "We'll call the insurance company and see what they say."

The next day, Gene said the insurance company told him they needed to file a police report, so she talked to the police staff at Quantico, and an officer took a loss report from her, which they submitted to State Farm.

"It was more reasonable to think I had knocked it out of my purse and it was just lost, which could have happened anywhere between my office and the car," she later recalled.

The insurance company sent the Bennetts a $12,000 check.

That Christmas, Gene gave Margo a ring that looked exactly like the one that had gone missing. At first, she couldn't believe it.

"My ring!" she said.

"You don't know how much trouble it was to find one like yours," Gene said. Then, with amusement in his eyes, he added, "Try to hold on to it this time."

As Margo turned the ring in her fingers, she recognized that it had the same little scratches as her old one. How many other rings could have this unique design? She'd certainly never seen another one like it.

She'd already lost a tremendous amount of respect for Gene because of the house relocation scam, but this hit home in a different way. She couldn't believe her husband would do such a thing to her, but she felt in her gut that he had. After they were first married, he'd snooped around in her briefcase and found a letter she'd written to a fellow agent, complaining about her marital difficulties. Since then, she'd come to believe that Gene routinely went through her belongings. Now he was lying to her.

"This was perhaps the worst because he stole from me," she said later. "He went into my purse and got it, so this was personal. On top of that, he was laughing at it."

But Margo didn't let herself get angry at Gene. She put her disappointment into a box and stuck it in the back of her mind, reverting to the coping mechanism of denial she'd learned growing up.

"I didn't want to deal with it," she recalled.

In late 1987, Gene finally got out of the desk job he'd hated so much and was moved to the Soviet KGB Counter-Intelligence Squad. His new assignment was to try to "penetrate" KGB officers in the DC area, their missions, and the Soviet embassy. He didn't talk much about his work to Margo, except that he was excited to have landed a new undercover operation called Operation Bootstrap, which lasted until early 1989.

But Bootstrap wasn't enough. It didn't take long before he was antsy again for more of the autonomy and the flashy undercover excitement he'd experienced in his Nickelride days.

Chapter Four

Uncomfortably Numb

Two months after Margo and Gene were married, he surprised her by suggesting that they take their sexual practices in a direction she didn't want to go.

"Would you be willing to do a threesome?" he asked. "Wouldn't you find that exciting?"

Stunned, Margo didn't say anything for a minute. "No, I don't think so," she said, carefully.

Margo didn't want to touch that subject with Gene. She wanted to leave her past behind her; she also didn't see a ménage à trois as a healthy step for their marriage.

Within a couple months, Gene started incorporating porno movies into their sex life. His favorites were those with lesbian scenes.

Over the next two years, Gene's interest in watching these movies increased. Then, while they were making love one day in late 1987, he asked her to do something new once again.

"Tell me what it would be like to be with a woman," he said.

When Margo didn't answer, he continued asking questions. "What does a woman feel like? Taste like?"

"I don't know," she said, trying to sound as if she didn't even want to imagine that scenario. She'd never told him that she'd been with a woman, and she didn't intend to talk about it now.

"I felt it was dangerous territory. Something was telling me, 'Don't expose that part of you to him,'" she later recalled.

But because he was so insistent and she wanted to please him, she went along with his request and described "fantasies" for him based on her memories with Donna. She assumed that he had no idea that she was speaking from experience, because when he asked, she denied it.

"Have you ever wanted to make love with a woman?" Gene asked.

"No," she said firmly.

She was relieved when he finally let it go, but she later wondered whether he'd picked up that she'd been lying.

Amid Margo's deepening discontent with Gene, Allison provided a bright spot for her, especially when the toddler uttered her first expressive phrase right around the age of two. She was not so pleased, however, with Allison's word choice.

Allison was sitting in her high chair in the kitchen, holding a two-handed sippy cup full of milk. She took a long slug, then set it down with a sigh of pleasure.

"Ah, shit," she muttered.

Margo took one look at Gene and said sarcastically, "Some things have got to change around here."

Gene just laughed. Whenever he talked on the phone, particularly with Jerry, it was "fuck this" and "fuck that sumbitch," so Margo decided she'd better start taking the child out of the room when Gene was on the phone.

Around spring 1988, Linda and Leon Blakeney, a married FBI couple the Bennetts had worked with in Atlanta, came to the area on bureau business and stopped by the house for a barbecue.

As the two couples were catching up, the Bennetts explained that they'd purchased the land in Manassas, about two hundred acres of farmland in Kentucky, two four-wheelers—one for the Nokesville house and one for the Kentucky farm—and a giant truck that was parked in the driveway when the Blakeneys pulled up. Margo was wearing about $25,000 in gold jewelry and diamonds; she and Gene also had on their Rolex watches.

After dinner, Margo and Linda were cleaning up after their steak dinner.

"Where are y'all getting all this money?" Linda asked. "I mean I know what you make. I just don't understand."

Margo shrugged and said they'd been saving for years. They never took extravagant vacations. They just worked and hung out with Allison.

"Gene handles all the finances," she told Linda.

But to herself, Margo acknowledged that Linda had a point.

"I really hadn't thought about what it looked like," she later recalled.

Margo and Gene started trying to get pregnant again in March, and by May they were successful. Their second daughter, whom they named Lindsey, was born on January 17, 1989.

On Margo's second day in the hospital, the doctor said he thought Lindsey had a heart murmur.

"They heard a swooshing sound," Margo said later. "Gene used to say it sounded like a sump pump."

The doctor referred them to Children's Hospital, where they did an echocardiogram and discovered that Lindsey had two holes in her heart, one in the ventricular wall and the other in the atrial wall. While they were examining her, they also discovered she had pneumonia, so they admitted her. She stayed there for ten days, with Margo at her side, sleeping in a cot next to the bed.

Every day, Gene would bring Allison to visit, and Margo would play with her for a little while in the waiting area.

Margo was worried because the doctors were saying Lindsey might need surgery. "This was my baby, and she was sick," she recalled.

Lindsey's heart defect wasn't fatal, but Margo was worried that her daughter would grow up with a disability that would limit her life. At the end of the ten days, however, she felt somewhat reassured. The doctors said the holes often closed up by the age of two, so surgery might not be necessary.

For the next two months, Margo took Lindsey to the pediatrician once a week for a checkup, and for the next two years, she took her to the cardiologist once a month. Margo had to quit breast-feeding so that they could put Lindsey on a high-calorie formula. They also gave the baby medication to help regulate her heartbeat and a diuretic to keep fluid out of her lungs.

"She was a mess, but she was a happy baby," Margo said.

By the time Lindsey was two years old, one of the holes had closed up and the other had shrunken enough to stave off the need for surgery. The doctor suggested that they continue to monitor Lindsey's heart on an annual basis, but Margo was relieved they were over the hump, at least for the time being.

In July 1990, Gene and Margo decided they needed to set up some financial and legal protections to provide for their children and each other, so they wrote up a will and set up a trust for the girls. They also took out separate $1 million life insurance policies, naming each other as the beneficiary, and signed power of attorney documents for each other.

"This was all done with the understanding that if anything happened to either one of us, the remaining person would be able to make financial transactions," Margo said later.

As Gene grew disillusioned with his assignment with the Soviet squad, he began looking for a new position. When he learned that a spot had opened up in the Management Science Unit at Quantico, a sister unit to Margo's, where they taught leadership, management techniques, and agent supervision, he asked Margo what the job would be like and whether he should apply for it.

Margo explained that he would be teaching at the National Academy and encouraged him to go for it.

"I knew he was very unhappy, and I felt the academic challenge at the academy would channel him in a different direction. But at that time, that wasn't what he was looking for," she recalled. "I think he was looking for an environment where he could do whatever he wanted."

Margo knew that unlike an undercover operation, where Gene was in charge and could spend time in bars and nightclubs as part of his job, a teaching position at Quantico would seem overly structured and restrictive to her husband.

"You can't afford to go out and bounce around and play outside for the entire day, not when you have to be prepared for a four-hour class," she said later.

The day before Gene's interview, he was feeling pretty confident. After talking to Dick Ayers, who was in charge of the Management Science Unit, Gene was expecting an easy afternoon of talking to a panel about himself and his background.

"Sounds like a piece of cake," he said.

But Margo knew better: he was going to have to give a presentation to show his teaching skills.

"What are you going to talk about?" she asked.

"Dick Ayers said I can just get up there and wing it," he said.

The next day, Gene came by Margo's office after he'd finished his interview. He was agitated because they'd asked him to give a twenty-minute presentation.

"Dick told me that I didn't need to prepare for the presentation, and I feel like I was set up," Gene said as they walked to their cars.

Margo was embarrassed about how badly Gene had done in his interview, but she felt she could be honest with John Hess.

About a week after Gene's interview, she asked, "Gene didn't do too well on the presentation, did he?"

"No, no he didn't. He just didn't come in prepared."

It wasn't until a few years later that John Hess told her what John Velier, an instructor who would later replace Ed Tully as their boss, had said about Gene: "He struck me as the kind of guy that you couldn't trust," John Velier said. "I would always have to lock my desk when I left the room if he was my office mate."

Dick Ayers, who rode with Ed Tully to work every morning for seventeen years, felt the same way.

Ed later recalled, "Dick Ayers thought he was a complete phony, and he was right on the money. Dick had him pegged from day one. . . . He was a bullshitter, and they don't really garner a lot of trust."

In September 1989, Margo, Gene, and the girls went back to Champaign, Illinois, where Gene was born, to see his widowed mother, Alene, who was dying of breast cancer. Gene returned to Champaign in mid-November and got a temporary transfer to the bureau office there so he could stay and take care of her. Margo and the girls stayed behind in DC.

Alene was about five feet four inches, and had a soft look about her. Like Gene, she battled with her weight. At one point she'd been heavy, then lost quite a few pounds, evidenced by the loose skin hanging from her arms. A sun worshipper, she baked herself in shorts and tank top whenever possible, so her face was always tanned. The pack of cigarettes she smoked every day only deepened the wrinkles.

Alene shared a modest lifestyle with Gene's sister, Linda, in a ranch-style house with three bedrooms and one bathroom, built in the 1950s. Alene operated a child-care business out of their living room, so it was cluttered with baskets of toys.

Linda, who was three years older than Gene, was an elementary school teacher and spoke in a high-pitched, childlike voice. She had gone away to college, then came home to live with her mother, who treated Linda more like a sister than a daughter.

Unlike Gene, Alene didn't use profanity, and although she didn't go to the local Baptist church while Margo and Gene were visiting, she did attend regularly. Gene told Margo he was raised Baptist, but he never wanted to go to church.

Alene's family had grown up poor in rural Kentucky, living in abandoned houses and playing in the woods. She and Hazel, one of her younger sisters, once told Margo they used to climb onto people's roofs to watch where the road workers put their lunch pails, then stole their food.

"We were just terrible," Alene said, nodding.

"I wonder if they ever figured out where their lunches were going?" Hazel asked rhetorically.

Alene turned to Margo and said, "We didn't have any food. That's how poor we were."

After Gene's mother died in December 1989, he came back to Virginia around Christmastime, planning to return to Illinois to settle the estate after the holidays. On his first night back, he complained to Margo about Linda.

"I hate her," he said. "I thought of sneaking back and releasing cockroaches under the house." Then he laughed and said, "She's terrified of cockroaches. That would really show her."

Gene had told Margo that he'd never gotten along with his sister. "He always felt that she was a goody-two shoes and a stick in the mud," she said later.

When he went back to Champaign the first week of January, he immediately sued Linda, accusing her of draining their mother's bank account. The estate and lawsuit were all settled in a short trial at the end of the month, when the judge ordered all assets to be split between the two siblings.

All told, the estate was worth about $150,000, including cash and proceeds from the sale of the house. Gene packed up a bunch of his mother's belongings into boxes, shipped them back to Virginia, and came home.

Hazel and her husband, Harry, called Gene on his first night back. Apparently, they found Linda in a flutter and the house a mess when they returned from dropping Gene off at the airport in Indianapolis. Linda said Gene was responsible and accused him of taking all kinds of family photographs and other items of sentimental value to her.

"Can you believe it? That crazy bitch blamed me for trashing the house," Gene told Margo, laughing.

He explained that he'd taken Hazel and Harry through the house before they'd gone to the airport, and it had been in immaculate shape. "She didn't think I would have shown the house to

Hazel and Harry. She must have come in, pitched a fit and trashed the house and then blamed it on me."

At the time, Margo believed Gene's story. But years later, she figured that Gene was spinning legends again, that he must have booked a later flight so he could sneak back to trash the house and make Linda look like she was nuts.

Linda got married, moved to Florida, had a family, and, as far as Margo knows, never spoke to Gene again.

In mid-1991, Margo started talking to Gene about wanting a third child, which she thought might help her stay engaged in the marriage. But he said no.

"I want to make sure that we can provide for our kids and ourselves," he said, explaining that he couldn't see putting three kids through college. "Having a third child will put a strain on us financially."

Margo accepted his answer, but figured it was still up for discussion.

Around the same time, Gene finally got the new challenge he'd been seeking. He was transferred to the Public Corruption Squad in Tyson's Corner, an arm of the Washington field office, where he was assigned to ferret out elected officials who were taking bribes, exchanging favors for votes, or manipulating land transactions or rezoning efforts.

On July 15, he received a commendation letter from Washington's special agent in charge, Thomas DuHadway, for his recently approved Operation Doubletalk, an undercover case resulting from more than two years of investigative work.

Gene asked his old Army buddy, Donald Albracht, who had also joined the bureau, to help with the operation. Steve Spruill, who would become a friend, was Gene's contact agent.

As Gene was setting up his undercover office in Fredericksburg, Margo began to notice that he was taking their old household items, such as the vacuum cleaner and TV, putting them in his office, and replacing them with new ones at the house.

She'd never liked his jewelry business. She didn't like the way he'd staged the loss of her ring or coerced her into the home re-location scam. And now that he was back working undercover full-time, she was worried that things were going get even worse.

"I just got the sense that he was using undercover operations as his own personal expense account for clothes, dinner, and drinks, creating a lifestyle for himself," she said later.

Like Margo, many bureau supervisors saw undercover work as potentially dangerous for some agents.

"You're hanging around with the bad guys, talking the talk. The problem is that you're trying to act like one of them," George Murray, Gene's partner on Nickelride, said recently. "It's a tricky business that is the reason for many divorces."

Margo and Gene's sex life cooled off after Lindsey was born. As the emotional distance between them widened, Gene became more frustrated and short tempered with Margo, who often went to sleep while Gene watched porn in bed next to her.

But they really didn't fight much because Margo had learned how to avoid conflict with Gene and keep the peace between them.

"Gene was very controlling, and I realized I had slowly evolved into having a household where I was doing my best to keep the kids quiet and behaved," she recalled later. "I didn't argue with Gene; I did pretty much whatever he wanted. . . . If I did anything that he didn't like he gave me the cold shoulder. Things had to be his way. I gave up trying to be my own person at home. I was highly successful at work and was a good mother, but I was getting nothing from my relationship with Gene. Frankly, I wasn't putting anything into it either. I gave up trying. I was sleeping for a couple of years, going through the motions. Days turned into months. I just was numb, thinking I could live my life like that."

But she couldn't stay quiet when she saw Gene disciplining Allison in a way that she thought was too harsh. Remembering the premeditated spankings her father had given her and her siblings,

Margo was determined not to let Gene do the same thing to their daughter.

When Allison was about two years old, he gave her a spanking that Margo saw as far too hard for such a small child. About ten minutes later, Margo checked the girl's bottom and found the red imprint of his four fingers and top of his palm still on her right butt cheek. She carried Allison downstairs and showed Gene the marks.

"Don't ever do this to her again," she said.

Gene just looked blankly at Margo.

Margo had finally begun to admit to herself that her marriage wasn't going to work, but she still thought she could tolerate the situation until the girls were older. Like her mother, she didn't want to go through a divorce, she didn't want to disappoint her family, and she certainly didn't want to bring on Gene's wrath.

"I knew how he was when people turned against him."

Chapter Five

Prolonged Embraces

Margo and John Hess developed an even closer professional and personal relationship after Lindsey was born. Together, they rounded out a trio with instructor Ed Sulzbach, who had worked as an undercover agent and as a serial-killer profiler in the Behavioral Sciences Unit.

The three of them were kindred spirits, sharing many of the same views on life and the bureau, although Margo and John used to tease Ed for being such a Pollyanna. While Margo and John taught Interviewing and Interrogation to new agents, Ed waxed poetic about the history and soul of the FBI, about fidelity, bravery, and integrity, as the bureau's motto goes.

"We'd just shake our heads," Margo recalled fondly. "He's a patriotic God-fearing man who believes there's goodness and nobility in everyone, even though he's seen horror through profiling crimes."

By 1991, Ed had transferred back to the field office in Richmond, but he stayed in touch with his buddies, for whom the admiration and respect was mutual.

"Margo was willing to speak up if something was wrong," Ed said recently. "She's also extraordinarily intelligent."

On June 17, 1991, Ed showed up at Quantico with a couple of boxes of books and his friend, an up-and-coming novelist named Patricia Cornwell, who, like Margo, had grown up in the South. She went by the nickname Patsy.

Ed had met Patsy a decade earlier in Richmond, when she was a data processor at the Office of the Chief Medical Examiner, trying her hand at writing crime novels. Hearing about Ed through the grapevine, she'd called to pick his brain and gain some insight into the criminal mind. They became close friends, and he introduced her to his profiler colleagues. Because she'd spent a good bit of time with them doing research for her novels, she wanted to repay them with some free books.

Ed had been talking up Patsy to Margo for six months. He told her a week beforehand that Patsy was coming to Quantico, so she went out and bought Patsy's first two forensic thrillers, *Postmortem* and *Body of Evidence*, so that she could get them signed.

Ed introduced the women to each other in an empty classroom, where Patsy had been autographing books.

"This is my great and good friend, Patsy Cornwell," Ed said.

Patsy gave Margo a firm handshake. Margo thought she'd probably never see this woman again, but she did notice that Patsy was attractive and about the same age as she. Patsy's light-blue eyes were inquisitive, and she had a pretty smile with straight white teeth. She was about five feet five inches, slightly shorter than Margo, with short, highlighted blond hair.

"It's great to meet you," Margo said, handing her the novels. "Ed has talked so much about you."

"Maybe you can teach Scarpetta a thing or two," Patsy said.

Margo laughed. "I doubt it, but I look forward to it," she said.

Later, Margo recalled, "When Patsy shook your hand and she looked you right in your eye, you knew you had all of her attention."

Back in her office, Margo flipped open the covers to see what the author had written.

In *Postmortem*, she'd written, "To Margo, A real character. Such a pleasure meeting you at Quantico. Warmly, Patricia D. Cornwell."

And in *Body of Evidence*, she'd written, "To Margo, Perhaps you can give Scarpetta and Benton a few tips! Warm Regards, Patsy."

Margo took them home to read, then brought them back and put them on a shelf in her office.

In January 1992, Ed told Margo that Patsy was coming back to Quantico, this time to audit her first weeklong National Academy course, where authors were rarely allowed. Ed asked Margo to make her feel welcome.

Margo found Patsy during a morning break in the Hall of Honor, a squared-off area with a sunken floor, built-in brick benches with seating pads, and walls lined with bronzed plaques of agents killed in the line of duty.

"Hi, I'm Margo Bennett. I don't know if you remember me," she said.

"Yes, of course, I remember you."

"Ed Sulzbach called and asked me to touch base with you to see if you needed anything while you're here."

They talked for a few minutes before Patsy had to go back to class. She seemed far more interactive and animated than when they'd met back in June.

One night that week, Margo was working as the on-duty agent, which meant she had to stay in her office until midnight and in the dorm overnight, so that she could respond to any crisis or medical problem.

Patsy stopped by around nine that night, and they hung out in the Ant Farm, getting to know each other better.

But with all the electricity in the air, this was not ordinary girl talk. As they sat in chairs next to each other, Patsy kept swiveling around and touching Margo's leg with the toe of her shoe. With only some of the fluorescent lights on, it was about as intimate as an office at night could be.

Margo saw Patsy as a commanding figure in her pants, tweed jacket, leather closed-toe shoes, and neck tie, which she wore in a Windsor knot. Margo had on her typical work uniform—a long-sleeved blouse, a skirt, nylons, and pumps.

Patsy talked mostly about Patsy. She told Margo she'd gone to Davidson College in North Carolina, where she'd met Charles Cornwell, one of her professors, who was seventeen years her senior. They were married, then he left academics to join the seminary and, at one point, was offered a job in Texas.

"She was interviewed by a group of wives from the church, and she told them, 'I'm not a preacher's wife,' and that's kind of what set her on the path to divorce," Margo said later. "That's what made her realize that her life was not heading where she wanted."

Formerly a police reporter for the *Charlotte Observer* and a police department volunteer, Patsy told Margo that she'd published a biography on Ruth Bell Graham, the wife of evangelist Billy Graham, before she'd started writing crime novels. She'd failed to get her first few published, but then took someone's suggestion to try a female protagonist. The new formula worked, and since then, her career had really taken off. She was learning to enjoy success and the luxuries that came with it, buying a nice house and a Mercedes for herself, and also leasing Mercedeses for her staff.

Patsy said she loved Ed dearly, explaining that she'd drawn on his vast knowledge and experience as an agent and profiler to create two of her male characters. Some of his qualities showed up in Benton Wesley, an FBI profiler who worked with her protagonist, Dr. Kay Scarpetta, Virginia's chief medical examiner; others ended up in Pete Marino, the gruff but endearing homicide detective who smoked, drank, and solved crimes with Scarpetta.

As they talked, Margo felt the blood coursing through her veins, very aware of the close proximity of her body to Patsy's. It felt dangerous. Wrong. Thrilling.

But at the same time, Margo also respected and admired Patsy for what she'd accomplished, and that feeling seemed mutual. That part of it didn't feel wrong at all. In fact, it was quite seductive.

As their conversation progressed, Margo began to pick up that Patsy wasn't heterosexual, not just from the leg touching, but also from the way she talked about the women in her life. She could also tell that Patsy had suffered a lot of emotional pain.

"She was very quiet, soft spoken. She seemed to have a lot of hurt in her life," Margo said later. "She wasn't clingy or needy; she just was very intense. She seemed to have a lot of depth in her, a lot of experiences."

Patsy told Margo a story about a woman who used to work for her. After Patsy fired her, she brought something of Patsy's back to her house and left it on the front step.

"That's something you'd see in the breakup of gay people," Margo said to her.

Patsy looked at her with surprise, and Margo could tell she'd hit a nerve. She later decided that Patsy either hadn't realized how she was coming off or was testing Margo's reaction.

Patsy also told Margo about a homeless person who'd yelled at her and a friend as they were getting off an escalator in DC.

"He yelled out 'Butch' at us," Patsy said. "It was scary."

Time flew by. When Margo looked at her watch, it was 11:45 PM. She suddenly realized she had to close up the building, check in with the front desk, and send the late drinkers in the Board Room to bed.

After their lengthy chat, Patsy started calling Margo a couple of times a week. Soon Margo felt comfortable calling her, too.

Initially their phone conversations were brief. They were both very busy. Patsy was doing a lot of book signings, so they'd talk about which city she was in, where she was traveling to next, and what Margo was teaching.

Later that month, Margo and John were visiting with Ed one morning at the Richmond field office, when he suggested that they drop over to see Patsy. They drove to Windsor Farms, the upscale subdivision where she lived, and sat on her leather couch drinking coffee, eating croissants, and shooting the breeze for nearly an hour.

Patsy's living room walls were made of dark stained wood, leading up to exposed beams that ran across the ceiling. There was a wet bar on one side and a massive stone fireplace on the other, framing a set of sliding glass doors that opened onto a nicely landscaped backyard lined with mature trees. At the time, Margo wasn't thinking about Patsy's protagonist, Kay Scarpetta, but later, as she read more of Patsy's books, she felt that Scarpetta's house seemed very familiar, as if she'd been there before.

Margo felt content to be at Patsy's, playing a game of hide-the-attraction from her male colleagues. "At that point, we had not progressed much further, so it was a mutual infatuation," Margo said later. "It was interesting being in her house because I was with John and Ed, when I would have much preferred to have been there just with her."

In February, Patsy came to Quantico regularly to hang out with the profilers, often checking in at Margo's office.

One day, she came by wearing a black Escada silk tie with a pattern of small white flowers, Greta Garbo style.

"That looks very good on you," Margo said.

Patsy pulled it off. "Here, why don't you take it?"

Margo thanked her and wore it to work the next day.

A few days later, Patsy bought a Mont Blanc pen-and-pencil set at the academy store. She gave Margo the pen later that afternoon, drawing Margo into the gray area where Patsy's life and her fiction intersected. In *Postmortem*, Benton Wesley, the married agent who becomes Scarpetta's lover in her later books, is described as "slowly turning his Mont Blanc pen end over end on the table top, his jaw firmly set."

Margo wanted to share more with Patsy, so she invited her over to the house for dinner with the family, driving her there in the Bennetts' van so that they could talk on the fifteen-minute trip over.

"She was very successful, well respected, and it was a nice feeling to know that someone who was that nice of a person, and also that important, was interested in spending time with me, wanting to meet my children, wanting to meet my husband," Margo said later.

But she also felt a little self-conscious about her attraction for Patsy in case Gene picked up on it. "I was a bit apprehensive about bringing my submerged feelings into the house. I didn't know where it was going with Patsy, and I didn't want to expose that."

After the meal, they all went onto the back deck, which looked out into the woods, so that Gene could show off his new night goggles. Gene took the opportunity to pull the top of his sweatpants open and look down.

"Yeah, everything is still there," he joked.

Mortified and humiliated, Margo turned and walked into the house.

"He must have felt something was weird, something was different, about Patsy, so he was exerting his passive-aggressive behavior, calling attention to the fact that he was a man with a penis," Margo recalled later. "To some degree, I believe that his embarrassing me made him feel better."

Patsy handled Gene's strange behavior graciously, laughing at his jokes and questioning him about his undercover activities.

Margo apologized on the drive back to Quantico, where Patsy was staying overnight.

"I'm sorry about the way Gene acted."

Patsy took Margo's hand gently and said, "Don't worry. It's okay."

Patsy continued to hold her hand as they drove the rest of the way in silence.

Back at the academy, Margo walked Patsy up to her room in the Washington Building, where they chatted for a few minutes.

"When we hugged goodbye, she liked to be held until she was ready to let go, and I would just hold her until it felt like she was ready to let go," Margo said later.

Margo enjoyed having this private time with Patsy, behind that closed door.

"I'll see you tomorrow?" Margo said, assuming they would run into each other.

"Yes," Patsy said.

Margo invited Patsy back to the house for dinner in early March. Patsy stroked Margo's hand in the van coming and going, which Margo found extremely erotic.

"She was making love to my hand," Margo said later. "It was like my whole system was in overdrive."

Back at Quantico, they had another prolonged embrace. When they parted, Margo saw a look of longing in Patsy's eyes, the same look she was sure Patsy could see in hers.

Margo felt herself getting increasingly caught up in her physical connection to Patsy, but she still didn't intend to take any action on it.

They started talking on the phone every day, and Patsy faxed her book tour itinerary to Margo every couple of weeks so that she could reach Patsy at any time. They exchanged such sentiments as "I miss you," "I've enjoyed my time with you," and "I'm looking forward to seeing you again."

On March 20, Patsy showed up in Margo's office with a surprise.

"I have something for you in my car," she said.

In the trunk of her Mercedes was a framed poster-size copy of the *Postmortem* book jacket, signed, "To Margo, a special woman and wonderful friend. Love, Patsy."

They took it back to Margo's office, where Patsy pulled two of her books off the shelf and wrote new inscriptions with that day's date under the ones she'd already written on the front pages.

"Why don't I sign your books every time I visit?" she asked. "Sooner or later it will fill out the book."

Patsy underscored that sentiment with the message she wrote in *Postmortem:* "If I sign this every time I visit, yours will be the rarest of 1st editions. Warmly, Patsy."

She also signed *Body of Evidence* for the second time, writing, "To Margo on the day I fell from Grace. Well, it may not get better with me, but it will always get different. Love Patsy. (I did inscribe it after all, but I'm going to do it again. What a special pleasure to be your friend.)"

Patsy was referring to the fall she'd taken during a run that day with some agents on a path at Quantico known as the Yellow Brick Road, a three-mile obstacle course, which made for a nine-mile run if the agents started from the gym.

A few days later, Margo was telling Patsy about a tour of Quantico she was giving that week to a group of about thirty kids with cancer, called Camp Sunshine. The children were in grades four through six.

"Is there something I can do to help?" Patsy asked. "Can I buy them FBI hats?"

Margo was happy to take her up on the offer. "Would you like to join us and meet the kids?"

"That'd be great."

So Patsy met up with Margo and the children, some of whom were rail thin and bald, but all of whom wore smiles and exuded courage. Together, they explored Hogan's Alley, a two-block area comparable to a Hollywood movie set, with buildings and two grassy common areas that look like a small town square, where new agents train to respond to bank robberies or hostage situations.

In addition to a phony bank, Hogan's Alley has mock townhouses and a fake bakery, drugstore, and hotel. It also has a reproduction of the Biograph Theatre, complete with a marquee advertising *Manhattan Melodrama*, starring Clark Gable and Myrna Loy. The Chicago theater has historic significance for the bureau because that's where fifteen agents gunned down bank robber John Dillinger on July 22, 1934, right after he'd watched this movie.

Patsy put her arm around Margo, and they posed for a few photos on the sidewalk. The snapshots show how very comfortable they were together—two slender and athletic thirty-something blondes, standing hip to hip.

Patsy continued to give Margo presents, sometimes in a gift box, for no other reason than that she felt like it. A black-and-red silk Nicole Miller blouse, for example, was "just because."

In early April, Margo invited Patsy over for a third family dinner while she was attending another seminar at Quantico.

This time, Patsy brought presents for Margo's three- and five-year-old daughters: two dark-brown mink teddy bears she'd picked up in New York City. They were six inches tall and extremely soft.

Margo found the gifts a bit extravagant, given that her girls were at the age where they were pulling off the heads of their Barbie dolls, but she appreciated Patsy's generosity.

After dinner, Margo went out to the van, thinking Patsy was right behind her. Patsy got in a couple minutes later and was quiet all the way back to Quantico. A month later, she told Margo that Gene had grabbed her ass on her way out, saying, "Call me sometime." Patsy was disgusted, and Margo was embarrassed once again by her husband's behavior.

Margo walked Patsy back to her dorm room as usual, only this time she sensed that the dam was about to burst on her will power. The emotional walls that had been straining to contain her attraction for Patsy were collapsing as the two of them made their way down the hallway.

In the room, their embrace lasted even longer than usual while Margo leaned against an armoire, with Patsy's head on her shoulder.

"I can feel your heat," Patsy said. "I can't believe how hot you are."

Margo reached down and started kissing her on the jaw and neck, moving slowly over, finally and at long last, to Patsy's lips.

"This is crazy. I'm sorry," Margo said.

"No, don't be sorry," Patsy replied.

They kissed again.

"It was a total sensual bath of feeling," Margo said later. "Plain nerve endings going Fourth of July bonkers. I was not there. Time wasn't there. It was so astounding. Took my breath away. Up to that point in my life, that was the most tender kiss I had ever had, and yet at the same time, it was the most ferocious in the intensity of it and what it was doing to the inside of me. I was mush. The hardest thing I had to do was let go of her and say, 'I have to go home.'"

When Margo finally did get home, reality smacked her in the face. Gene was pissed. She'd been gone for over an hour.

"Where have you been?" he snarled at her. "You needed to be at home to put the kids to bed."

So Margo did her motherly duties, then got into bed with Gene, who was still pouting. She gave him the usual goodnight kiss on the cheek while he channel surfed, but he didn't kiss her back. That was fine with her. She needed time to think.

"It took me a long time to fall asleep that night," she recalled later. "I rolled away from him and just lay there, wondering what the hell was going on in my life."

The next morning, she went to straight to Patsy's dorm room to apologize. She was a married woman, after all.

"Patsy, I'm sorry," she said. "I didn't mean for that to happen last night."

As their eyes met, Patsy softly said, "Margo, I wanted that to happen."

Margo later said, "Then it was like the cards were out on the table. I knew we shouldn't be doing this, but sometimes people do stupid things. I admit I should have turned and run down the street. Why? Because I was married, if for no other reason. I should not have walked into that, but I did because, frankly, it felt good, and it was the first time I had the sense of being appreciated for what I brought to the table."

Over the next two hours, Patsy unveiled some of her more personal struggles. She seemed tired and fragile.

Patsy talked about growing up with her mother, who had suffered from mental illness. She explained how her brother had kept a gun in their bedroom in case their mother came in again, acting crazy. How she'd been molested as a child by a security guard. How her dog went missing when she was in elementary school, and when she came home one afternoon, her mother was burning something in the fireplace that looked and smelled like meat.

Patsy also told Margo she'd recently come out of a relationship that broke her heart, but she didn't elaborate. Margo took that to mean that Patsy was ready to feel something for someone again. Margo's own heart had felt frozen for a long time, but she was ready too.

After they hugged goodbye, Margo left, confused. She really wasn't sure what she was doing or what it all meant.

But she was quite sure of one thing: the desire for more was entirely mutual.

On April 15, Patsy extended a welcome invitation to Margo over the phone.

"Would you like to spend some time together?" she asked. "I'll come and pick you up and bring you back."

Clearly, Patsy meant intimate time.

"Yes, I would," Margo said, scared but forging ahead nonetheless.

Margo was expected to be at Quantico all day, but nobody kept close tabs on her. So they made arrangements for Patsy to come by two mornings later, then bring Margo back around three in the afternoon so that she could check her messages and be available to students.

Over the next two days, Margo let herself remember the satisfaction and completeness of being with a woman. It was a feeling she'd thought she'd left behind more than fifteen years earlier.

To have that memory reawakened after all that time, coupled with the physical attraction and passion she felt for Patsy, was a heady experience. She was not thinking rationally at this point. She was enjoying being in the moment too much for that.

She'd felt passion and lust for Gene in the beginning, too. She'd even grown to love him, but it was different. Being with a woman was more of an emotional experience for her, an intermingling of spirit and soul, something she'd never felt with Gene or any other man. She didn't think Gene had ever fully let go of control over his emotions, and neither had she, so they had sex. When she'd been with Donna, they both had let go. To her, that was making love, and she expected it to be the same with Patsy.

When the morning of their rendezvous arrived, Margo was ready.

"I've got some things to do," she told John Hess as she left the office around ten that morning. He had no idea what was going on and frankly wouldn't have cared anyway.

Patsy was waiting for her at the parking circle, dressed in a white pantsuit. She handed Margo a toasted bagel, doused with olive oil and wrapped in foil, for the hourlong drive to her house.

"I'm glad you could get the day away," she said.

"Me, too," Margo said.

"Are you sure you want to do this?"

"Yes," Margo said definitively. "I'm sure."

From that point on, Margo felt no guilt or confusion, only nervous excitement about consummating her feelings for Patsy.

During the drive, they talked about Patsy's writing, how she drew her ideas from conversations with police, news events, and her own imagination. She said she'd sit down to write, blocking out the world, not knowing the end of her own plots until she got there, which made for rapid, unexpected endings.

Despite the difference in their incomes, Margo didn't feel any socioeconomic divide or awkwardness between them. Patsy may have chosen a Mercedes or an Escada tie to make a statement, but Margo was wearing her three-carat diamond ring, her diamond earrings, and her Rolex watch. Patsy was a successful author, but Margo saw herself as a success in her own right: she was an instructor at the FBI academy. The degree of emotional risk between them felt equal as well.

"It wasn't her chasing me, or vice versa," Margo said later. "It was a mutual attraction."

Patsy drove through her secluded, affluent neighborhood, with its expansive homes and well-groomed lawns, and up the driveway to her large ranch-style house. They entered through the garage, then Patsy led her into the kitchen, through the living room, and into the bedroom, which had a queen-size bed directly in front of the door.

Patsy went over to the vanity and started taking off her rings and jewelry. She seemed a little nervous and unsure of how to proceed, so Margo took the lead.

Margo came up from behind and put her arms around Patsy. Patsy looked up at their reflection in the mirror, where their faces and blond heads were side by side. Now they could both see their expressions of longing.

"It was a perfect picture," Margo recalled. "It just felt right. She turned around in my arms, and I held her. And then we kissed."

When they'd first kissed in the dorm, Margo had felt an urgency of passion. But this time, it was soft and gentle, and it built from there. They lingered on every touch, not wanting to miss a beat. This time they had all afternoon, and Margo wanted to draw out every moment of it.

Margo found Patsy's vulnerability, openness, and desire seductive.

"It was a very special and magical, unique moment," Margo said later, "not something I'd ever felt before, nor did I have any idea that I would feel this again."

They undressed each other and got into Patsy's bed, a soft, inviting sea of powder blue, where they made love for more than an hour. Margo wasn't looking at her watch, but time didn't seem to be moving. She was suspended in the sensation of it all.

As they lay together afterward, quiet, letting the sweat dry, Margo felt calm, complete, and satisfied.

"That was wonderful," Patsy said. "I've never felt that before."

"Thank you," Margo said. "Loving you is easy."

By this, Margo wasn't saying she was in love with Patsy; she was merely thanking her for sharing a unique lovemaking experience.

"I'll be right back," Patsy said.

She returned a few minutes later with a bottle of spicy red wine from her cellar in one hand and two short glass tumblers in the other, the way real Italians drink wine. She mentioned that the wine cellar had come fully stocked by the home's previous owners.

Margo had never celebrated making love before, but that's exactly what they were doing. "I didn't hold back with Patsy," she said later. "My heart, my soul, my guts were right out there, experiencing her."

They lay there, caressing each other as they sipped their wine, and Patsy told Margo about her first affair with a married woman. Patsy said she'd fallen in love with the woman, but she wouldn't leave her husband. Patsy also said that she and this woman had messed around, but they'd never made love.

Margo took this to mean that Margo was Patsy's first female lover, although later she wasn't quite so sure.

"Patsy was the only other person I had been with since I'd met my husband," she later said. "I'd never strayed, never even thought about it. So it was touching to me that she was that trusting of me, just as she should have been that I was that open with her."

About forty-five minutes later, they looked at the clock and decided they should get dressed and go.

"I have a surprise for you," Patsy said, turning the car toward an older part of Richmond, where she pulled up to a small house with peeling paint. There they were greeted by a woman in her early sixties, whose living room was dusty and cluttered.

Patsy went to another room while the woman sat Margo next to a small wooden desk, where she'd cleared a space in the middle of her things, and started shuffling a stack of cards that were white on both sides.

"When I touch the cards, I see things," she said in a kind voice with a southern Virginia accent. "I pull from the cards what I'm supposed to see. They weren't blank when I got them, but they turned that way."

The woman pulled cards from the deck one at a time, moving them around, putting some aside, and reshuffling. When she was satisfied, she laid three down on the desk.

"I see that you are going through a defining time," she said. "You are making decisions and are under a lot of stress. You're worried about people getting hurt. You have some tough times ahead, but don't worry, you are doing what is right."

Patsy came in for her own reading, and about twenty minutes later, they headed back to Quantico.

"She told me you're going to have a difficult three years ahead of you, but after that you'll be okay," Patsy told Margo, though she didn't mention anything about her own reading.

Margo was surprised to hear that Patsy saw this psychic regularly. She also saw the reading as a strange way to end an otherwise memorable day.

"It spoiled the intimacy, calm, and peace I'd felt," Margo said later.

Back in Margo's office, Patsy signed her books again. "I'm back. And it's better every time. Love, Patsy," she wrote in *Postmortem*.

In *Body of Evidence*, she scribbled, "Hello again. It is a gorgeous spring day and I've had a terrific time with my friend. Love, Patsy."

That same April, Margo and Gene were in the van with the girls, about to pull out of their driveway, when she realized that she'd forgotten to put on her jewelry.

Gene went inside to get it for her, but when he came back, he had only her watch and rings.

"Where are my earrings?" Margo asked.

"I brought everything that was up there," Gene said, referring to the crystal dish on her nightstand.

Margo went inside to look for herself, but Gene was right. The diamond earrings were nowhere to be found.

"I can't find them," Margo said as she got back in the van.

"C'mon, let's go," Gene said. "We'll look again when we get home."

After the Mexican ring incident, this seemed all too familiar to Margo. When the earrings didn't turn up, Gene filed a claim with the insurance company.

Although they had been appraised at $9,000, the company issued a check to the Bennetts for $11,000, the earrings' current value.

Shortly after receiving the check, Gene went on a visit to Atlanta. He'd used the insurance money to pay off one of their lines of credit, and had left virtually nothing in the household bank account.

Margo was frustrated.

"I don't have any money, and I have to go to the grocery store," she told Gene when he called from Atlanta.

"Write a check off the line of credit," he said.

When Gene returned from his trip, he gave her a pair of "replacement" earrings, which came in a similar gold setting and looked remarkably like the ones that had disappeared. Margo knew they didn't have the money for new earrings, so she figured Gene had done it again. This time, she could no longer deny what was staring her right in the face: her husband was a crook.

"For so long, I had my head in the sand, but I couldn't hide this," she said later.

On April 23, Margo went to an early release party for Patsy's latest book, *All That Remains*. She and twenty other agents had dinner with Patsy in the back room of a bureau hangout called the Globe & Laurel, which, with its plaid carpets, was reminiscent of a small hunting lodge.

The owner, Major Richard Spooner, was a former Marine with a near obsession and deep respect for the military and law enforcement. He had blanketed the walls and ceilings of his restaurant with memorabilia, patches and shoulder epaulettes from around the world, and glass boxes displaying commemorative and actual guns.

Nobody brought their spouses that night, and Gene, who had been showing signs of jealousy at the attention his wife was paying the famous author, hadn't wanted Margo to go. He'd always had a way of isolating her, which had previously discouraged her from making close friendships outside their nuclear family.

That night, Patsy signed Margo's copy of *Postmortem* once more: "Next time we'll do the Yellow Brick Road (try to make me sweat). Love, Patsy."

Patsy and Margo posed for another photo in their matching Nicole Miller silk shirts and ties. Patsy's outfit was an aquamarine version and Margo's was in red, Patsy's most recent gift to her.

As soon as Margo got a copy of the photo, she put it in a frame on her desk.

Patsy called Margo at home as soon as she'd learned she'd won a Prix du Roman d'Adventure for *Postmortem*, and invited Margo to fly to France with her to accept the literary award.

Margo wanted to go, but she declined.

"I don't even have a passport," she said.

Gene came into the bedroom as they were talking, and wouldn't leave.

"He just came into the room, didn't he?" Patsy asked.

"Yes, why?"

"Because your voice changed."

The real reason Margo said she couldn't go to France was Gene.

"I knew he wouldn't approve of me going," she recalled.

In early May, Patsy had a signing at a bookstore in Richmond. She invited several dozen friends and acquaintances to dinner afterward at Ruth's Chris Steak House next door.

Among Patsy's guests were some local political figures, including an aide to Governor Douglas Wilder. This time, Gene, who was still working the public corruption case, accompanied Margo and embarrassed her and Patsy by telling dirty jokes to the politicos at his table all night.

About a week later, Patsy started backing away from Margo, saying Gene made her uncomfortable.

"He scares me," Patsy said. "I don't trust him."

"I understand. Whatever you want to do is okay," Margo replied.

Patsy also told Margo that a friend had spent the weekend at her house right after she'd slept with Margo. The friend woke up in the middle of the night in Patsy's bed and couldn't get back to sleep after dreaming that it was soaked in blood.

"Whatever is going on," Patsy quoted her friend as saying, "be very, very careful."

Two weeks later, Patsy audited Margo and John's class, and afterward, the two women agreed that they needed to talk. They decided to meet at the gym and take a run over to the reservoir, which was about a mile away.

Patsy teased Margo that she was in better shape than Margo as they jogged along the tree-lined shore. They found a bench and sat facing each other so that their knees were touching.

Margo told Patsy that she'd come to realize she needed to deal more directly with ending her marriage; getting involved with someone else wasn't the way to do it. Patsy said she understood.

"He's dangerous," Patsy said. "He's got all these antennae out there, gathering all kinds of information. You may not know that he's picking up on things, but he is."

"I know that," Margo said, her mouth suddenly going dry. Patsy's words only underscored what Margo had been feeling in her gut all along. "I realize I may be signing my own death warrant by asking him for a divorce."

"You may be right," Patsy said.

"But I can't live with this any longer."

Although they both had their own reasons, Margo figured they'd come to the same conclusion: it was time to stop the sexual part of their relationship.

Margo reached over and touched Patsy's hand, wishing things could be different. "I think we should just be friends," she said gently.

Patsy looked down at her lap and then up at Margo. "You're right," she said, sighing. "I think we can do this."

Margo sensed that Patsy had been scared that Margo was going to say she wanted to keep the affair going, so she seemed relieved when Margo let it go without a fight.

"I think she was worried that I was going to push back and that it would become ugly," she recalled.

Margo was sad to let Patsy go; Patsy had brought her joy during their time together. But more than that, Patsy had made her feel more alive than she had in years.

Still, Margo said, "I felt good. It kind of ended out that chapter. We were very sincere and respectful and honest about what we wanted out of life. She didn't always want to be looking over her shoulder. I had things I wanted to do. She thought I was a great person; I thought she was a great person."

Margo had told Gene in advance that Patsy was coming to town that week, and had asked him to suggest a restaurant because he knew the area around Quantico better than she did. Gene suggested an Italian place in Fredericksburg that he'd been frequenting as part of his Doubletalk undercover work, the same place where he and Margo had gone for their anniversary a few months earlier. It was a quiet spot with white napkins and candles on every table.

All told, the night with Patsy lasted about two hours, including the half hour of drive time to and from Quantico.

Later, Gene claimed to have followed them and seen them kissing and fondling each other at the restaurant and in the parking lot, so Margo figured he'd been outside, watching them. But, she said, he fabricated the level of contact he saw between her and Patsy that night. Since their discussion by the reservoir, there had been no more touching or romance between them.

Over dinner, the two women talked about Patsy's next book project and the upcoming challenges Margo faced with Gene.

"I'd pretty much come to the realization that I couldn't stay in my marriage any longer, but I didn't really know how to get out of it, and I felt that I needed to see an attorney," Margo recalled later.

Patsy said she would help her find a good one.

A week later, she called with a name: Betty Thompson, who was reputed to be among the top ten divorce attorneys in the greater metropolitan DC area.

In early June, Margo went to see Betty, whose high-rise office in Arlington had heavy glass doors and felt like money.

"Most men put up a good front and threaten and really act like a bully, but bullies are really timid. When push comes to shove, they really fold," said Betty, who had been a divorce attorney for more than half of the forty-two years that she'd been a member of the bar.

"You don't know Gene," Margo replied. "Gene Bennett is going to look at you like a snack before lunch."

"Oh, no, I've dealt with guys like this before."

"Don't underestimate him," Margo said. "It's not going to be easy."

Betty advised her to copy all the records of their marital assets, including money market accounts and land purchases.

"Once you decide to leave, you won't have a chance," she said.

So when Gene was away on a trip to Atlanta in mid-June, Margo made copies of their financial files, which he kept in his home office, and put them in her desk at Quantico.

After Gene came back from Atlanta, they had an argument that marked the beginning of the end.

Margo had always hung up his pants, regardless of where he'd dropped them, but this time, she'd tossed them on his side of the bed. He called her at Quantico first thing the next morning to complain.

"What's your problem—can't you hang up my pants?" he snapped.

"Work is not the place to talk about this," she retorted. "We'll talk later."

When she got home that night, Gene ignored her until they went to bed. The bedroom was his battleground, the place where he seemed to feel that he could get Margo under control.

"What's your problem?" he repeated, sitting up in bed.

"I just can't do this anymore," she said. "I want a divorce."

Gene was wearing his poker face. "Are you saying you don't love me anymore?"

"No, Gene, I don't love you anymore," she said softly. "I don't love you in the way I need to love you to stay married to you."

Margo smelled fear on him that night, an acrid, sweaty odor that she'd never smelled on him before. For the first time, he didn't seem to know what to say. He just sat there, speechless.

"Maybe he, in his own way, loved me," she later said. "Maybe I was upsetting his apple cart. There were a lot of things, really, with the land deal and what was going on in his undercover operation. Maybe he thought I could hurt him. Maybe he thought it was risky to let me go."

The next day, Gene sent Margo a large bouquet of red roses to the front desk at Quantico, with a card that said, "I love you."

"Ooh, you got flowers," the clerk said when Margo came to pick them up.

"Yes, it's amazing what happens when you say you want a divorce," she said, then promptly tossed them into a nearby garbage bin.

In early July, Patsy called Margo to say she was having a book launch party at her house at the end of the month and asked if Margo would come and stay the night. Margo said yes.

When Gene asked if he could come too, she said no.

"Don't you realize that Patsy's just using you?" he said. "When you can't offer her anything more, she won't give you the time of day."

There were about thirty people at the party, including Ed Sulzbach, John Hess, and Dianna Beals, Margo's agent friend and a firearms instructor at Quantico.

Patsy handed out T-shirts to the partygoers under a big white tent in her backyard, and at the end of the evening, she sent her out-of-town guests to a hotel by limo. After they'd all left, Patsy signed another copy of *All That Remains* for Margo.

"To my good friend Margo," she wrote. "There is not enough space here to thank you for all that you do, or to say how much I enjoy you! Love, Patsy."

By the time she and Margo got to bed, it was close to midnight, and Patsy was worn out.

They started making love, but Patsy kept drifting off.

"I'm sorry; I'm exhausted," Patsy said.

"That's okay."

Margo had already realized that it wasn't working between them, so she just went to sleep.

The next morning over coffee and bagels, they agreed it wasn't a good idea to try that again. They would keep their relationship strictly platonic.

Looking back later, Margo thought she might have developed deeper feelings for Patsy if they'd spent more time together.

"But it was over almost as soon as it started," she said.

If it had continued, Margo said, "Gene would have killed us both, in bed, which probably would have been condoned in Virginia."

Coupled with the diamond earrings caper, her affair with Patsy was the final push she needed to decide to leave Gene.

"It kind of awakened inside me a part of me that didn't go away," she said later. "That need to connect at that level with another woman. It made me realize that I was just fooling myself."

Chapter Six

The Divorce Battle Begins

The night in June 1992 that Margo told Gene she wanted a divorce, he suggested going to marriage counseling.

"I'll go, but it won't make any difference," she said. "It's too late."

Gene found a counselor, Julie Hoxie, and they saw her one evening after work. She asked them both what they hoped to get out of therapy.

"I'm not happy, and I want to understand her needs better," Gene said.

He sounded genuine, but Margo sensed that his statement was more for the therapist's benefit than hers, although he did seem to want to try to prevent Margo from leaving him.

"I'm here because I want to be able to dismantle this relationship in a way that causes the least pain to us and our children," she said.

At the end of the session, Julie recommended that Margo and Gene see separate therapists and said one of them could stay with her. Gene decided to find a male therapist, while Margo continued to see Julie. Over the next eight months, Julie helped her understand that the failure of the marriage wasn't hers alone and that it was okay for her to try to stand on her own two feet.

About a month into the sessions, Gene suggested they go to a matinee at the mall, leaving the kids with their nanny. Afterward, they went to the food court to talk.

"I know you're very confused and need some time to get your thoughts straight," he said. "If what you need is space, we can get you an apartment."

Margo just looked at him, so he kept talking.

"You can move into this apartment and the kids can come visit with you, but there's no way you're taking the kids with you."

"That's not what I want," she said. "What I want is to share custody of the kids."

"Well, that's not going to happen."

Seeing they had reached an impasse, they got up and went home.

"That's when I knew this divorce was never going to happen. He was just going to jerk me around," Margo later said.

When Margo next met with Betty, her new divorce attorney, she told Betty about the conversation, and Betty explained that in Virginia, parties had to live apart for a year before one of them could be granted a "no fault" divorce, regardless of whether the other party wanted it. Betty said Margo could get a divorce immediately if she could prove desertion, adultery, or physical or mental cruelty, but cruelty was hard to prove.

"If you're waiting for your husband to give you permission to divorce him, then you're going to wait a long time," Betty said.

"What am I supposed to do?"

Betty told her to wait for him to go to work one day and move out.

"I'm not leaving my kids," Margo said.

"Then you'll have to take them with you. We'll get a quick court date and have a temporary custody arrangement set up," Betty said, adding that she would file divorce papers and send a letter notifying Gene of their actions the same day that Margo left.

Betty reminded Margo to take anything important or that had sentimental value because she wasn't going to get a second chance.

Margo started looking for a rental in nearby Woodbridge, a bedroom community for government workers in DC, about seven miles from Nokesville. She also began compiling a list of items she would put in a U-Haul, such as her grandmother's handmade quilts.

In August, she found a townhouse and signed a lease effective September 1.

She planned to put her belongings into temporary storage, then sneak off with the girls while Gene was at work and hide them away for a week or two in a rented trailer at Colonial Beach, a seaside resort about seventy-five miles south, until they could get a custody hearing. Gene would never think to look for them there.

"If Gene knew where I was, then he would come and physically take the kids from me," she later said.

Margo told the girls' nanny, Brenda Sue Nuss, about her plan and asked if she wanted to come along or return home to Nebraska. Brenda, who was attending the local community college, said she wanted to help the kids through the transition. While Margo was away visiting her parents in Tuscaloosa over Labor Day weekend, Brenda agreed to quietly take some of the girls' toys and other things over to the townhouse.

Meanwhile, Margo went to the Nations Bank branch office at Quantico, where she thought she would have some degree of privacy, and set up a new account in her name. She and Gene already had a joint account with the bank, but he did his transactions at the branch near the supermarket in Woodbridge.

Margo set it up so that her paycheck would be directly deposited into the new account, rather than the one she shared with Gene. She asked John Hess to take that same amount from her new account and deposit it into the joint account while she was in Tuscaloosa. Figuring that Gene would freeze her out of those accounts as soon as she'd moved out, she also asked John to deposit a check for $18,000 out of one of their money market accounts, which was half the balance of their savings.

Margo told John she didn't think it was safe to leave the Bennetts' financial records, which included the real estate documents

Gene had dummied up for the home relocation scam, in her desk. So before she left for the weekend, she moved them into John's filing cabinet.

Margo and the girls arrived in Tuscaloosa the Thursday before Labor Day weekend. She and her mother talked while they were fixing dinner that night.

"Mom, I'm not happy, and I'm going to leave Gene."

Dean was quiet for a minute, then said, "I want you to be happy. What are you going to do?"

Margo laid out the escape plan for her matter-of-factly.

"Are you going to be okay?" Dean asked.

"Yes, I think everything is going to be fine."

After dinner, Margo went out to her father's woodworking shop to fill him in, too.

"You know, I always felt that something was missing with you and Gene," he said.

"Yeah, real love," she said. "I've been unhappy for a long time, and I really tried to make it work."

"Well, baby, you do what you need to do."

Letta was waiting in the car to drive Margo to the airport that Sunday, when Margo came out and saw her mother crying in the driveway. She gave Dean a hug.

"Mom, everything is going to be fine," she said again.

"I'm just so worried that someone's going to get hurt."

Margo was puzzled. Gene had never threatened to hurt her. She figured her mother was simply being overprotective.

Gene picked Margo up at the airport, and on the way back, he told her that Brenda had gotten a call from her brother, who was in some kind of trouble, so she'd flown out to help him. Margo saw no reason to doubt what he said and hoped that everything was okay. Brenda's sudden departure put a crimp in her plans; she hoped Brenda would be back in time to help her slip away.

Margo and Gene spent Monday cleaning out the garage, but there was still no sign of Brenda.

Margo got to Quantico around 8:30 AM on Tuesday, and as soon as she sat down at her desk, she knew something was wrong.

The framed photo of her and Patsy at the Globe & Laurel, which normally sat on the rear left side of her desk, was missing. She pulled open the top drawer and found that the Mont Blanc pen Patsy had given her was gone, too. So were the thank-you cards from her students.

She immediately suspected that Gene had rifled through her desk over the weekend, but before she had a chance to tell anyone, her phone rang. It was Peggy, one of the tellers at her bank at Quantico, and she sounded concerned.

"Margo, something strange is going on," she said.

Peggy explained that Gene had asked to speak to the Woodbridge bank manager on Friday about the new account Margo had opened. He said Margo had set it up for both of them because they'd "messed up" their joint account, but he couldn't access it because Margo had left town without leaving the signature card for him to sign. The manager pulled up the new account, and Gene asked her how many checks had been drawn on it. When she realized she may have said too much, she told him she needed to have Margo present to say anything more, and immediately called Peggy.

"Did he get copies of the bank records?" Margo asked.

"No."

"Thank you," she said. "I appreciate it."

Margo's stomach was in knots. She was pretty sure he'd figured out her plan, or was at least suspicious of it. The unknown factor was Brenda.

Margo called Brenda's mother, who had no idea where her daughter was, but said her son was not in any trouble as far as she knew. After talking to her son, she called back to say they were both worried now because neither of them had heard from Brenda.

Margo called Gene and told him she thought something had happened to their nanny.

"Maybe she's in trouble and she's off getting an abortion somewhere," he said. "It's not our place to get involved."

Learning more about Brenda's disappearance and Gene's meddling at the bank had only heightened Margo's anxiety. By that point, she was scared to go home.

Katie Land, one of her former students, who was assigned to the Richmond field office, was taking an in-service class at the academy that week, so Margo asked if she would stay the night at the Bennetts' house. They worked out a story for Gene—that Katie was in the area working surveillance—and planned for her to arrive about an hour after Margo.

When Margo got home, Gene was in the living room, hiding behind the newspaper in his easy chair, and didn't look up. She went to look for the girls and started to panic when she couldn't find them anywhere.

"Where are the girls?" she asked.

"I don't know," he said, still hiding behind the newspaper. "How does it feel not knowing where your kids are?"

Margo finally found them laughing behind the bed in Lindsey's room, where Gene had told them to play a game of Hide from Mommy.

Margo took them downstairs, where she started fixing a dinner of tuna salad and rolls. Gene joined them in the kitchen.

"How does it feel not knowing where your kids are?" he asked again.

When Katie arrived, she put her gun on top of the fridge next to Margo's. The Bennetts always put their weapons there, out of the children's reach.

They'd just sat down to eat at the kitchen table when the doorbell rang. Margo opened the door to find a man in a tacky plaid jacket, holding some folded-up papers.

"Are you Marguerite Bennett?" he asked.

"Yes, I am."

The man handed her the papers and said, "Have a nice evening."

Gene had served her with divorce papers, accusing her of abandonment and desertion. Margo saw the girls standing on the stairs, looking at her, confused about what was going on, so she started toward them.

Gene met her at the foot of the stairs, leaned into her face and growled, "Did you think for a minute that I was going to allow you to take my children away from me?"

Margo took the girls upstairs, then came back to the kitchen table. She was reading the papers when Brenda knocked at the back door. Gene unlocked it, then followed Brenda into the kitchen. She looked frazzled and pale as she mouthed to Margo, "He knows everything."

Gene told Brenda her parents were looking for her and said she could use the phone upstairs in the bedroom to call them. Brenda did as she was told, then retreated to her basement apartment.

Gene switched his attention back to Katie. "How dare you act like our friend and break bread at our table," he said. "Do you think I didn't call and check? I knew you didn't have to be up here."

Katie just sat there. She correctly assumed that the best way to deal with Gene was to say nothing.

Gene started disassembling Katie's gun into pieces—the spring, the slide, the frame, the barrel, and the magazine—and took them into the front yard. Margo could see him through the open garage door, throwing the bullets into the surrounding wooded area. He came back inside, handed Katie the pieces of her gun, and said, "Get the hell out of my house."

"She doesn't have to leave if she doesn't want to," Margo said. "If she wants to stay, she can stay."

But Margo could see that Katie was uncomfortable being in the middle of such a volatile domestic situation, especially when it involved two highly trained FBI agents who had guns within easy reach. So Margo told her she could go if she wanted, and walked her outside to her car.

Katie sped back to the academy, where she immediately called John Hess.

Meanwhile, Gene had taken Margo's house keys and removed her gun from the top of the refrigerator. He told her he'd locked her weapon away in the safe upstairs, along with her FBI-issued gun, and then changed the combination so she couldn't get into it.

Margo went upstairs to give the girls a bath and put them to bed. Afterward, she was walking by Gene's office and heard him talking on the phone, so she stopped to listen.

"Your daughter was going to take my kids," he was saying. "Can you believe that?"

"Why are you talking to my parents?" Margo asked.

Gene ignored her.

"I want to talk to my parents," she said.

"I'll let you talk to them when I'm done."

When Gene decided to give up control of the phone, Margo tried to calm her mother, who was in tears and sounded very fearful.

"It's okay, Mom," she said, trying to reassure her, but the damage had already been done.

John Hess called around nine, and Gene answered. John said he wanted to hear Gene say he wasn't going to hurt Margo.

"I'm not going to do anything like that," Gene said, explaining that Margo had tried to steal his kids.

"Can you believe what she was going to do to me?" he asked.

John later told Margo that he thought about calling the police as soon as he hung up, but he determined it might only escalate the situation, so he didn't.

Gene spent the rest of the night screaming at Margo, belittling her about what a horrible mother she was, how she didn't care about the kids, how she was a horrible housekeeper, and how bad she was in bed.

"You're a dried-up, flat-chested whore," he said. "I'm going to ruin you. You will have nothing. How dare you think about taking my children! Who in the hell do you think you are, you stupid cunt?"

Allison, who was about to turn six, and Lindsey, who was almost three, stayed upstairs, where Allison would always remember telling Lindsey to hide in her toy chest, a plastic green tub with a red top, to try to shield the toddler from all the yelling.

Anywhere Margo went in the house that night, Gene was right there with her.

"How stupid did you think I was?" he demanded. "And how stupid are you to think that you can get away with this?"

Margo started washing dishes, trying to shut out Gene's voice.

"Now you want to clean the house?" he said.

"I have always cleaned the house," she said quietly.

Margo was feeling somewhat defiant, determined not to crack. She knew he wanted her to cry and beg forgiveness, but she wasn't going to give him that. She also knew that the less she engaged him, the better.

After doing the dishes, she sat on the sofa, and he plopped himself down so that their bodies were touching. She scooted over, and so did he, until she was crammed into the corner, his body pushing against hers.

"You know, you're very lucky you brought the kids back and didn't leave them in Alabama," he said.

Gene explained how he'd caught Brenda trying to move some of the kid's things into the townhouse, how he'd figured out that Margo had set up the new checking account, and how he'd immediately called an attorney to beat her at her own game.

After Gene's forty-minute tirade, Margo got up to grab a pillow and blanket, then tried to curl up at the other end of the sofa so she could get some sleep. But Gene wouldn't let up.

"Oh no," he said. "You're not going to sleep tonight. I've been up for two nights making sure you couldn't do this."

He took the remote control for the TV, found a war movie, and turned up the volume.

"You're going to wake up the kids," Margo said.

Gene turned it down slightly, but every time she'd start to drift off, he'd yell at her again.

Finally, at 3 AM he went upstairs, and Margo turned off the TV, but Gene came back downstairs twice to turn it back on, taking the remote with him.

Ultimately, Margo got a couple hours of very light sleep, and when it was time to go to work, she felt barely alive.

Gene continued screaming obscenities as she was getting dressed. He said he was going to take off work for as long as it took to keep his daughters safe.

"You won't have another chance to take them," he said.

Margo stumbled into the office, her eyes bleary, her shoulders slumped, walking like a zombie.

She'd already confided in John earlier that summer about the home relocation scam, the missing ring and earrings, how Gene had swapped out the vacuum cleaner and color TV, and about his general emotional abuse. So John was not surprised to hear about the Night from Hell she'd just endured.

"Margo," he said. "You should not be covering up for this guy anymore."

Margo called her divorce attorney to tell her what had happened. Betty changed course from her previous advice and told her that she now needed to stay at the house until the court settled the custody battle, or she would fall into the trap he'd set for her by filing for divorce on the grounds of abandonment. Otherwise, she'd hurt her chances of getting shared custody of the girls. In the meantime, Betty said she'd call Gene's attorney and try to get her house keys back.

Next, John told Margo she should go talk to Tony Daniels, the top official at Quantico, and tell him that Gene had taken her keys and FBI-issued gun.

Margo went to Tony's office that morning, closed the door, and sat in a chair facing him across his rather expansive desk. She explained that she was in the process of divorce and that things had gotten a little out of hand the night before.

"He took my guns," Margo said.

"Why does he have the right to take your guns? Is he your supervisor?"

"Well, no, he has no right to take them."

"That's the point," he said.

Tony could see the fatigue on her face and heard the tension in her voice. Normally, he thought Margo appeared very self-assured, but this morning she didn't seem like herself. He was concerned about the well-being of Margo and her daughters, but he was also concerned that Gene had taken possession of FBI property without going through the proper channels.

"Where are the girls?" he asked.

"They're with him. I don't think he would hurt the kids."

Tony had never met Gene. All he knew was that Gene was the kind of undercover operator whom supervisors had to monitor closely. Tony hadn't known the Bennetts were having domestic problems, but it was not uncommon for married employees to have such disputes.

"FBI agents are people too," he said recently.

Tony recalls that Margo started to tell him about the fraud and other activities that morning, but he stopped her before she got into specifics, cautioning that he would have to report such activities to headquarters. Margo simply remembers Tony asking her to come back at three o'clock to check in, after he'd made some calls to see what he could do.

Margo went back to her office, and when John could see that she was in no condition to teach her class, volunteered to do it for her.

Just before she headed to Tony's office for their afternoon meeting, John said, "You ought to go in there and tell him what it's been like. Tell him the truth."

She knew that she had some legal "exposure" for her involvement in the home relocation scam, but she and John naively thought she wouldn't be in any trouble because she'd been coerced into it. They both figured the bureau would see that she'd had limited choices being married to Gene, with small children to care for.

After talking to Margo that morning, Tony had called the bureau's legal counsel and the firearms people at Quantico, along with Gene's supervisor and the head of the Washington field office. The consensus decision was that Gene should bring Margo's guns to Quantico, where Margo should leave them, secured, in the vault. If she brought them home, Gene had threatened to take them away again. Gene had also told his coworkers and superiors that his wife was unstable and shouldn't have access to a gun at home.

"We wanted things to cool off," Tony later recalled. "She didn't really need a gun. . . . If she'd insisted on having it, we probably would have let her take it."

Margo decided to take John's advice and tell Tony about Gene's extracurricular activities.

"Tony, I've come to the realization that I'm married to a crook, and I can't live like this any longer," she said. "He's a cheat, a liar, and a thief."

"Whoa, whoa, time out, Margo," he said.

But Tony got quiet and listened once Margo started listing specific examples—the home relocation scam, which involved Gene's informant Jerry York; insurance fraud involving the missing diamond earrings; the new color TV and vacuum cleaner; and a $100,000 investment Gene had made in Jerry's trucking business in Atlanta.

Tony was shocked to hear the allegations Margo was making about another FBI agent, but he didn't ask a lot of questions. He just treated it like any other interview and took notes to send to the Office of Professional Responsibility (OPR), an internal affairs unit that investigated allegations of wrongdoing by FBI agents.

Margo went home that night to another evening of torment.

She and Gene were arguing in the kitchen after the kids had gone to bed when they heard Lindsey screaming and crying upstairs. Margo got to Lindsey before he did. She'd had a bad dream, so Margo comforted her, tucked her back in, turned off the light, and went to leave, but Gene blocked the doorway.

"What did you do with the money?" he asked, referring to the $18,000 she'd taken from the money market account.

When she tried to squeeze by him, he picked her up and threw her on the empty bed next to Lindsey's.

"Where's the money?" he demanded. "Don't you ever push me or shove me again."

Margo got up and went downstairs to call John.

"Things are getting bad here," she said.

They discussed whether one of them should call the police, but Margo told him she thought she could deal with this on her own. This time, John called the police anyway.

Gene had overheard Margo's conversation with John, so Gene called a buddy of his to tell him that Margo had shoved him. Then he called 911.

"My wife and I are having a disagreement," he told the dispatcher. "She's getting abusive."

He listened for a minute and said, "You should know we're both FBI agents and have guns in the house."

Margo and Gene went downstairs to the living room, where they waited in silence for the police to arrive.

About ten minutes later, an officer showed up and asked Gene what had happened. Gene told him they'd been upstairs comforting Lindsey when Margo started a fight with him.

"She kept asking me, 'Where's the money?' and then she shoved me against the wall."

"What did she specifically say?" the officer asked.

Gene wasn't prepared for the question. He stuttered and said, "What did you do with the money?"

When Margo told her side of the story, she sensed that the officer knew Gene was lying, but couldn't do anything.

"Do you guys think you can go to separate parts of the house and behave for the rest of the night?" he asked.

Margo and Gene both said yes.

Unlike the previous night, Gene let her go to sleep on the couch without incident. Nonetheless, she woke up exhausted, feeling like an emotional punching bag.

Her unit chief, Ed Tully, called her into his office first thing.

"Tony's in a bind here," he said. "Based on your conversation yesterday, he is obligated to report this, unless, of course, you misspoke and he misunderstood what you said. Tony is very concerned with how this is going to affect you."

Tony and Ed were clearly trying to give Margo an out, but she was determined to proceed with what she'd started.

"The truth about Gene Bennett is going to come out, now or later, and if I take this back now, it's going to be much worse on me later."

"Is this really what you want to do?"

Margo nodded. "I made a decision. I'm not going to lie anymore. If it hurts me, then it hurts me."

Tony subsequently wrote a memorandum to David Binney, the head of OPR, officially outlining Margo's allegations and his conversations with other bureau officials about Gene.

"When questioned as to why she had waited until now to surface these allegations, SSA Bennett replied that she was trying to 'hold her marriage together' and that she was fearful of retaliation," he wrote. "She emphasized that the reason she is seeking a divorce is that she can no longer tolerate her husband's illegal and unethical activities."

That same day, Gene fired Brenda, told her to get out of the house, and put her belongings in the driveway. He called a cab to come get her, but he wouldn't let her take her things with her.

Margo later learned that while she and the girls were in Alabama, Gene had spent the weekend intimidating and frightening

Brenda into confessing Margo's escape scheme into a tape recorder. He'd told her that if she didn't fess up, he was going to call the police and have her arrested for stealing his property. Then he sent her to a hotel room, which he made her pay for, and forbade her to call Margo or her own family.

On Friday, September 11, Gene requested the help of the FBI's Employee Assistance Program and was assigned to Steve Spruill, a counselor who was Gene's contact agent on Operation Doubletalk. The program also referred Gene and Margo to a crisis counselor, with whom they met that night to set up a system of boundaries within the house so that they could coexist in an environment that was less chaotic for the girls.

At first, the counselor tried to get Margo to live in the basement, but she refused to be relegated to servant's quarters. Instead, she agreed to sleep on the couch in the living room, but to shower and get ready for work in the basement apartment.

While Gene was with the kids in the evening, Margo often went for a run, which she would spend praying, crying, and begging God for the strength to get through this ordeal. Once, when she returned from her run, she found that Gene had removed the last check out of her checkbook. She figured this was retaliation for withdrawing the $18,000 from their savings.

Margo and Gene had registered Allison at the local public school, but he wouldn't let her go because he thought Margo was going to steal her away while he was at work. For that matter, Gene refused to go to work for the next three weeks, telling his supervisor that he needed to stay home so Margo couldn't abscond with his daughters.

Margo called the school to tell them Allison would not be attending after all, which ultimately resulted in a truant officer's coming to the house and informing Gene that he could not keep Allison at home. Gene finally relented and enrolled both girls at the private Appletree Preschool, where Allison had gone the previous year. Every day, he sat outside in his car for the duration of the four-hour program.

At a September 18 hearing, a judge ordered a temporary custody arrangement that gave the girls to Margo from Saturday morning until she dropped them at school on Monday and to Gene for the rest of the week.

Margo's attorney thought it would be better not to fight Gene on this arrangement and to try to get through the divorce as quickly and with as little rancor as possible. But Margo knew that nothing was ever easy with Gene Bennett, who was taking even more joy in playing head games these days.

"I don't think any court's going to give a cunt-sucking whore like you custody of those kids," he said to her one morning, revealing for the first time his strategy to paint her as a lesbian so that he could get full custody of the girls.

"What are you talking about?" Margo asked.

Gene just smiled and walked away.

Another morning, he stood watching as she filled her travel mug with coffee. Margo noticed that it had an odd chemical smell, so she didn't drink it. She asked her colleagues to sniff it, and although they, too, noticed the strange odor, some could not accept that Gene would intentionally try to poison her.

Next, Gene complained that his Jeep wouldn't start because someone had been messing with it, and he accused her of unhooking his distributor cables to harass him. One morning she got in her car and found that someone had turned up the volume full blast on her radio, which gave her a jolt when she fired up the motor. Gene had the only other set of keys.

All these psychological tactics kept Margo off balance.

As soon as the custody arrangement went into effect in mid-October, Margo moved into the townhouse she'd rented in Woodbridge, ending thirty-seven days of domestic battle. But because she had to leave the girls with Gene, the war was far from over.

On October 22, 1992, Margo had her first interview with two agents from OPR, John Roberts and Phillip Reid, in DC.

At first, it seemed like an informal meeting, not an interrogation. She sat on a couch as the agents asked her to clarify the allegations in Tony's memo and to walk them through the home relocation scam.

"You realize you have exposure in this case," John Roberts said.

After he'd issued this warning for the third time, Margo suddenly realized what he was saying—that the bureau was not going to be as understanding as she'd initially anticipated and that she probably should talk to a lawyer.

"Look, this interview is over," she said. "I want you to understand that I am fully committed to telling the truth, but I need to seek guidance from someone first."

Margo immediately called Betty.

"I think I need an attorney," Margo said.

"I think you do too."

Betty gave Margo the name of a criminal defense attorney, but he was too busy to take her case, so he referred her to another lawyer, Brian Gettings.

Brian was in his late fifties and, after smoking for most of his life, had developed throat cancer. He'd recently undergone surgery that left a hole in his throat, which he sometimes covered with his hand when he talked. His voice always sounded hoarse, as the air whistled through his windpipe, even more so when he was tired.

When they first discussed her case, Brian was frustrated because she refused to take his advice and stop talking to the investigators.

But Margo felt that she was in a no-win situation. She'd made a commitment to herself that she wasn't going to lie anymore, and now telling the truth was causing her problems as well.

Brian finally accepted her position.

"Okay," he said. "But if this is the route you want to take, you have to let me help you."

Brian negotiated an immunity deal with OPR so that nothing Margo said during her interviews could be used against her in court as long as she agreed to help them build a case and testify against Gene if necessary. Margo fully cooperated with the investigators, providing copious documentation, much of which would have disappeared when Gene raided her desk if she hadn't moved the materials to John's filing cabinet.

Brian accompanied Margo on the three interviews she had with investigators. Federal prosecutor Marcia Isaacson also attended the interviews, which took place in the Department of Justice's Public Integrity Section in DC. Marcia, who looked slightly younger than Margo, seemed to empathize with her plight.

On December 23, Gene sent an eleven-page memo to Robert Bryant, the special agent in charge of the Washington field office, launching a counteroffensive against Margo and giving the FBI a very different version of events.

He accused her of exhibiting "peculiar behavior, odd personality swings and medical abnormalities." He also claimed she'd accused him of being "a psychotic undercover agent with multiple personalities," a claim that would prove to be wholly ironic three and a half years later.

Margo did not see this memo until her attorney gave it to her several years later as part of the divorce proceedings, but she was not surprised by its contents.

In his memo, Gene said he felt required to report a number of illegal or actionable activities on Margo's part. (He would be found guilty of committing at least two of these himself in the coming year, and, according to Margo, committed some of the others as well.) Gene accused her of falsifying bureau documents, having lesbian affairs with women in and out of the bureau before and after she joined its ranks, failing to notify the bureau that she had mononucleosis and bulimia, committing insurance fraud, stealing bureau funds, abusing illegally obtained prescription drugs, illegally wiretapping their house using FBI equipment, stealing things from their home, and failing to pay off debts.

"I approached this situation from the beginning by being honest and upfront with everyone about my personal and family

situation, as I knew it would be foolish to try to handle this situation alone," Gene wrote, commending his counselor Steve Spruill
for helping him through it.

In the midst of all this nastiness, Margo managed to have a bit
of fun on a girls' night out in November with her friend Dianna,
Patsy Cornwell, an agent who worked in the Behavioral Sciences
Unit at Quantico, and a Richmond police officer.

Since the night of Patsy's book party in July, she and Margo
had been chatting once or twice a month, either by phone or when
they'd run into each other at Quantico.

Patsy wanted to do something nice for Margo's birthday, so she
had them all meet at her house, where she had each of them wear
something of hers. One wore her mink stole, Margo sported one of
her jackets, and Dianna put on her sapphire necklace.

Patsy had rented a limo for the night and poured each of them
a glass of champagne as they were driving to dinner at Ruth's Chris
Steak House.

"You deserve to have a good time tonight," she said to Margo.
"You've been through so much crap."

Patsy had just returned from a trip to Hollywood, where she'd
been trying to drum up interest in making a movie based on her
books. Patsy suggested they stop at Blockbuster Video to rent Eyes
of Laura Mars, starring Faye Dunaway, whom Patsy was courting
to play the role of Dr. Kay Scarpetta, along with Demi Moore
and Jodie Foster. Patsy really had a thing for Jodie Foster and was
frustrated that she couldn't seem to finagle a meeting with the
two-time Oscar winner.

Patsy, who was in a bit of a manic mood that night, decided to
call Faye Dunaway from the limo. She couldn't reach her, so she
left her a message.

When Margo first met Patsy, she seemed down to earth. But
Margo sensed that her friend was getting caught up in a frenzy
and was losing her equilibrium, which sometimes caused bizarre
behavior. Several months later, Patsy told her about the day she

drank Bloody Marys, followed by wine with dinner, then flipped her Mercedes on the Pacific Coast Highway in Malibu. Margo was worried that her friend was spinning out of control, with no one to ground her. Patsy was ultimately diagnosed as bipolar.

After dinner and more drinks on Margo's birthday, they piled back into the limo and went to a nightclub, where they danced with each other and puffed on the little cigars that Patsy liked to smoke, another affectation of the Greta Garbo image she was cultivating at the time.

They stayed over at Patsy's, where Margo slept on the large U-shaped couch. Patsy left for a while, then came back with a woman and waved at Margo in the darkness as the two of them went into her bedroom.

Margo felt no jealousy. She and Patsy had turned the corner and were comfortable being just friends. She was happy for Patsy that she was so successful and had so much money to spend on limos and the best steak house, and to lease cars and buy clothes for her friends. But Margo had come to realize that they wanted different things out of life. Margo didn't want or need all that flash. She also didn't want to be one of the leeches she saw clinging to Patsy.

"I realized that we weren't compatible anyway, and that was OK. We could still be friends," she said later.

By the next morning, Patsy's two miniature dachshunds had pulled her mink stole into their crate and shredded it, but Patsy just laughed and shrugged it off.

In early December, Patsy brought Demi Moore to Quantico, calling Margo in advance to arrange a tour and get them single rooms in the Jefferson Building.

They ended up in the Board Room that night, which was filled with police chiefs, lieutenants, and assistant chiefs who were attending the National Academy. After the women had been sitting in the corner for about fifteen minutes, some of the men started coming over and asking if the dark-haired woman was really Demi Moore.

Demi was worried that she wasn't going to be able to get out of the bar without being mobbed by drunken men, so she and Patsy sneaked out while Margo stood guard in the doorway, stopping the men and asking them to leave Demi alone. By the time she managed to leave the bar, Demi and Patsy had gotten themselves stuck in the elevator.

Apparently, Patsy had been eager to get back to her room, so she'd hit one button at the same time that Demi, who'd wanted to wait for Margo, had hit another one.

"We're getting a little nervous," Patsy said through the doors. "Demi doesn't like being in here."

"It's okay, relax, we'll have you out of there in no time," Margo called to them, then left to alert security.

The women were released within ten minutes.

Around the same time, Patsy threw out a suggestion that Margo leave the FBI to come work for her.

"I could really use someone with your experience, taking care of my security," she said.

"There's no way you could afford me," Margo replied.

"How much are you making?"

"$86,000."

"Wow, you're right, I can't afford you," Patsy said, chuckling.

Patsy told Margo she wanted to make her a ring out of the gold coin-shaped award the bureau had given Margo in 1991 for her ten-year anniversary. Margo agreed and received the gold ring as a Christmas present from Patsy. But it felt so heavy and masculine on Margo's hand that she couldn't wear it.

On March 24, 1993, Brian Gettings called Margo to tell her that a federal grand jury had indicted Gene, along with Jerry and

Brenda York, in the home relocation scam. Gene, who was indicted for conspiracy and theft of government property, entered a plea of not guilty and was released on his own recognizance.

Margo knew this was coming, but she dreaded the thought of having to get up on the stand and dredge up the whole mess in public.

"Even though I was committed to getting all of this behind me, I knew it wasn't going to be pleasant," she later said.

The next day, the bureau placed Gene on administrative leave.

Gene sought counseling for six months from psychiatrist Alen Salerian, who later mentioned his former client in an op-ed piece he wrote for the *Washington Post* in 2001, with the headline "Diagnosis Missing: The FBI Should Monitor Its Agents' Mental Health."

"Bennett clearly knew he was in trouble," he wrote. "Like any good spy, he had done his homework—checked out my background and security clearance, concluded that he could confide in me. Also true to form, he maintained outward control: When he called me, his voice was a monotone, his words cryptic. And during our meetings, his face would remain expressionless. . . . I can say he was a dangerously volatile character."

The bureau suspended Gene from its rolls on June 11, 1993.

On the night of Thursday, June 17, Gene called Margo to say he needed to change the time for her to pick up the girls that Saturday from 9:30 AM to 7:30 AM because he had an early meeting with his attorney. His trial was set to start the following Tuesday.

For about six weeks, Margo had been bringing Dianna along when she picked up the girls so that she didn't have to face Gene alone. However, because 7:30 was such an early hour, she decided not to bother her friend that week.

Later, in retrospect, she chided herself for not realizing that on this weekend, above all others, she should have had her guard up. She knew better than to forget that Gene never did anything without a reason.

Chapter Seven

Abduction

Margo arrived at the Nokesville house on June 19 at 7:30 AM as arranged. The sun had already burned off the haze that often hung over the woods behind the house at daybreak, and the sky was the perfect bright blue for a lazy Saturday with no real plans.

She was looking forward to a relaxing day with her daughters after weeks of endless meetings with prosecutors to prepare her testimony against Gene at his trial. Maybe she'd take the girls to the park or to the playground with Daisy, their new fourteen-week-old miniature dachshund. She opened the trunk of her Geo Prizm, letting Daisy roam as far as the leash would take her, and waited for Gene to come out of the garage with the girls' backpacks.

Some months ago, Gene had changed the Saturday pickup routine by bringing out the girls and their stuff in separate trips. He'd raise the garage door, hand the backpacks to Margo, head back into the garage, lower the door, then open it a second time to bring the girls out. This seemingly inefficient practice, she later realized, was to train her not to be surprised or alarmed when the door opened and he came out with just the backpacks.

On this beautiful June morning, Gene opened the garage and sauntered over to her with a pack in each hand, giving off his usual air of superiority and disdain. Gene made as if he were going to hand them to her, but instead, he dropped them on the driveway, revealing a blue plastic taser, slightly larger than a pack of cigarettes, in his right hand. He'd shown it to her once years before, describing it as a toy dating back to his Army days, when he'd spent several years working for the Criminal Investigation

Division. But she now knew what it was—a device used mostly by correctional officers to incapacitate prisoners by temporarily turning their muscles to mush.

Margo didn't have time to think before her body instinctively started to run up the inclined slope of the driveway toward the street, letting go of the puppy in the process. But she barely got two steps away when she felt Gene grab the back of her T-shirt and get a hold of her arm. He pulled her body against his side and dragged her into the garage as she twisted and kicked, trying to get away.

Once he got her inside, he picked her up and slammed her body onto the cement. Her upper back and shoulders hit first, landing between his Jeep Cherokee and the garage door. With the adrenaline rushing into her system, she didn't feel any pain from the impact, although fist-size bruises erupted later on each shoulder and smaller ones along the middle of her spine.

Her thoughts were focused mainly on trying to escape. She wasn't worried about the girls because she figured they weren't home; Gene would never risk letting them see this.

Go, go, go, she told herself. You've got to get out of here.

She tried to scream, but no sound came out. It was like a bad dream, the kind where her vocal chords constricted, but her voice would not respond.

Gene was twice her size, but she was putting up a good fight. He had to lie on top of her to pin her to the floor. As she arched up against him, he wrapped his legs over hers, shifting his upper body so that he could trap her head in the crook of his arm.

Suddenly, Margo saw the garage door start to roll down toward the cement floor. Gene must have grabbed the remote while they were struggling. Somehow, with a Herculean twist and pull, she got one leg free of his grip and kicked wildly at the rubber safety strip on the bottom of the door. If she couldn't get her foot on that strip, she knew she was in big trouble. With the door closed, there would be no chance for anyone to hear her calls for help, let alone see what Gene was doing to her.

She sensed her foot making contact with the safety strip and felt a small but temporary victory as the door began inching its way back up. Finally, she found her voice.

"Gene don't do this," she said hoarsely. "Don't do this. Don't do this."

Gene said nothing. He dropped the taser, scrambled for the remote, which had skittered across the floor, and hit the button once more. As the door started coming down again, he grabbed the taser and shot her above the right eye, sending at least fifty thousand volts through her skull.

Margo heard a loud buzzing as the dizzying jolt shot into her brain. She felt confused and off balance as she thrashed around.

He shot her again, twice on the crown of the head and once a little over to the side.

She'd lost count by the fourth or fifth jolt. Her head was throbbing now, and she knew she couldn't withstand another huge electrical charge. Finally, she let her body go limp.

As she lay flat on her stomach, her cheek resting on the cool cement floor, Gene wrenched her arms behind her and snapped on a set of handcuffs, pinching a nerve that would cause her thumb to remain numb for six weeks. Then he rolled her over and pulled her to her feet.

"Now we're going to have a talk," he said.

Taking her by the shoulders, he lugged her up the four steps that led into the kitchen. Margo stumbled, feeling disoriented, weak-kneed, and depleted of every ounce of fight she'd once possessed. He pushed her shoulders down toward the floor and her face into the cream-colored tiles.

"Gene, why are you doing this? Please don't do this," she pleaded. "Please don't do this."

Gene got up and started moving around the kitchen, but all she could see were his tennis shoes and white ankle-high athletic socks.

"There's some people who want to talk to you," he said. "They're not happy with the mess you've caused. Ralph's probation is going to be revoked unless his girlfriend testifies that we never lived at the house."

Margo assumed he meant Ralph, the boyfriend of Brenda York's sister, Jeanette, and by "some people," he meant Jerry York and his associates. Gene said "they" were not happy with the trouble Margo had caused over the scam involving the Lake Capri house and wanted to talk to her. He didn't elaborate, but this gave Margo some hope. She had to be alive to talk to these people.

"Where are the kids?"

"They're asleep upstairs. I'm going to bring them down here and tell them exactly what their mother has done," he said, referring to turning him in to the FBI for fraud.

Margo still didn't believe he would do this to her with the girls around, so she figured they had to be somewhere else. The question was where.

Gene was a frenzy of movement as he talked, although much of what he said made no sense. It felt like pure chaos. If he was trying to keep her off kilter, he was definitely succeeding. Gene paced from one counter to another, then stooped down and started frisking her through the side pockets of her white sweat shorts.

"Are you trying to shoot me?" he screamed. "Where's your gun?"

Obviously, he could see that she had no place to put a gun. She wasn't even wearing a fanny pack, where agents often carried their weapons. And why was he yelling at her like that? She wondered if he was going to shoot her and then tell the authorities he'd acted in self-defense because he'd thought she had a gun.

"Are you going to kill me?" she asked, her voice tinged with fear and bewilderment. She hoped she could reason with him, understand what he was doing. Didn't he love her once?

"You're not worth killing," he said flatly. "You're not worth the bullet it would take to put in your head. If I was going to kill you, I would've done it before the indictment. In a couple hours, this will be over."

Gene started to calm down as he meticulously bound her ankles and knees together, first with a bandanna, next with an Ace bandage, and then with multiple layers of duct tape; she later realized that he had used the padding to avoid leaving any sticky residue on her skin as evidence of the abduction.

"I have something pretty for you," he said, dropping a heavy canvas belt on the floor next to her face.

It was a yellow bellyband, a belt typically used to restrain criminal defendants for safe transport by keeping their arms secured at the hip, each wrist attached to a ring by a separate set of handcuffs. He kneeled down and rolled her over so that he could get the band under her. He attached her wrists, then closed the band in the back with a Velcro fastener.

Unable to move, she felt completely helpless. His surprise attack had caused her to fall back into the mental space of doing what he said to avoid making him more angry.

He's going to kill me, she thought.

Gene picked up the phone, which was on the kitchen counter, and punched in some numbers. It sounded like he was calling 911.

"Somebody's trying to kill me," he said, his words clipped, as if he didn't have much time to talk. "I need help."

It didn't register with her at the time, but Gene was doing his usual number again, anticipating the allegations she would make against him and claiming that he was the true victim. Nonetheless, she figured she'd be safe if the police came and caught him trying to kill her.

He paused, as if he were listening to the dispatcher, then said, "Can you send someone right away?" He paused again. "I'll lay the phone down," he said, setting the receiver down on the counter. He never gave the address, and Margo later realized that there probably hadn't been anyone on the other end of the line; the "call" was just another ploy to confuse her.

Gene wet a paper towel and wiped her forehead where he'd hit her with the taser. The spot must have been bleeding because a triangular scab eventually formed there.

"We don't want you to look messy," Gene said patronizingly, as if he were getting a child ready for church.

After that, he went into the garage, leaving the door open so that he could keep tabs on her. Margo heard scuffling sounds, as if he were trying to catch the puppy. Meanwhile, she wriggled around on the floor, testing to see if she could stand up. But it was no use.

Gene must have heard her handcuffs rattling against the tile because he charged back into the kitchen.

"If you try to get up again, I'll put a bullet in your head," he said. "Frankly, Margo, I don't care what happens to you."

Margo knew there were about thirty-five guns in the house. Aside from the sixteen her father had given them for safekeeping a year before she and Gene had separated, there were the machine gun, revolvers, semiautomatic pistols, shotguns, and rifles that Gene had collected over the years. If he didn't have a weapon within reach on the counter, all he had to do was go upstairs to the office safe and get one.

Gene went back into the garage and returned a few minutes later to grab her car keys from her shorts pocket. He pulled her to her feet, then guided her back down the steps to the garage. She could manage only slow little hops.

He pointed to a large sheet of plastic that was bunched up in a heap by the Jeep.

"That's what they wanted me to wrap you in," he said.

Clearly, he was talking about her dead body. The only reason he would wrap her in plastic would be to prevent her blood and other bodily fluids from making a mess.

Gene had backed her car up so that it was parallel to the garage door. The trunk was open, and he told her he was going to put her inside. She figured he was going to take her somewhere to die. If he wasn't going to kill her, then Jerry York would.

Gene sat her on the back rim of the trunk, then swung her legs up and turned her body so that he could lower her in. He laid her on her side with her head facing the rear of the car, rolled up a lavender bandanna, and tied it around her mouth. Then, without another word, he slammed the trunk lid down.

Margo's world went completely dark, but that only heightened her other senses. The air was heavy and still and smelled of rubber from the spare tire. The carpeted floor was scratchy and rough on her face. It was going to be an eighty-degree day, and by 8:30 AM, the temperature was already well on its way up.

Margo felt him pull out of the driveway and start driving as she slowly adjusted to the reality that she'd never see her children again. She'd never watch them graduate from high school, get married, or have families of their own. Not only that, but they would have to grow up without a mother.

She started praying that God would show her a way out of this horrific situation, because she couldn't see one for herself. She felt lost and defeated, which were new feelings for her. She'd always considered herself a pretty capable person, tough even. Certainly all her law enforcement training had instilled the technical skills to fight back, but she'd always possessed the determination and stamina not to give up. Somehow Gene had found a way to break through all that.

At one point, she heard him open a door and drop something into the bushes, then heard the crinkling of leaves. Later, Gene told her he'd stopped to throw the puppy out into the woods. Rather than tell the girls the truth about their father, Margo would later say she'd lost Daisy.

After driving on the highway for forty-five minutes, he pulled off, opened the trunk, and told her to roll over and face the other way.

"Ralph's watching the car," he warned, then slammed the lid again.

"If she makes any noise, drive her off a fucking cliff," he shouted to someone, whom she figured was Ralph. Throughout her ordeal, however, she never heard another voice but Gene's.

He stopped a third time for gas and then, after she'd pleaded with him to stop because she was going to throw up or pass out, he pulled over one more time to give her some fresh air.

Once they arrived at their final destination, Gene opened the trunk and pulled the gag away from her mouth. She couldn't see anything from her vantage point but him, standing against a blue sky.

"Here's the deal," he said. "They've got the kids."

"Who's got the kids?"

"Jerry and Brenda. If we don't do exactly what they want, we'll never see the girls again."

At that point he had her. She knew that Jerry was an ex-con and that he, Brenda, and Gene had been indicted in the home relocation scam, so what would the Yorks have to lose by kidnapping the girls if it saved Jerry from going back to prison? She believed Gene and was willing to do whatever he said.

"What do you want me to do?"

"I've got to get you in the van," he said.

She was a little perplexed because she'd left the van, which became hers in the separation, at Quantico. It hadn't been running very well, so she preferred driving the Prizm.

Gene looked down and noticed that she'd torn the tape around her ankles.

"You got your ankles undone," he said with surprise. "Well, it doesn't matter."

He helped her out of the trunk, feet first. Feeling light-headed, she was able to get only a quick glimpse of her surroundings. They were parked next to the van in a large, empty lot, surrounded by red brick buildings. She didn't recognize the area, but because it was deserted, she thought they were probably somewhere in downtown DC.

A white sheet covered the van's back bench, where he had her lie on her side while he sat on the floor, facing her.

For about thirty minutes, he talked and she listened. What he told her only increased her emotional buy-in that he, too, was a victim in this mess.

He said the Yorks had come over to the house Friday night. Brenda told him she was taking the girls out for a Slurpee while Jerry took him for a ride somewhere to talk. But Brenda, he said, never came back with the girls, and he got "busted up" in the ribs and knees by two "professionals" who worked with Jerry. Considering how hard Gene had fought Margo, she figured he was exaggerating. But it sounded as if Jerry had set him up to be jumped so as to prove that "they" meant business.

"We need to call the police," Margo said.

"If we call the police, they'll walk away and we'll never see the kids again."

Gene said Jerry didn't want to hurt the kids, but he wasn't willing to go back to jail. "Everybody" thought Margo was the key witness in the fraud case, so they didn't want her to show up in court. If Margo wouldn't agree not to testify, Jerry told him, "they" would have to kill her.

"If there's no other way to save the kids, then you should go ahead and kill me," Margo said.

"They said I could shoot you in the head and make it look like a suicide," Gene said. "But now you're all banged up, and I can't do that. I can't kill the mother of my children."

He paused. "Frankly, Margo, you can shoot me to save the kids if that's what it takes, because they're the most important thing."

At the time, Margo thought he really meant it.

"When this is over, Jerry and Brenda are dead," he said. "I will hunt them down."

"I'll be there to help," Margo said, exhausted and befuddled.

Gene loosened the handcuffs because they were hurting her. Then, after rewrapping her ankles with tape, he threaded the seat belts between her legs and clicked them shut, wrapping tape around the latch. He pulled off another piece and went to put it over her eyes.

"Please don't do that," she said.

Gene reached for another bandanna instead. Then he repositioned the gag over her mouth and told her not to move around in the van.

"If they see anything out of the ordinary, they'll just leave, and we'll never see the kids again," he said.

Gene said he was late for his appointment with his attorney and had to go. It was about 9:30 AM.

For the next several hours, Margo felt woozy, sweating profusely as the sun beat down on the van, which grew hotter and muggier by the minute. She felt stiff and crampy from being all tied up. Her upper back hurt where Gene had thrown her down on the concrete. Her wrists were sore from the handcuffs, and her thumb had gone numb.

As she went in and out of consciousness, she wondered what she was going to have to do to keep the kids safe. When she felt she had to shift her body, she tried to do it gently, because the handcuffs kept rattling, and she didn't want to anger whoever was watching the van.

Gene came back a few hours later with a hot can of Sprite, which apparently had been riding around in his car. He didn't detach the handcuffs from her bellyband or remove her blindfold, so she had to bend over to take small sips while he told her how mad at himself he was for letting Brenda take the kids. He sounded as if he were crying.

"I let them go," he said, his voice cracking.

He checked her bindings and told her that "they" had ordered him to remove her watch because it beeped on the hour. He also said they had offered him two options: he could either kill her or hide her on a boat until the trial was over.

"You can go ahead and shoot me. Just don't put me on a boat. I won't make it on a boat," she said, thinking they would leave her there to die.

Gene tried to calm her down: "They haven't decided what they're going to do yet," he said.

Then he left.

Ever since she'd moved out of the house, she'd gotten used to thinking of the girls as "her" daughters. But over the past few hours, the girls had become "theirs" once again because she and Gene shared the common goal of rescuing them. The soft drink seemed to have revived her a bit, and she wondered if she was going to die or if Gene was going to keep her in the van until the trial was over.

Eight years earlier, in summer 1985, Margo had taken a two-week seminar on hostage negotiations at Quantico.

Within a couple of weeks, she was able to exercise her new skills as the secondary, or backup, negotiator on a plane hijacking case. In such cases, the primary negotiator generally talks to the suspect, while the backup feeds him or her information and tracks what's been said, sometimes making suggestions and also taking over when the primary negotiator needs a break.

Judson Dean Talley had just gotten out of the military and had drunk quite a bit on the plane. He told the flight attendant he had a bomb in his carry-on bag and wanted to hijack the aircraft, but he didn't say why. The Delta pilot landed in Atlanta as scheduled, then let the FBI take over.

When the primary negotiator asked Talley to explain his motivation, Talley said he was upset that his girlfriend had just broken up with him. However, he didn't make any demands that the agents could respond to, which made it more difficult to negotiate with him. He had no plan.

The primary negotiator stirred up the hijacker by repeatedly calling him Judson, when he wanted to be called Dean. So Margo took over, used the name that he'd requested, and later earned kudos and a bonus check for her role in getting the passengers and then the flight crew safely off the plane.

"The goal was to get him to focus on the here and now and how to resolve the issues, not to dwell on those things that made him angry or fall apart," Margo said later.

After double-teaming Talley, they persuaded him to surrender so that they could get him the help he needed. Talley, who was in his twenties, came down the stairs in a cocky stance. But when he reached the tarmac, a SWAT team member knocked his legs out from under him, threw him to the ground, handcuffed him, and took him to jail.

During her hostage negotiations training, Margo had been taught to be aware of Stockholm syndrome, in which captives develop a bond with their captors. But while she was tied up and blindfolded in that hot van, waiting for Gene to return with news of their children, she didn't realize that she was exhibiting textbook symptoms.

Gene seemed to be in good spirits upon his return around six o'clock.

This time, he brought her a hot can of Coke, but it still tasted good. He also brought her a mini Reese's Peanut Butter Cup and a couple of small hard candies. She wasn't hungry for real food, even though the last thing she'd eaten was a hamburger and chips at a neighborhood cookout almost twenty-four hours earlier.

"Two cars are in the lot watching us. They told me to keep you healthy and mark free," he said.

He also told her "they" had let him talk to the kids.

Margo noticed that "they" had now become a separate and distinct entity from Jerry and Brenda. Gene said he could hear water splashing when they let him talk to Allison and Lindsey on the phone, so he thought the kids were at a pool somewhere. Allison, he said, told him she and her sister were "on vacation" and assured him that they were using plenty of sunscreen.

Margo felt a little relief. At least the kids were okay for the moment.

"Why can't we call in the FBI?" Margo asked.

"If we call the anyone, they'll just leave, and we'll never see the kids again."

They started talking about their lives together, the breakup of their marriage, and how they'd gotten into this mess.

"I don't know how our lives got so off track when what we should have been doing is helping our kids get through this," he said, referring to the divorce.

Margo agreed. "It's not right that our kids are being torn apart," she said. "They ought to have parents who can sit down and have a meal together."

"Are you saying you want to get back together?"

"No," she said firmly. "What I want is a healthier relationship between us for the sake of the kids."

If they both got through this ordeal alive, she thought the kids deserved better than to see their parents fighting all the time.

Then Gene asked a question he'd obviously been wanting to ask for months.

"What about Patsy?"

Margo knew how jealous he'd been, but she wanted to tell him that she didn't want a divorce so she could be with Patsy, that their affair didn't mean she was gay, and that there weren't going to be any other women in the future. At the time, this was what she believed.

"I was only with her twice," she said.

"Okay," Gene said, as if he had accepted it.

Looking back later, Margo suspected that Gene had been fishing for even the smallest confirmation so that he could use it against her in the divorce.

Gene told her he was going to leave the Prizm at Quantico so that it would look like she'd swapped cars. Then he was going to drive his truck to the Nokesville house and come back for her in his Jeep.

"I have to wait until dark before I can move you," he said.

Margo hadn't been to the bathroom all day. About three hours after he'd left, she couldn't wait any longer. Her movement was limited because of the handcuffs, but she was able to inch her pants down slowly and bunch up the sheet so it was under her. After she relieved herself, she pushed the sheet onto the floor so she didn't have to lie in her own urine.

Gene finally showed up around 1 AM.

"There was a bad accident that stopped traffic," he said.

He cut the tape off her ankles, but left the other bindings in place. Then he put her, still blindfolded, onto the backseat of the Jeep with a water bottle and some saltine crackers, covering her with a tarp. They arrived in Nokesville about an hour later.

Gene let her go into the bathroom by herself, then took her upstairs and told her to lie on a quilt he'd laid on the closet floor. After he turned out the light and shut the door, Margo could hear him lie down just outside. She woke up every time he rolled over or her handcuffs clinked together.

The next morning, she heard Gene washing at the sink.

"My knees hurt," she said when he opened the closet door. The Ace bandage had slipped down, and her skin had been rubbed raw.

Gene had her roll onto her side so that he could cut the duct tape, and in so doing scratched her on the back of her thigh with the scissors, deep enough to draw blood, which he mopped with a tissue.

"Your feet smell," he said, coming back with clean pairs of socks.

Then he rewrapped the Ace bandage, fastened it with new tape, and put her back in the Jeep, retying the gag and blindfold. He had her back in the van before he ran off to a 9 AM meeting with his attorney, leaving her a plastic water bottle with a straw and a big box of graham crackers shaped like teddy bears.

"I'll try to get back at noon," he said.

Gene didn't return until six that evening, when he removed her gag so that they could talk about his upcoming trial.

"I'll lie on the stand if you need me to," Margo volunteered.

Gene left again briefly, then came back saying he'd just talked to "them."

"They've given us three choices: we can tuck you away until the trial is over. You can get up on the stand and lie. Or I can put a bullet in your head."

"I can lie on the stand. I know I can do that," Margo said, trying to convince him.

Gene drove them to a smaller parking lot nearby. Then he took off all her bindings and removed the blindfold. The van clock read eight.

Gene told Margo to follow him in the van, while he drove the Jeep. He gave her only a minute or two to stretch, which wasn't enough. It hurt just to stand up straight. After being bound, gagged, dehydrated, and starved for two days, she wasn't sure she could move her limbs enough to drive at all.

Around eleven, they stopped at a Chevron station in Wood-bridge, where Gene told Margo to withdraw $150 from the nearby ATM. From there, they went to her townhouse, where he asked whom she was planning to see the next day. He instructed her to leave messages for each of them, specifying what innocent explanations she should offer for why she was bruised, scraped, and cut up, or not coming to meet them.

Margo did as she was told; she didn't feel that she had the freedom to question Gene's directives. She later realized that he'd told her to make the calls so that no one would believe her if she tried to claim that he'd caused the injuries.

"I may be late for tomorrow's meeting because I was out jogging and fell down, but I'll be there," she said in messages she left for her attorney Brian Gettings and prosecutor Marcia Isaacson.

"The kids aren't going to be at school tomorrow," she said in her message to Nancy Waugh, who ran her kids' nursery school but was also a friend. "Gene has the kids, and we've swapped week-ends."

She also called and left a message for John Hess, with whom she was supposed to team-teach a course that week, then made a reservation for that night at the Keybridge Marriott in Arlington, Virginia.

Gene told her to gather up the clothes she'd need for the week. Because she thought she'd be testifying on Tuesday, she brought her best blue linen Jones New York suit and, for her meetings on Monday, a green one she also liked.

By this point, Gene apparently believed that Margo was fully buying into the plan and would heed his warning about calling in the authorities, so he felt it was safe to let her go alone to her hotel. Margo was also sure that he or Ralph would follow her there.

Before he left, Gene told her to page him from a pay phone at the Marriott at 3 PM the next day.

When Margo expressed some concern about the cost of staying there, Gene said he would look into less expensive accommodations. He took off in his Jeep, and she arrived at the hotel just after midnight.

As she lay in bed, she had fleeting thoughts of calling the police and worried about what would happen to the girls if she couldn't lie convincingly on the stand. She figured that the people who knew her would empathize with her reasons for lying and that the rest of her FBI colleagues would likely think the worst. But what she struggled with most was the prospect of swearing to God and then lying under oath.

"I felt that only God would understand why I was doing this. I felt like God was going to forgive me," she later said.

On Monday morning, June 21, Margo and Brian Gettings met with prosecutors Marcia Isaacson and Bruce Reinhart. They gave her an outline of the questions they were going to ask her, which Margo tucked away to share with Gene. Marcia was still acting concerned, viewing Margo as a victim, but she had put her trial game on. Bruce, whom Margo had met a couple of times during trial preparation interviews, treated her more objectively, as a witness he needed to win his case.

After Margo called Gene's pager from the Marriott around 2:45 PM, he told her to meet him at a Wendy's in Alexandria, and from there, he led her to the Giant grocery store, where he told her to leave the van and get in the Jeep with him. It seemed important to make her drive around and switch cars, so she followed him, clutching Marcia's outline. Once they got to the Old Colony Inn, he took her to his room.

"Strip down to your bra and panties. I need to check you," he said, indicating that he wanted to see if she was wearing a wire.

Margo handed him the outline and took off her suit. After he was satisfied, she dressed again, and for the next hour, he directed her how to answer questions on the stand. Gene said she should change her testimony to say that she had in fact lived in the Lake Capri house and commuted to work from there.

While they were talking, there was a knock at the door. It was a Latina hotel maid who asked if Gene wanted the room cleaned. He said no.

"That really wasn't a housekeeper," Gene said after the woman left. "She's one of them. They sent her over to check on us."

He and Margo talked a while longer about the people who had ordered the abduction of her and the kids. "They" had now become a group of Mexicans or Colombians who were somehow connected to Brenda and Jerry. Gene had mentioned the Latin connection to her on Saturday, so this provided some confirmation that Jerry had other people working with him.

"Tomorrow I want you to clean the van. They want it cleaned inside and out," Gene said, telling her to page him at noon for further instructions.

Margo left around seven that evening and headed back to the Marriott, where she went in and out of sleep all night, startled awake by the tiniest of noises.

Tuesday was the first day of Gene's trial at the federal courthouse in Judiciary Square in DC, starting with jury selection and a motions hearing. Gene went on his own, and because Margo was a prosecution witness, she didn't have to go until she was called to testify.

When Margo talked to Gene around noon, he told her to go to the bank after cleaning the van, and to withdraw $3,000 by putting a cash advance on her credit card.

"We might have to leave at any moment to go and get the kids, and we need to have enough cash," he said.

They met up again later that day at the Holiday Inn in Manassas, where he had them swap vehicles. He was wearing blue cotton gloves, which, she later figured, was to keep her van free of his fingerprints.

Gene led her back to the Giant in Alexandria, where he told her to buy some wine, then they went back to the Old Colony Inn.

When he opened the door to the room, Margo saw the king-size bed and felt an immediate sense of dread.

"This was the only room they had," he said. "I'll sleep on the floor."

They left to get some dinner, which consisted of a chicken sandwich at Wendy's. They both had some wine, then Gene climbed into bed with her around 9:30. So much for the floor.

"Let's have sex," Gene said.

"No, I don't want to."

"C'mon, it'll help us both relax."

"I'm not on the pill. I don't want to do this."

"C'mon, help me come," Gene said, pulling her hand under the sheets toward him.

At that point, Margo was weak and weary, and she felt she had no choice but to do what she was told. She had no idea where her children were, and she didn't know whether she was going to be dead or alive after she testified at Gene's trial the next day. So she finished her task as quickly as possible. She felt sick to her stomach and a little lost as she lay there, pretending to be asleep until she finally drifted off.

On Wednesday, Margo and Gene left the hotel around 9 AM so that he could get to his attorney's office by 9:30. She took the Metro from National Airport to Brian Gettings's office.

Once she got there, Brian told her she wouldn't be called to testify until after lunch, so she went to the cafeteria. Feeling nervous, she paged Gene from a pay phone. She needed him to calm her down, to tell her she was doing the right thing by lying on the stand.

"You're okay because you have a letter of immunity. Be tough. Don't worry," he said.

After lunch, Margo learned she wasn't going to be called until Thursday, so she went back to the Old Colony Inn to wait for Gene.

He took her to Wendy's again for dinner, then drove them to a notary at the airport. Gene said Jerry had told him to draw up some papers that promised Margo full custody of the girls and possession of the Bennetts' co-owned property as insurance that Gene would indeed persuade Margo to lie on the stand; if he didn't, she would get everything. As implausible as this promise may sound in hindsight, Margo didn't question it at the time. She simply signed on the dotted line.

Next they stopped so that Gene could buy some deodorant, but once they got back to the hotel, Margo was disheartened to see that he'd bought a box of condoms instead.

She felt the emotional and physical strain of the last few days taking its toll, and started to worry that she would crack during her false testimony.

"Why do I have to lie on the stand?" she asked. "Why can't I just tell the attorneys I'm going to change my testimony?"

"Recanting your story has to be done publicly, so you have to be on the stand," he said.

When they got into bed, Gene tried to pull Margo to him, but she resisted.

"Gene, I don't want to do this."

"It'll help us relax," Gene said again. "And I have a rubber tonight."

Margo felt even more tired and drained than she had the night before. Feeling like an empty shell of a person, she stopped protesting as he climbed on top of her.

"Talk to me," he said. "You know what I like to hear."

As beaten down as she felt, this was one small battle Margo was determined to win. She remained silent as Gene did his business. The experience was more unpleasant than it had ever been. Margo felt as if she were outside her body, watching and waiting for him to finish his dirty work.

He never put on the condom.

And she never had sex with a man again.

The next morning was D-Day.

Margo was finally going to testify.

After Gene left the hotel at 7:30 AM, Margo didn't have anything to do before testifying but wait.

Gene told her to page him at 11:55 AM to make sure her head was clear. She took the Metro into DC and called him before she met up with her attorney.

"You doing okay?" Gene asked.

"Yes," Margo replied. "I don't really want to do this, but I'm okay."

By 12:30, she'd arrived at Brian's office, riddled with apprehension.

"Are you nervous?" he asked, glancing over at her as he drove them to the courthouse. She was sitting on her hands, which got cold when she was anxious.

"You're going to be just fine," he said, reassuringly.

"Do you promise to stand by me no matter what?" she asked.

Brian, who had no idea how loaded her question was, looked at her and smiled. "Of course," he said.

To Margo, the courtroom felt old and on the smallish side. Only six or eight people were sitting in the gallery, including Brian, who was in the front row behind the prosecutors. A couple of people she didn't recognize, whom she later learned were reporters, were in the back row. Gene was at the defense table with his lawyer Reid Weingarten, a former trial attorney for the DOJ's Public Integrity Section.

After lunch, around 1:30 PM, Margo was the first witness to be called to the stand, which was only seven or so feet from the judge.

She was sworn in while the jury was in the room. But as soon as prosecutor Bruce Reinhart started asking questions, Reid objected, saying her testimony should be precluded by spousal privilege, the legal mechanism to exempt information passed between spouses.

U.S. District Court Judge Thomas Penfield Jackson excused the jury so that he could hear enough of Margo's testimony to rule on Reid's objection.

"Did there come a time in late September of 1986 when you overheard a conversation between your husband and Jerry York?" Bruce asked Margo.

Gene stared straight at her as she answered. Her mouth was dry and she was trembling.

"Your honor, let me clarify," Margo said. "I am under oath still, correct?"

"Yes, you are," the judge said.

"Actually, the time period was in August of 1986. My husband and I entered into a financial agreement to purchase the house from Jerry and Brenda York. Up until this time, up until today, I have misled Mr. Reinhart and Ms. Isaacson, and I would like to explain what's happened. . . . No one has done anything wrong here, your honor. To my knowledge, the transactions that we entered into with Jerry and Brenda were entirely legitimate.

"What happened is in September of 1992, September 8th, my husband served me with divorce papers. . . . A lot of terrible things were said to one another. We were both up all night. My husband was threatening to take my children from me. I went into work the next day to try and get away from the hostilities that were going on at the house, and I was exhausted. I was a mental basket case. I was confused."

"Let me stop you just at this point," the judge said.

Hearing a dramatic reversal in the direction of her testimony, he asked if she'd conferred with her attorney about her statement.

"No, sir, I have not."

"Well, I'm not sure that I want to hear it before you talk to Mr. Gettings," he said.

"Well, your honor, I mean, where I'm coming from is that this is the first time I've ever been placed under oath and under threat of perjury, and I'm not going to sit up here and perjure myself."

The judge reiterated his strong suggestion that she talk to her attorney before saying anything more under oath, then called a recess.

Brian Gettings took Margo by the arm and led her into the room just outside the courtroom where defendants generally consulted with their attorneys. Margo sat at the table while Brian paced around her.

"Why are you doing this?" Brian asked.

"I wouldn't do this if it wasn't important," Margo said, looking him in the eye, "but I can't tell you."

"Wait a minute," he said, and left the room.

When he came back, Brian said he'd told the judge he needed a recess for the rest of the day.

"Let's go," he said.

As they were leaving the courthouse, Margo was met by a *Washington Post* photographer whom someone, presumably Gene, had tipped off. The photo he took of her that afternoon not only ran with a story in the *Post* the next day, but with articles in numerous national publications for years to come. Margo's hair was blown back by the wind, and she looked gaunt and haunted. She'd lost almost a dozen pounds during her harrowing week with Gene Bennett.

Neither she nor Brian said a word as he drove them back to his office, but Margo could sense that he was quite frustrated with her.

He took her to a conference room and rolled his chair right up to her, their knees practically touching.

"Margo," he said, "you've got to talk to me."

"Brian, I can't," she said shakily, agonizing over what to do.

"I know you. You wouldn't do this. What is going on?"

But Margo couldn't jeopardize the lives of her children. She felt frozen. Gene had only prepped her to the point of lying on the stand. Now she was on her own.

"What's it going to take for you to talk to me?" he asked.

Margo felt that one person, and one person only, could help her figure out what to do next: John Hess.

"I've got to talk to John," she said.

Brian didn't much like this idea. He didn't know John, had never met him.

"I don't want you talking to anyone else," he said.

But after considering his options, Brian gave in and called John at his home in Fredericksburg.

"It's against my advice that Margo speak with you, but she's insisting," Brian said. "She says she won't talk to anybody else."

With that, Brian handed Margo the phone and walked a few feet away to give her some space.

Margo began to babble as she tried to explain what had really happened with Gene so far. It took her about five minutes to tell a story that many of their colleagues would not believe. It was such a crazy tale, some dismissed it out of hand. Many couldn't believe that an undercover agent for the FBI would ever do such a thing to one of his own, especially his wife. Further, they thought, if Gene had really wanted to kill her, he could easily have done so. Others found it hard to believe that a trained agent like Margo would have bought into a ludicrous story about Colombians ordering the kidnap of her and the girls. For most of them, the coup de grace was that she'd had sex with Gene in the hotel room. Twice. That eliminated any remaining shred of her credibility.

But not for John.

John had never liked Gene and thought he was a sociopath. That said, John was amazed and frustrated with Margo for forgetting all her training and falling victim to Gene's manipulative tactics. However, John cared very much for Margo, so he listened, trying not to interrupt.

"The kids are gone, and they're in danger. If I testify, they say they're going to hurt the kids," she said.

That's when John couldn't stay silent any longer. "My God, Margo, listen to what Gene is saying to you," he said, his words clipped. "You know this is not true."

"John, I don't know what to do," Margo said weakly. "I don't know where the kids are."

"For Christ's sake, you've got to tell the truth," John said. "Tell them the truth."

As Margo felt herself coming out of the surreal fog she'd been in for the past week, she slowly began to accept the possibility that she'd been duped. After they hung up, Margo told Brian the whole story.

When she was finished, Brian went to get his partner, Frank Dunham, and had her tell the story all over again.

"My God, Margo, this is crazy," Frank said.

Margo put her head down and parted her hair.

"Give me your hand," she said, placing Frank's fingers on the burns and scrape marks on her scalp. "That's from the taser."

"Oh, my God."

Brian called prosecutor Marcia Isaacson, gave her a brief recap, paused and then repeated everything he'd just said.

Afterward, Brian told Margo that he'd run through the story with Marcia, but she'd held the phone out to her partner and said, "I can't deal with this. Here." So Brian had to tell it again.

For the next hour, Margo and Brian waited for two FBI agents to arrive and take her statement.

"In my entire career, never have I had anything as bizarre as this," Brian said.

Margo was still unable to let go of the possibility that Gene was telling some piece of the truth. "I don't know where my kids are. I need to know my kids are okay."

"Margo, can't you see that Gene's lying?"

"I just need to know that my kids are okay," she repeated.

After discussing the best way to check on the girls, Frank and Brian suggested that Margo call the Prince William County police. She persuaded the police to go to the Nokesville house, but when they called back fifteen minutes later, they said the house was dark and no one was home. This did little to reassure Margo.

It turned out that the girls had stayed the weekend with Tracy, the baby-sitter Gene had hired. But it would be two more days before Margo would learn that the kids had never been in harm's way.

Agents Charlie Price and John Roberts interviewed Margo at Brian's office for the better part of three hours, until close to midnight. At one point, John Roberts left the room, and his partner looked at Margo with utter scorn.

"You don't believe me, do you?" Margo asked.

"I've got to tell you, Margo," he said. "If I had done to my wife what you say Gene did to you, she would not have had sex with me. She would have taken my gun and blown a hole in my head."

Margo didn't say a word. She could see what was happening.

Oh, God, she thought, her heart and stomach dropping to the floor. *Nobody believes me.*

Margo went out to the lobby and found Brian pacing near the elevators, rubbing the back of his neck and looking as if he wished he could smoke a cigarette.

"Margo, I don't know what we're going to do," he said. "But whatever we do, it will be the right thing."

Charlie Price and John Roberts took Margo to buy some makeup and clean underwear before they dropped her at a Holiday Inn in downtown DC. They had offered to take her back to her townhouse, but she said she was too scared to sleep there alone, vulnerable to another of Gene's attacks. Their offer only reinforced her sense that they didn't believe her story.

Gene had said that her testimony was crucial and that if she testified that they really had lived at the house at Lake Capri, the whole case would crumble and he'd be acquitted, but they'd never discussed what might happen after she lied on the stand. Now, as her mind roamed through the possibilities, she pondered whether the judge would order a mistrial and she'd get fired for lying on the stand, not to mention destroying the Feds' case.

She had no idea what was going to come next.

Chapter Eight

Mitigating Circumstances

On Friday morning, June 26, the *Washington Post* hit the stands with a headline that read, "FBI Agent Withdraws Charges Against Spouse: Woman Testifies Husband Not Guilty of Theft." To Margo, it might as well have said, "Agent Lies on Stand."

The story cited statements from court papers filed by Gene's attorney, Reid Weingarten, saying that "the marriage broke up because Marguerite Bennett was having an affair with another woman. That fact, the papers said, also was central to her having made the accusations against her husband."

Even though Margo disagreed with that statement, she was relieved, at least, that Patsy's identity had not been revealed.

Brian Gettings and Frank Dunham took Margo back to the courthouse around 9 AM Friday so that they could advise the judge that Margo had given false testimony under duress.

As they were riding up the escalator, they saw Gene standing at the top, leaning against the wall with an amused smirk.

"I wonder what that was all about," Frank said.

Afterward, Brian told her to go see her doctor, because none of the federal authorities seemed interested in documenting her injuries, which included multiple bruises on her forehead, back, and knees; the cut on the back of her thigh; her numb thumb; and the scalp burns.

The doctor told her she was lucky she didn't have more serious problems from the taser.

"Those things aren't meant to be used on someone's head," he said.

Margo got to Quantico around three that afternoon, feeling like a leper. When she walked into a room, everyone stopped talking. In the halls, her colleagues looked down or away, anywhere but her eyes.

After the other instructors left for the weekend, she sat in her empty office, alone with her thoughts.

Margo was concerned about drawing Patsy any further into this mess and thought it would be best in the long run if she could say she had no ties to the famous author. Margo could only imagine the next set of headlines. She didn't feel right, knowing she could expose Patsy—and her own family—to more bad press.

She'd thought her friendship with Patsy would go on for years and years. But since the attack, she'd realized that Gene was going to try to use Patsy to damage her, that he was willing to do anything to make Margo look like a nut who was unfit to raise their children. Given Patsy's international celebrity status, she thought it was dangerous and foolish to maintain their friendship.

"This was Virginia," she later said. "They would not have tolerated a gay relationship like that, with a woman who had two small children. Had I maintained a relationship with Patsy, it would have been harder for me to say 'I'm not living a gay lifestyle,' and there was no way I would have gotten custody of my children. I wouldn't have even gotten visitation rights. So I was willing to take that part of my life and put it on a shelf, because I had to."

Margo called Patsy and laid out a condensed version of what Gene had put her through over the past week.

"I told him we were together twice, but that it was over and it was not what he thought it was," Margo said. "Gene is trying to use you to get to me, and I think it would be best for you and for me if we had no further contact."

"Do you think he would ever try to hurt me?" Patsy asked.

"No, it's me that he wants. So it's in your best interest to disassociate yourself from me."

"Are you really sure this is the right thing to do?" Patsy asked, her voice reflecting her gradual acceptance of the situation.

"Yes."

"I'm sorry to hear that, but I know that you're right," Patsy said. "Good luck."

Later, Margo recalled, "It was a very realistic decision to make, and unfortunately that's what we had to do. She was a megamillions book writer and I was still very focused on getting my life back in order."

Brian was frustrated that the FBI wasn't investigating Margo's allegations or making any move to protect her from Gene, so he arranged for a former Fairfax County police captain to give her a polygraph on Saturday morning. She passed.

The next day, Margo met with the same two FBI agents to finish giving her statement. She tried to give them as many specific details hoping to give them verifiable proof that she was telling the truth, and also the ammunition they needed to prosecute Gene for the abduction. She said, for example, that on Tuesday, while she was waiting for Gene to finish in court, she'd written a letter to John Hess and a chronology of the events so far. She'd put it into a stamped envelope addressed to John, but never sent it. Gene took it from her that night, saying she could have jeopardized the kids' safety if "they" had seen her mail it.

On Monday, June 29, Brian called the prosecutors to report that the polygraph proved Margo was telling the truth and that if the bureau didn't start taking more aggressive action, he was going to send his own people out on the street to do it for them.

Attorney Reid Weingarten filed for a mistrial that same day, saying he could not respond to Margo's latest allegations in a timely fashion. The judge granted his request and scheduled a new trial for the end of July.

Over the next couple of weeks, the FBI sent agents to Atlanta to look into Gene's past activities there, and by mid-July, the bureau had gathered enough information that they posted two agents at Margo's house from sundown to sunup in case Gene showed up. One stayed outside in his unmarked car; the other sat on the couch all night. This lasted a couple of days, until Margo told them that she found this approach too intrusive.

So she and the bureau worked out another arrangement: during the week, she stayed the night in a secure part of Quantico, an area in the Jefferson Building usually reserved for high-profile or foreign counterintelligence informants. Then, on the weekend, Margo took the girls—along with two agents from the Washington field office—to Dianna's house. Margo was still too scared to stay at the townhouse alone.

Dianna, who had learned about the kidnapping from another agent the week it happened, was devastated. "I almost felt guilty because I hadn't been there," she said later. "Of all the times for me not to have gone with her, and then this was the time he pulled this stunt."

Tony Daniels, the top official at Quantico, believed the kidnapping story. So did Caroll Toohey.

"I had no reason not to believe it," Tony later said. "Margo didn't seem to be the type of person to fabricate something like that."

Caroll thought it was understandable that a hostage in her situation, who was under Gene's power and had fallen victim to Stockholm syndrome, would give in to sexual manipulations like Gene's.

"It's completely reasonable that she'd go along with sex or anything else really," he later said. "It's not even out of the ordinary."

But the rank and file felt differently. While the agents were staying at Dianna's house, they waited until Margo left the room to express their disbelief to Dianna that Gene, a respected FBI agent, would do such a thing to his estranged wife.

"Do you really believe her?" they kept asking.

Margo and Dianna felt frustrated with the sexist nature of their questions.

After two weeks of alternating between strange beds at Quantico and Dianna's house, Margo could no longer deal with the instability, so she asked her sister Jackie to come up from Tuscaloosa to be, in effect, her emotional bodyguard for a while.

Jackie was the first family member or friend in whom she confided about her affair with Patsy, although she didn't name names.

"I want you to know that Gene's accusing me of being gay and that I did have a very brief involvement with someone," Margo said.

She was scared to hear her sister's response, but Jackie didn't even blink.

"That doesn't matter," she said, waving it off with her hand.

Gene's second trial was delayed until August 17.

On August 13, Margo got a call from Brian Gettings, saying that the prosecutors wanted to know how she would feel if Gene got a year in prison for pleading guilty to two felonies—filing a false claim with the federal government and obstruction of justice—but was not charged with a violent crime.

"I would feel like my life isn't worth very much," she said.

"I understand, but by going forward with this, it would mean you don't have to come back into court. Can you deal with this?"

"Yes," she said. "Tell them to do what they're going to do and get this over with."

Margo felt she was powerless to say or do anything more to force the prosecution, so she tried to accept the fact that Gene was getting off easy. She figured that the prosecutors had determined that the abduction was too difficult to prove with no witnesses and little, if any, physical evidence. Gene had cleverly made sure of that.

Tony Daniels later speculated as to why Gene was not prosecuted for the kidnapping: "You basically had a he-said, she-said. . . . Nobody saw the assault in the garage, so how do you prosecute a case like that?" Even given the scrapes, burns, and bruises on her body, he said, "There's a hell of a difference between injuries and a kidnapping."

As Brian briefed Margo on the plea agreement, she was irked that Gene had made a special point of telling investigators that he would never testify against her if the government tried to prosecute her. They had already told Gene that Margo was not a target in the investigation, yet he continued to insist that the agreement include his statement. Margo saw this as simply a ploy so that he could claim in the divorce proceedings that he was trying to be reasonable and nice, even after his wife had leveled such horrible allegations against him.

Jerry York's case was transferred to Georgia, and his wife, Brenda, was granted immunity. Both of them agreed to testify against Gene.

Before he'd abducted Margo, Gene had told George Murray, his former Nickelride partner, that he was innocent of the original two charges involving the home relocation scam, and asked George to be a character witness at his upcoming trial in June.

"You got to tell me you didn't do this," George said.

"No, I didn't do it. They made this up to try to get me," Gene replied.

George agreed to testify but was never called.

After the kidnapping, Gene called George at his office in Atlanta one afternoon and told him he was accepting a plea bargain.

"Look, I want to let you know I'm pleading guilty," Gene said.

"What?" George said. "You're telling me you did this? You swore to me you didn't."

George, a Vietnam veteran for whom loyalty to a comrade means everything, was so angry that he spewed expletives at Gene and told him he never wanted to see or talk to him again.

"I'm probably the last person he'd call if he was on fire because he'd know I'd throw gasoline on him," George later said. "I saw this as a blatant betrayal of trust."

On August 19, Gene went to court to plead guilty to the two new charges and to officially accept the plea agreement, under which he agreed to resign, "to provide truthful, complete, and forthright information to the FBI at all times during the debriefing" of his crime, and to serve one year in prison. He submitted his letter of resignation that same day.

"It has been a pleasure serving with you in happier times," he wrote to Weldon Kennedy, an associate deputy director for administration at FBI headquarters.

The *Washington Times*, which covered the hearing, ran a story the next day, saying that Gene had pleaded guilty to defrauding the government and coercing his estranged wife into testifying falsely. The story mentioned that Margo had recanted her original statement about the Lake Capri house "because her husband had abducted her and improperly pressured her." It also quoted Reid Weingarten as saying that Margo initiated the criminal fraud case against Gene to retaliate against him for suing her for divorce.

Even though Gene was not charged with kidnapping, Margo's allegations were included in Gene's presentencing report, which was written by federal probation officer Michelle Merrett. She recommended a longer sentence because of the violent means he'd used to obstruct justice and because of his continued denial that he'd abducted or even threatened to harm Margo. She also said she found a "preponderance of evidence" that the abduction had occurred, referring to the sealed reports of Margo's interviews with the FBI, medical records from the doctor documenting her injuries, and her truthful polygraph test results.

Allison and Lindsey had been seeing a therapist, Molly Ellsworth, since Margo had moved out in October 1992. Although the girls continued their sessions with Molly, Margo relied mostly on her friends Dianna and John for her own emotional support. Julie Hoxie, the counselor Margo was seeing before the abduction, had moved away, and Margo felt that it would be too overwhelming to start over with someone new. John kept her focused at work and listened whenever she needed to talk; Dianna took her shopping, cooked her meals, and generally took care of her.

Margo got some help through the Post Critical Incident Trauma Program, a weeklong group therapy session for agents and nonsworn employees who had been through work-related or personal crises. This was the first time she had to tell her story to strangers, which proved to be a very difficult task.

Afterward, a man whose daughter had died of AIDS came up to her.

"I don't know how you did it, being put in the trunk of a car," he said. "I would go crazy."

Margo replied, "I don't know how you did it, burying your daughter. I'd go crazy."

In early September 1993, Dianna was selling her house and proposed moving into the basement of Margo's townhouse, but Margo felt that Dianna should know the truth about her and Patsy before Dianna made her final decision.

Margo, who was still working through her sexuality issues, no longer felt she was heterosexual, but she was still trying to find a way not to be a lesbian. She figured she'd just remain celibate, work hard, stay home, and take care of the kids. Embarrassed and fearful of rejection, she got up the nerve to broach the subject as they were driving to the townhouse one day.

She was surprised and relieved by her friend's response.

"I don't give a rat's ass what anybody says," Dianna said.

For six months after Gene pleaded guilty, his attorneys wrangled with federal prosecutors over whether he was complying with his pledge to take full responsibility and exhibit adequate contrition for the charges against him.

Because of Gene's refusal to fully admit to his crimes—namely, the abduction—prosecutor Marcia Isaacson pushed for a longer prison term at his sentencing hearing on February 11, 1994, citing the probation officer's recommended sentence of fifty-seven to sixty-seven months. The maximum penalty for each of the two charges against Gene was five years in prison, a $250,000 fine, or both.

However, Judge Jackson decided to give Gene only one year in prison, the term Gene had agreed to accept in the plea bargain.

The judge faulted attorneys from both sides for putting together such an ill-formed plea agreement, saying he was in the frame of mind to put "a plague on both your houses."

But, he added, "I find that there is sufficient acceptance of responsibility here, barely sufficient but sufficient nevertheless, to give him credit for acceptance of responsibility and to do so in connection with both of the offenses."

Before he imposed sentence, the judge asked Gene if he wanted to make a statement, which he did.

"Judge Jackson, I just again want to apologize for all the trouble I have caused," Gene said. "My life is in ruin. It has ruined the possibilities of me doing too much with my life from now on with the two felony convictions on my record. I have to live with that. What I did back in 1987 was done in anger and with greed and I deeply regret that and I am having to pay for it now. I have had to pay for this with my career, my family situation, everything else. I don't know how many other ways I can say that I am sorry, but I accept responsibility for what I did. I don't blame anybody else. . . . The sooner I start it [the sentence], the sooner I can get it over and have some chance to get my life back together and get back to my children."

A week before Gene was to report to prison, Margo heard someone pounding on her front door one night while she was in the kitchen talking to her father on the phone. She peered through the blinds and saw Gene standing on her front doorstep with a woman.

"Dad, it's Gene," she said, her heart pounding so loudly she felt as if it were in her throat. She knew that Gene had seen her looking at him.

"What's he doing there?" her father asked.

"I don't know. I'll call you back."

Margo's mind raced with possibilities. Had he come to hurt her? Was the woman there as a witness because he wasn't going to hurt her, or was she there to help him?

"Margo, come to the door," Gene yelled from outside. "I know you're in there."

Paralyzed with fear, Margo didn't say anything.

"Come to the door," he said again. "I need to talk to you."

"I am not coming to the door," she yelled. "Just go away."

Margo was about to dial 911 when they left. She called her father to let him know she was safe, but it took her all night to calm down.

About a month later, Margo received a letter from the FBI's retirement fund administrator, notifying her that Gene was cashing out his account. Margo talked to her attorney about trying to stop him, but they learned that Gene could cash out as long as he advised her of his intention beforehand. Apparently that's what he and the woman were there to do that night at the townhouse.

During the negotiations for the plea agreement, Gene had requested that he be allowed to serve his time in a minimum-security prison camp in Petersburg, and the prosecutors agreed to make that recommendation to the judge. Before he left, Gene told his daughters that he was going away "to camp."

Margo told them the truth, albeit in simple terms because of their age. "I told them Daddy had signed some papers he wasn't supposed to sign, and the judge said he had to go away for a year," she later said. "I told them Mommy knew Daddy signed the papers and Mommy knew it was wrong."

As it turned out, Gene was put into solitary confinement, apparently at the federal prison in Petersburg, next door to the camp. This was for his own protection, a standard precaution for former law enforcement officers, who are considered more vulnerable if housed in the mainstream population. A month later, he was moved to a prison in Atlanta, then was driven to the federal prison in Sandstone, Minnesota, staying anywhere from a day to a week in three prisons along the way. He spent the majority of his term in Sandstone.

In late April, a bank official informed Margo that fore-closure was about to begin on the Nokesville house and that in about a week, a sheriff's deputy would dump all its contents on the street.

Betty, her divorce attorney, said Margo could go and salvage her belongings before they ended up on the sidewalk, because the house was still in her name.

So Margo called a locksmith to meet her there. He picked the lock and opened the door for Margo once she showed him her ID and the deed with her name on it.

"Good luck," he said.

When she'd left the house in October 1992, Gene had allowed her to take only her clothes and makeup. This time, she brought a moving van and a crew to box up the rest of her things. She also brought John Hess for emotional support in case Tracy, the baby-sitter Gene had used during the kidnapping, who was living in the house while he was in prison, was home.

Margo took the girls' bedroom set, the blanket chest her father had made for them, her grandmother's cedar chest, the tables and chairs from the breakfast and dining room, the sofa, and two TV sets. She also cleaned out the garage. Many of her things were missing, such as her wedding dress, family photos, and several of her grandmother's handmade quilts.

Among some papers, she found Gene's presentencing report, which outlined a chronology of the investigation, the charges against him, and many biographical details he'd provided that would be completely contrary to what he would claim about his family and his mental health history several years later.

For example, the report said that Gene "described his upbring-ing as a very wholesome, loving family environment. He noted that there was never any type of mental or physical abuse imposed on family members. . . . [He] noted that his family was 'poor,' how-ever, all his material and emotional needs were provided for. He indicated that [he and] his sister . . . had a normal relationship that most siblings experience."

Margo had the moving crew box up Gene's clothes, which she gave to his attorney, but she sold his tools at a church yard sale, along with much of their furniture, china, crystal, and linens, using the proceeds for living expenses or to pay off the debts with which he'd saddled her. She also got rid of a whole slew of picture frames, which she'd emptied, as if she were trying to free herself of her past life with Gene.

All the financial records that she and Gene had kept in two filing cabinets in his office had also disappeared. He would later say that Margo stole these documents that day, using this as an excuse when he didn't want to account for or explain certain transactions he made after he got out. He later admitted to making a number of such transactions by using the power of attorney she'd signed back in 1990, including borrowing money on the lines of credit they'd obtained before she left.

When Gene found out about Margo's visit to the house, he told Tracy, the baby-sitter, to call the police. After he was released from prison in April 1995, he contacted the police himself to report that Margo had stolen $15,400 worth of his property, then filed a claim with the insurance company. The police didn't pursue the matter, and the insurance company rejected Gene's claim after Margo explained the situation.

For Margo, the foreclosure brought back childhood memories of her parents' money problems back in Trussville, Alabama, when she heard her father crying to her mother in the bathroom about how he'd tried to stop the bank from taking their house. She also remembered being thirteen and seeing her mother tucking away the baby-sitting money Margo had given her, then looking embarrassed when Margo saw her pull it out of her lingerie drawer later to pay bills.

Margo didn't want her children to have the same kind of memories, but she didn't know how she was going to deal with the awful financial mess that Gene had put them in.

She felt overwhelmed as the debts began to mount. Gene had taken out loans on the van and the Jeep Cherokee, which she still co-owned, but he'd stopped making payments once he went to prison.

The repo man called in November to tell Margo he had to take the van, so she told him where it was parked, and he picked it up. The Jeep went next.

Margo found it strangely coincidental that on April 4, 1994, the same date that Gene reported to prison, she was informed in a letter from Ed Leary, the bureau's personnel officer, that the agency was strongly considering firing her. She was given ten days to respond.

Among the reasons he cited were that she was involved in a scheme to defraud the government and had filed false joint tax returns in 1986 and 1987, made false statements on joint loan applications, perjured herself at Gene's trial, and exhibited conduct unbecoming to an agent.

"Employees must not, at any time, engage in criminal, dishonest, immoral or disgraceful conduct prejudicial to the government," he wrote.

Margo felt that the bureau had used her to prosecute Gene and then discarded her. She also felt that Gene's allegation about her homosexual activities, which had been publicized in the newspaper, was a silent but contributing factor in her current predicament.

FBI officials today say that as late as 1991, bureau policy concerning sexual conduct was that "an applicant or an employee must be reliable, trustworthy, of good conduct and of complete and unswerving loyalty to the United States," conduct that, whether heterosexual or homosexual, would be considered in judging any applicant or employee on a case-by-case basis. Margo says she never saw a written policy explicitly about sexual conduct. All she knew was that for some time, the bureau had considered being a homosexual a security risk.

During the spring and summer of 1994, Margo and her attorneys wrote many letters, arguing that there were mitigating circumstances to her situation. For one, she knew nothing of the couple's tax returns and financial activities, which Gene controlled. She argued that, under the law, testifying falsely in court under duress was not considered perjury. She also claimed protection under the federal Whistleblower Act, noting that other agents hadn't been punished as harshly for far more egregious violations. Take the husband and wife team at the Washington field office, for example. He had rammed his wife's bureau-issued car with his own vehicle, then beat her up, and the bureau did nothing. The wife told Margo that FBI officials said, "You're an FBI agent; you shouldn't have let things get to this stage."

By that summer, Brian Gettings's cancer had come back, so Frank Dunham took over her case and requested an extension for her appeal.

"Ms. Bennett's cooperation with the bureau . . . helped secure the exposure and conviction of Mr. Bennett, an FBI agent who is a sociopath," Frank wrote. "She voluntarily came forward and blew the whistle on his conduct to the detriment of herself and her family. . . . She subjected herself to near continuous harassment from Mr. Bennett, subjected her children to an almost intolerable situation, and subjected the family to financial difficulty."

Margo and Frank tried pleading her case to top officials in the bureau and the Department of Justice, even to one of the congressional judiciary committees.

To D. Jerry Rubino, security officer for the Office of Security and Emergency Planning Staff for the DOJ, Margo wrote,

> Many people question how an agent of the FBI could allow themselves to be victimized in such an abusive and controlling relationship. My only response is to urge those people to look around. This world is filled with women in successful careers who have fallen victim to this type of relationship. Carrying the credentials of an FBI agent does not make me any more immune to this type of victimization than the average female. To be told that female agents can't be seen as victims (as one female agent was told by her

SAC [Special Agent in Charge] when her agent-husband beat her) is an unbelievably insensitive position to take.

Looking back, I can see how Gene's control over me led me to do such stupid things, I can see how I made bad choices, and I can see why it took me so long to make the decision to get out. What I don't understand, is why, after all the sacrifices I have made, and after the physical and emotional terror I have been through, does the bureau think that my actions call for this type of discipline?

One of the last things Ed Tully did before he retired was to write a memo to Tony Daniels, trying to defend Margo. He felt a great deal of sympathy for her because he understood and supported her motivations.

Ed argued that the bureau hadn't had female agents around long enough to understand the actions of a mother who was under duress and was following the very natural instinct to protect her children from harm.

"If I were in such a position, I'd hire her again," he said recently.

Margo appealed her termination on May 10. Nine days later, she was told that her "Top Secret" security clearance, "a condition of employment," was going to be revoked.

As she and Dianna were leaving Quantico to go to lunch one day, Margo could see her bleak future before her. She felt powerless to change it.

"Why are they doing this to me?" she asked.

Dianna had tears in her eyes. "Margo, I don't know."

Margo's only hope was that she could drag out the process, but even that seemed like a long shot. Louis Freeh, who had just been appointed director, had instituted a zero-tolerance approach and was taking a hard line on disciplinary issues. Some agents described him as Hoover without the compassion. Margo tried to get a meeting with him, but was unsuccessful.

"I felt like if someone would just stop and listen to what I was saying, they'd see that I was okay, that I wasn't a horrible person, but nobody was willing to stop and listen," she recalled later.

Her security clearance was finally revoked, and she was placed on administrative leave for thirty days while the bureau made its final decision about her future employment.

Margo felt that she was losing her identity, bit by bit. But even as she beat herself up over the situation in which she found herself, she told herself she couldn't have done anything better. Most of all, she was frustrated that the FBI couldn't or didn't want to understand the dynamics of her marriage—that Gene was the one in control, and she couldn't do anything about his dishonesty because she didn't feel it was safe.

On September 2, Margo discussed her situation with Frank Dunham.

"I feel like I'm doomed," she said.

"Margo, you've been doomed ever since you said 'I do' to Gene Bennett," he said. "We can fight this if you want to. It will involve getting all the women's groups behind you, getting lots of publicity, and jumping on the FBI with both feet. We can fight it, and we might stand a good chance at winning, because you've been dealt a bum hand, but it's going to take its toll."

Margo wanted very badly to get past all this stress, to live a more peaceful life. She also knew that even if she won, she couldn't stay at the FBI.

"I don't know if I have the strength to get through that," she said.

"Then, frankly," he said, "the best thing for you to do is cut your losses and start over."

Margo had to agree. So she decided to give in and give up. She resigned for "personal reasons" on September 6, 1994, forfeiting her $86,000 salary and the job she'd always loved.

Looking back a decade later, her former colleagues Ed Sulzbach, Ed Tully, Caroll Toohey, and Tony Daniels all sympathized with her situation, although Tony said he had mixed feelings because of her involvement in the home relocation scam.

"The overwhelming attitude was that she knew what was going on for a long time," he said. "She benefited from it financially, materialistically. . . . If they were able, through their investigation, to find that she was coerced, she was forced, she was intimidated to participate, I would like to think they wouldn't have [wanted to fire] . . . her."

Ed Sulzbach, however, felt that the bureau's treatment of Margo was outrageous. "She was a victim of a brutal psychopath," he said. "They should have taken care of her."

Gene, he said, was an embarrassment to the FBI.

In summer 1994, Margo went on a weekend church retreat for women called Walk to Emmaus. The retreat was named after the biblical story of a three-day walk two disciples made, during which they met the resurrected Jesus Christ. He then helped them break through their own feelings of helplessness and sadness so that they could see God's redemptive purpose in the bad things that had happened to them.

During the retreat, the sponsors delivered letters to each participant. Margo received notes from friends, family, and total strangers offering words of hope, inspiration, and strength. Margo began to cry as she read the first letter, which was from John and said it was no coincidence that their paths had crossed; everything was going to be okay. Dianna's letter reinforced Margo's own belief that they were involved in something bigger than they were and that they each offered something special to one another.

That fall, Margo went to another of the retreats, this time as an organizer. Her role was to share her own journey and what she'd learned from her experiences with Gene.

As she spoke to fifty women in a crowded meeting room, she felt empowered, as if every word was critically important for them to hear. If any good was going to come of what she'd been through, she felt it would be by talking about it to help others.

"God gave us the ability to make choices in our lives," she told the group. "If you allow someone else to make your own choices, then, in fact, you have made a choice. It is a choice to not be in control of your own life. The loss of this responsibility for your own life invariably has negative consequences and requires pain and massive effort to overcome."

She told the group that by allowing her marriage and Gene's activities to contaminate her, she'd made a bad choice and needed to correct it. As she described the divorce, Gene's attack, the trial, and the loss of her job, she emphasized how difficult that correction turned out to be.

Many of the women cried as she spoke, and at dinner that night, some came up and hugged her, saying that her words had touched and motivated them. The speech left Margo emotionally drained, but it felt good to know she'd made such an impact.

From the time she resigned until the following summer, Margo tried to make ends meet by substitute teaching at middle schools and high schools in Prince William County and by leading training courses at a nearby police academy. She was too exhausted to get a full-time job.

Dianna moved out in January 1995, which meant Margo no longer had help with the rent, so she cashed out her retirement account and used the $26,000 to finance her divorce and living expenses.

Gene had racked up at least $350,000 in debts. He had maxed out the half dozen lines of credit they had taken out to invest in Jerry's business, and now the banks were demanding payment from Margo. Gene later said he'd spent $340,000 on attorneys' fees, after paying for Brenda and Jerry York's legal expenses as well as his own.

Margo tried to use this time to heal from the damage Gene had caused and from the loss of her identity as an FBI agent. She tried to focus instead on the enjoyment she received from having her kids full-time, putting them on the school bus and volunteering in their classrooms. She also became more involved at the new church her neighbor had taken her to, the Prince of Peace United

Methodist Church in Manassas, where she taught vacation Bible school and helped build the membership.

"It was repair time," she said.

She talked to Betty about trying to change the custody arrangement while Gene was away so that she could continue to have primary custody when he got out, but Betty discouraged it. Betty said primary custody would go to Margo by default, and it would be better to wait to try to make the arrangement permanent until after she'd had the girls for a year. Margo didn't agree, but she deferred to Betty's long-time experience in these matters.

In his letters to the girls from prison, Gene described the snow and deer that frolicked in the fields around his "camp." He told them how much he missed and loved them and how they would always be his little girls.

By this point, Allison was in first grade, and Lindsey was in preschool. Because they couldn't decipher his handwriting, Margo read the letters to them, suffering through the nausea and repulsion this caused, because she felt it was the right thing to do.

Gene, who had helped out in Allison's classroom before going to prison, had told the teacher that he was afraid Margo wasn't going to allow his daughter to stay in touch, so once he was gone the teacher encouraged Allison to write him. When Allison told Margo about her teacher's unsolicited and unwelcome advice, Margo was irritated that they had to deal with Gene's manipulation even in his absence, so she told the teacher that it wasn't her place to interfere in this; Allison would write him from home.

Margo had never told the girls about the abduction because she didn't want to taint their memory of their father or their relationship with him. At the time, she still thought her children deserved to have two parents, no matter what.

"I knew he was only going to be gone a year, and I didn't want them to have to be torn with loyalties or to fear him," she later said. "But mostly I didn't want them to feel guilty about enjoying time with their father, yet knowing what he had done to me."

"It's time to write your dad," she said one evening before she put the girls to bed.

She gathered them around the small desk near her bedroom window, and as they each dictated their own letter, she typed up their sweet, innocent words.

"I felt they needed that contact, so I made myself do it. No wonder I'm all screwed up."

The only way she could get through this chore was to turn herself off emotionally and distance herself from the man who she thought would be so angry when he got out of prison that he would try to kill her.

Chapter Nine

Paranoia

In January 1995, shortly after Dianna had moved out, Margo received a letter from the federal Bureau of Prisons, notifying her that Gene would be released on April 2. Although she still had three months to go, Margo went from feeling safe and worry free to being stricken with the nagging urge to look over her shoulder.

She spent $500 to install an alarm system in her townhouse and made sure to have a gun on her at all times. A male former student who was worried about her safety had sent her a .38-caliber revolver with a three-inch barrel, slightly smaller than the four-inch-barrel revolver a law enforcement officer would normally use. Now that she was no longer a sworn peace officer, it wasn't legal for her to carry a gun without registering it with the state, but she didn't feel safe without it and hadn't gotten around to filing the proper paperwork. She also kept a can of pepper spray, which a friend from Quantico's firearms range had given her, in her purse.

Logically, she knew that Gene was in prison, but that didn't stop her from feeling paranoid. He had friends and associates from his undercover days, people he could call collect from a prison pay phone to come get her. She felt that she always had to be on guard.

In early March, Margo called the girls' elementary school to let them know that Gene was getting out and might show up to see his daughters. She told them that the existing custody order was still in effect, so if he tried to take the girls on a day he was allowed to have them, there was nothing anyone could do to stop him.

April 2 came and went, with no sign of Gene, but Margo's vigilance level had kicked up a few notches. She knew he was out there, waiting. Lurking.

About a week later, Margo got a call from Melanie, a secretary in the school's main office.

"I just want to let you know, he's here, and Allison is talking to him right now," she said.

Margo thanked her for the heads-up. There was nothing more she could do, really.

It's begun, she thought. *He's back.*

Lindsey's kindergarten program lasted only a half day, so Margo picked her up at the bus stop, and they ran some errands until Allison finished school at around three.

"Did you get to see your dad today?" Margo asked.

Lindsey said yes, then rattled on about something else. Margo didn't push for more details because she didn't want Lindsey to sense her anxiety.

Margo pulled into the parking lot at the mall, where they were going to buy some treats for Dianna's dog at PetSmart. Margo heard Gene's voice before she saw him.

"Lindsey!" he called out.

Margo scanned the area but didn't recognize the new Gene, with his thick beard and long, stringy hair. Lindsey, however, had seen him only a few hours earlier, so she ran over to meet his welcoming arms.

"Daddy!" she shrieked.

Margo stayed about twenty feet away while Gene bent over and hugged Lindsey, patting her on the back and glaring over at Margo with an expression that said, "I'm back, and you're going to have to deal with me."

As much as she'd tried to prepare for this moment, all the terror she'd experienced during his attack in 1993 came rushing back like a wave, almost knocking her over. It shook her to see him, waiting for them like that, knowing that he must have followed them from the bus stop and that she hadn't seen his car in her rear-view mirror. He clearly wanted her to know that he could show up at any time, anywhere, and take her by surprise.

She realized she needed to be even more vigilant as she prepared for his next attack. It wasn't a question of if. It was a question of when.

While he chatted with Lindsey, Margo stood there as patiently as she could, determined not to let Gene sense the emotional tsunami that was raging inside her. But finally she couldn't take it anymore.

"Lindsey, c'mon," she called out. "We have to run our errands."

As they finished their shopping, Margo did her best to keep her fear hidden.

After she and Lindsey got home, they walked the block and a half to meet Allison's bus. Then, as the three of them walked home together, Allison told her mother all about her father's visit at school that day. The experience made such an impact that Allison would write about it in a school assignment four years later.

Allison was called to the office over the intercom by Melanie, who told her that someone was there to see her. When Allison looked around the lobby, the only person she saw was a man with a beard and long, straggly hair sitting on the couch in what she thought was a blue one-piece janitor's jumpsuit. He didn't get up, so she went back into the office and told Melanie she didn't see anyone. Melanie told her to try again, so she took a second look at the man and realized it was her father.

"Daddy!" she yelled with glee. He was crying as she jumped into his lap, her Lion King shirt flying up. He seemed a lot smaller than when she'd last seen him, when he'd weighed about 250 pounds.

She told him all about school for five or ten minutes until he said, "Go on back to class, my big girl," and gave her a kiss. Allison had always been Gene's favorite.

Gene also wanted to see Lindsey, so he had Melanie call her to the lobby too.

Margo and Gene soon returned to their preprison custody arrangement. He would pick up the girls from school on Tuesday afternoon, and Margo would take them from Saturday morning until she dropped them at school on Tuesday morning. Gene also got the girls every third weekend.

The major change for Margo was that she insisted on picking them up in a very public place. Gene wanted to make the exchange in the police dispatch center parking lot in Woodbridge, but Margo refused because she knew it would be isolated on Saturday mornings. She decided on the much busier Food Lion parking lot in Manassas, where she would always park at least seven spaces away from his car. If he got there after she did and pulled up next to her, she would back out and drive to a spot further away. She wanted to be sure that the girls had to walk some distance across the lot to meet her.

Sometimes Margo brought Dianna or her neighbor Beth Carter to pick up the girls, and sometimes she didn't, so that Gene would never know whether she would come alone.

Gene had lost his confident swagger in prison. He always had dark circles under his eyes and seemed exhausted. His body looked softer and less physically fit than before, but the anger in his eyes was fiercer than ever. Margo could see the loathing there, and it scared her.

Pat Hammond, Gene's divorce attorney, arranged for him to live in the basement of a home in Manassas that was owned by a real estate agent she knew. Allison and Lindsey told Margo that the basement had only one large bedroom with three beds and that their father snored so loudly they had trouble sleeping.

Margo asked Betty to look into the living arrangements because she thought that the girls were old enough—Allison was now eight and Lindsey was six—to need some privacy, not to mention a good night's sleep. Word came back that Gene was going to be moving into a rental house after the girls' school year had finished. In July, he moved to a quiet cul-de-sac with a rural feel on Old Bushmill Court in Manassas. Margo immediately suspected they would have a problem when school started again in the fall because Gene's new house was about seven miles away from Westridge Elementary, where the girls had been going for the past year.

That summer, Margo and the girls got a new dog, a cocker spaniel that Allison named Pellet. Margo worked out an arrangement with her neighbor Beth, who would talk to Margo through the window while she walked the dog at night.

Other than that, Margo didn't leave the house after dark, not even if they'd run out of milk. Allison had a habit of leaving the front door unlocked, but Margo wouldn't go in without first yelling out her daughters' names or using her cell phone to call the house phone to see if anyone was home.

"I lived my life and I waited," Margo said later. "The healing time was over, and now it was time to get busy and try to watch out for myself."

Margo had begun to apply for jobs around the area that spring.

In July, she got a call from the police chief of the Northern Virginia Community College (NOVA) system, who was one of her former students. "I have a position I think you'd be perfect for," he said. "I think you should apply."

One of his lieutenants had just quit, and he thought Margo would be a fine replacement. She didn't ask how much the job paid. She knew the salary wouldn't be anywhere near as much as she'd earned at the FBI.

Margo got the $42,000-a-year job and started at the Woodbridge campus in August. It felt good to get back to her roots in campus policing.

"I needed to find consistent, steady employment," she later recalled. "I'd certainly been praying about it."

Margo traded in her old can of pepper spray for a brand-new one. It could shoot about ten feet and contained a 10 percent concentration of oleoresin capsicum, the main ingredient, versus the 2 percent a civilian could buy at a retail store. And now that she was back in law enforcement, it was legal for her to carry the gun she'd been toting around in her purse.

Meanwhile, the start of school was approaching, and Margo was growing increasingly concerned, not only because she figured Gene was up to something but also because his attorney had failed to respond to a dozen letters and inquiries from her and Betty.

Sure enough, when she picked up the girls the Saturday before school started, they told her they had already visited their new school in Manassas. She also found a note in their backpacks from Gene—their usual method of exchanging information about the girls—instructing Margo to take them to the new school, which, coincidentally, was called Bennett Elementary.

Betty said there was nothing they could do on a weekend, but because the girls were still registered at Westridge Elementary, Margo should take them there on Tuesday morning.

Margo alerted Westridge that Gene had changed the girls' registration to a different school at the last minute and that he might try to take them there. On Tuesday morning, she dropped them off at 8:45, but she was not surprised when the school called to say that Gene had arrived an hour later to pick them up. Betty filed a motion in court that day, and on Friday, September 8, they had a hearing.

The fact that Gene was a convicted felon just released from prison was apparently irrelevant to the judge. He ruled that the girls should attend the school closer to Gene's house because the existing custody order gave him the kids four nights a week versus Margo's three.

Margo was furious with the court, Gene, and her own attorney.

"This was so stupid and so unfair to the kids," she said later. "They did not deserve to be jerked around like pawns or yo-yos. The fact that Gene was willing to jerk them around, and waited until the last minute to do it, all showed that he didn't care about their best interests. It was my inconvenience and pain that most interested him."

Margo had long been troubled by the way Betty had responded to Gene's manipulative tactics, and now that the situation was affecting the children, she could no longer stand idly by. She searched around for a new attorney, and in mid-September she went to see a woman with a reputation for being tenacious. Her name was Kathy Farrell, and she agreed to take on Margo's case.

Allison described Gene's behavior during his postprison period as erratic, ranging from playful and loving to just plain mean.

Some days, he seemed to be the same man who had built her and Lindsey a big wooden jungle gym in their backyard in Nokesville, where he'd pushed them on the swings and ran around with them. The same man who used to lie on the ground and pretend to be asleep, letting the girls sneak up on him so he could grab and tickle them.

On his happier days, he would keep them home from school to watch TV or play with their dolls—for no apparent reason other than that he seemed to want the company.

"You don't seem like you're feeling that good," he'd say, or, "It's a special day."

He would take them out to the creek in the woods behind his house to collect frogs and lizards, which they would keep in jars, rubbing their fingers along the creatures' leathery skin. Gene liked to joke that he would turn the frogs into frog legs so they could eat them as the French did.

He would also take them to Baptist Sunday school at his church, where he introduced them to the Reverend Bill Higgins.

Allison and Lindsey called the pastor "Rubber Chicken" because his face was so red.

But then there were the days when their father wasn't so nice, when Lindsey and Allison cringed with fear at their father's flaring temper. It was always worse when it involved Margo.

One night, while they were still living in the basement apartment, Allison woke up, crying, after dreaming that her mother was running away from her. Gene showed her no sympathy.

"It doesn't matter; go back to bed," he said.

Lindsey would always remember the times Gene yelled at her for crying. She cried on the trip they made to Kentucky for the Bennett family reunion in 1995, for example, and he said, "I'll give you something to cry about," then spanked her.

Among her other medical issues, Lindsey had developed a nervous bladder, which often caused her to get up five times in the middle of the night, thinking she had to pee.

"He would yell at me [even though] the doctors had said it wasn't my fault," Lindsey said later.

Allison, like her mother, learned how to keep Gene's temper at bay. "It wouldn't be bad if we didn't piss him off, but God forbid if one of us said something wrong," she said.

She'd often give Lindsey a warning look, as if to say, "Stop talking." Then later she would direct Lindsey not to do or say whatever she'd been doing that had upset their father.

Allison did not think to tell her mother until much later about Gene's drinking or abusive behavior, how he would sometimes vomit from all the cheap wine he drank and how the recycling bin would fill up with jug wine bottles.

"He always had a glass of something, even during the day," she said later.

One night, she remembered him throwing up in the kitchen. All the lights were off in the house, and the girls were in the living room watching TV.

"Why don't you come over and help your father?" he screamed. "You just sit there like you don't even see anything?"

The two girls ran to his aid in the kitchen, but they didn't know what he wanted them to do, so they just stood there, feeling scared that he would yell at them some more.

Sometimes he told them he was happy that he was able to be there for them because he had been a teenager when his father died. But he had high standards he wanted them to meet.

"You're going to grow up to be something," he'd say. "No kid of mine is going to grow up to be a little half-ass."

In November 1995, Margo went to a retreat for Stephen Ministries training, a peer counseling program for nonordained church members, and ran into a minister she'd met at a friend's funeral a year earlier.

"How long did it take you to get your divorce?" the minister, Diane Lytle, asked.

"It's going on four years, and I still don't have it yet," Margo replied.

"It sounds like you have had some interesting experiences," Diane said. "I'd like to spend some time getting to know you. Give me a call, and we'll get together after the first of the year."

Margo called Diane a couple of months later, and they met at her church one evening in late January. Margo told her about all the struggles she'd been having with her sexuality, knowing deep inside that she was gay, but feeling so ashamed that she'd been living in denial. She also said she'd been realizing that she couldn't get rid of her feelings of attraction to other women.

"Does this thing inside me make me a bad person?" Margo asked.

"Who is God to you? What is your concept of God?"

"I believe in a kind and loving God. He is a forgiving God."

"Does God make mistakes?"

"No," Margo said.

"Do you believe God is perfect?"

"Yes."

"Then why do you think God made a mistake in creating you?"

Margo soon saw where Diane was going with this. "She was guiding me into realizing that God is loving, he is kind, and he is perfect," she said later. "Why would he create me and make a mistake, to be wrong, to be bad? No, God doesn't create us to be bad."

After all her years of struggle and shame, Margo finally accepted that God loved her just the way she was. She was also able to accept herself—and the concept that she was not going to hell for being gay.

"That was truly the moment of the liberation of my soul," she recalled a decade later, crying as she described this pivotal moment. "It was a very significant point in my life, when I realized I'm OK and no, it's not heresy for a gay woman to say, 'I believe in God; he made me and he loves me.'"

That said, Margo was still not able to share her newfound belief with other members of the congregation at Prince of Peace, because Methodist doctrine says that the only moral intimate relationship is between a husband and wife. For now, she felt she still needed to keep her sexuality a secret, because others would disapprove and think she was a bad person.

In November 1995, Lindsey had her annual cardiology checkup in Georgetown. As usual, they did an EKG, which showed no abnormal symptoms, and a color sonogram of her heart, which did. Her pulmonary artery had become enlarged, which suggested that a lot of blood was being recycled through her lungs.

Margo scheduled an angiogram for the following month, then put a note for Gene in Lindsey's backpack to explain what was going on.

The angiogram showed that the hole in the ventricular wall of Lindsey's heart had not shrunk as they had originally thought. It had grown to the size of a quarter, and a significant amount of blood was leaking through it into the lungs and overtaxing them. The doctors said this could become a fatal condition and recommended that Lindsey see a surgeon to repair it.

Easter 1960 in Athens, Georgia: Margo at age six (lower left) with her mother, Gerthaldean "Dean" Akers, and siblings Larry, Letta, and Jackie.
Courtesy of Margo Bennett

Margo went through orientation at FBI headquarters, known as the Hoover Building, 935 Pennsylvania Avenue NW, Washington DC, in October 1981.
By Caitlin Rother

Gene Bennett and Margo Akers were married in Atlanta in February 1984.

Courtesy of Margo Bennett

Margo and her parents, Ed and Dean Akers, at a Bennett family reunion in Kentucky in the late 1980s.

Courtesy of Margo Bennett

Margo says Gene abducted her from this house in Nokesville, Virginia, just days before his first trial in 1993.
By Caitlin Rother

John Hess, who taught Interviewing and Interrogation with Margo, here at Quantico, the FBI academy, in November 2006.
By Caitlin Rother

Gene was processing security applications at the White House when Margo took this photo of him and daughter Allison in the White House press room in 1987.
Courtesy of Margo Bennett

Margo with eighteen-month-old Allison in Nokesville in April 1988.
Courtesy of Margo Bennett

Gene holds daughters Allison (left) and Lindsey at the Prince William County Fair in 1990.
Courtesy of Margo Bennett

Gene, Allison, Margo, and Lindsey in March 1992.
Courtesy of Margo Bennett

Margo (left) and Patricia "Patsy" Cornwell in Hogan's Alley at Quantico in April 1992 during a tour for a group of kids with cancer.
Courtesy of Margo Bennett

Margo and Patsy decided to end the romantic portion of their relationship during a talk along this reservoir at Quantico in May 1992.
By Caitlin Rother

Mary Ann Khalifeh, the woman unknowingly hired to help Gene in his scheme to kill Margo, in November 2006.
By Caitlin Rother

Crime scene photo of the Rev. Edwin Clever's office at Prince of Peace United Methodist Church in Manassas, Virginia, where Margo took cover behind the desk in June 1996.
By Caitlin Rother, courtesy of the Prince William County Police Department

Crime scene photo of the chair to which the pastor was handcuffed and shackled in his secretary's office, which adjoined his, and the bag that Gene put over his head.
By Caitlin Rother, courtesy of the Prince William County Police Department

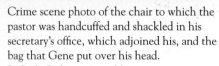

The Reverend Edwin Clever in November 2006, a decade after the crime, in his office.
By Caitlin Rother

Gene holed himself up in this house in Manassas, Virginia, during three-plus hours of 911 calls he made in the early morning of June 24, 1996, after fleeing from the church.
By Caitlin Rother

Gene's booking photo in June 1996.
By Caitlin Rother, courtesy of WRC-TV, Washington DC, and the Prince William County Police Department

Gene walks into the court-room during his trial in 1997 in Manassas.
By Caitlin Rother, courtesy of WRC-TV, Washington DC

Margo testifies for the pros-ecution on January 29, 1997.
By Caitlin Rother, courtesy of WRC-TV, Washington DC

Commonwealth's attorneys Paul Ebert (right) and Jim Willett, who prosecuted the Gene Bennett case together, in Paul's office in November 2006.
By Caitlin Rother

Margo in October 2006 at the University of California, Berkeley, where she works today as a campus police captain.
By Caitlin Rother

Lindsey (left), Margo, and Allison, pregnant with Serena, outside Margo's home in the Bay Area in October 2006.
By Caitlin Rother

Over the next few months, Margo's battles with Gene now centered around if and when Lindsey should have open-heart surgery. Margo wanted to move ahead as soon as possible, as the doctors had advised, whereas Gene kept pushing for a delay.

He took Lindsey to a new therapist, saying she was suffering from severe anxiety and nightmares, and insisted that Lindsey was in no emotional shape to go under the knife. He also insisted on participating in the sessions with the new therapist, Jennifer Levy, and with the surgeon as well. Margo didn't like being in the same room as Gene, but there was no way to avoid it.

In the year since Gene had been released from prison, Lindsey had gained thirty pounds, going from an outdoor sporty kid to a more rotund child. Allison told Margo that Gene had been feeding Lindsey bowls of peanut butter and ice cream. Margo could not figure out why Gene kept trying to stall the surgery and was feeding her such fattening foods, while at the same time, he was sending notes in the backpack, telling Margo to stop giving Lindsey so much "junk." Later she realized he'd been up to his old tricks trying to make her look crazy as part of an elaborate deadly scheme to capture all the marital assets, including the girls, for himself.

On February 11, 1996, he took out an ad in the classified section of the *Washington Post* that said, "SECURITY—FT/PT non-lic investigators for NoVA work. We will train for licensing." (In this case, "NoVA" was an abbreviation for Northern Virginia, not the community college system.)

A woman named Mary Ann Khalifeh, a former analyst for the Internal Revenue Service, responded to the ad and was hired by Gene, who was posing as a retired FBI agent turned private investigator named Edwin Adams. Gene told Mary Ann she was going to help him investigate an insurance fraud and embezzlement scam and gave her detailed instructions for a number of things he wanted her to do, promising her a lump sum of $35,000 once the job was done. One of those tasks was to open four bank accounts with $50 each, then use them to take out four $250,000 accidental death policies on herself, naming Marguerite, Allison, and Lindsey Bennett and Elizabeth Akers as beneficiaries. Marguerite Bennett, he told her, was one of the embezzlers.

In March 1996, Gene finally agreed to let Lindsey have the surgery after Jennifer Levy said she couldn't recommend postponing the operation. The procedure was scheduled for April 3.

Betty had submitted a list of divorce-related questions, called interrogatories, for Gene to answer in writing. But when Gene didn't answer the questions, Betty didn't force the issue. His foot-dragging routine didn't stop Kathy, though. She went to court and got an order to make him comply.

Gene's responses gave Kathy a chance to prepare a hard-hitting set of questions for Gene's deposition in June, where he would be sworn under oath to tell the truth and she could get an idea of his position before trial in divorce court. That was the point, at least theoretically.

The first question asked him to list the factors that had led to the dissolution of the marriage as well as the dates and descriptions of any postseparation incidents he planned to introduce as evidence.

Gene's responses painted Margo as a power-hungry, overambitious closet lesbian who shirked her duties as a mother and saw him as little more than a sperm bank. He said she repeatedly pushed him to watch lesbian porno and to bring other women into their marital bed. He claimed that he protested "on religious, family, moral and health grounds for Mrs. Bennett to forget about these sexually deviant behaviors."

As Gene described Margo's affair with Patsy, he mixed fact with fiction: "Mrs. Bennett became totally infatuated with Patricia Cornwell. . . . Mrs. Bennett would secretly meet with Cornwell for romantic candlelight dinners, would visit Cornwell's Richmond home, accepted expensive gifts and clothes from her and spoke with her on the phone constantly. . . . Mr. Bennett followed Mrs. Bennett to several of these rendezvous during this time and observed Mrs. Bennett and Ms. Cornwell hugging and kissing in their vehicles. Mrs. Bennett attended a book signing and dinner as Ms. Cornwell's guest and Mr. Bennett learned that Mrs. Bennett and Ms. Cornwell had spent the night together. The next day, after Mrs. Bennett returned to the FBI academy, Mr. Bennett checked the family van and removed Mrs. Bennett's lingerie, sex toys, lesbian pornographic material, etc. from the van for safe keeping and testing."

Gene later said he sent the lingerie to a forensic expert at George Washington University and then to a lab to get DNA proof of the affair. Margo told Kathy that Gene was "barking up the right tree," but that he was making up evidence to support his claims. She said she would admit under oath that she had been with Patsy on the night in question, but she never put any lingerie, sex toys, or lesbian porno videos in the van. When Gene produced a photocopy of a photo he took before sending the panties to be tested, Margo said she'd never seen them before, so if the lab found any female secretions they weren't hers.

In addition, he accused her of stealing everything she could from his house while he was in prison, blaming the foreclosure on her failure to pay the mortgage. He said she "actively blocked" him from contacting their daughters by phone or by mail while he was behind bars and insisted that she "never exercised any discipline or authority over the children . . . [and] tried to be a buddy or friend to the children instead of an adult with serious parental responsibilities." He said she frequently gave Allison and Lindsey prescription medications without sending them to a doctor and sent him notes asking him to do the same, another allegation that Margo denied.

"Mrs. Bennett's plan was to use their children as bargaining chips for a quiet divorce while ruining Mr. Bennett financially, emotionally and professionally," he wrote. "Mrs. Bennett in effect wanted everything, except their joint debt, and wanted Mr. Bennett to walk away from his family and assets."

In late April, Margo got a call from a private investigator, another former student. When he started his own business, she'd said she would do some small jobs for him and agreed to let him list her on his brochure. He called to say that a woman named Mary Ann Khalifeh had seen the brochure at a divorce support group meeting and wanted to meet with Margo.

Margo wasn't interested, but she agreed to call the woman. When they talked a week later, Mary Ann said she thought her husband was cheating on her.

"If you'll just meet with me, maybe you can help me," Mary Ann said.

Margo tried to be polite but firm, saying she didn't really want to get into this type of work and was very busy at the moment. "I'm willing to meet with you," she said. "I just want you to know that I don't know if I'll be able to help you."

They agreed to meet a week later at a restaurant-bar called the Polo Grill in Lorton around 6 PM.

Margo was still feeling roundly paranoid and fearful; she also felt that there was something odd about this woman. Since Gene's attack, she'd been skeptical about anyone who came into her life for no apparent reason. She was not in a risk-taking mode and wondered if Gene could be involved somehow, so she decided to bring her sister Letta, who had come up from Tuscaloosa hoping to find a job in the area, and her neighbor Beth to the meeting. The two women followed Margo in Beth's van, arriving fifteen minutes early so that Margo, like any good law enforcement officer, could make sure she didn't have to sit with her back to the door.

But when Margo walked into the dimly lit restaurant, the hostess was expecting her. Mary Ann had gotten there early, too.

"Are you here to meet someone?" she asked.

The hostess led her to a table where Margo was pleased to see that Mary Ann was already sitting with her back to the door. Letta and Beth got a table nearby so they could keep watch.

Mary Ann got halfway out of her chair to shake Margo's hand, then sat back down. She had reddish brown, shoulder-length hair, looked to be in her mid-forties, and was wearing dark slacks and a blouse, as if she had come from the office.

They both ordered sodas. Margo hoped to keep the meeting as short as possible, so she got right to the point.

"Why do you think your husband is cheating on you?"

"He comes home late at night, and one night I found match-books from bars in his pocket."

"What bars?"

"I don't know the names of them, but I can show you the matchbooks. I thought you could go to these bars and catch him."

"Have you driven by the bars and seen his car there?" Margo asked.

"No, I haven't," Mary Ann said. "He has a bad temper."

"Has he hit you before?"

"No."

Mary Ann said she didn't want to go to the bars alone and asked if Margo would come with her to help catch her husband in the act.

By this point, Margo's initial feeling about Mary Ann was re-inforced by her sense that the woman was, in essence, reading a script. She didn't sound sincere, and her story didn't ring true. There was no anger or fear in her voice, and she seemed to lack the conviction to go through with the plan she proposed. Margo also didn't believe that the woman was telling the truth about who she was.

In fact, Mary Ann was telling Margo the truth about her own marital situation. But, as Margo had picked up, she lacked convic-tion because the proposal her boss had told her to make seemed ludicrous. In addition, her nerves were on edge from having to carry out this exercise.

"You have to understand—I'm going through my own divorce, and I don't have time to take this on," Margo said. "I can't help you."

"All you need to do is go with me," Mary Ann pleaded.

"No, I just can't do this for you, but I'll help find someone to help you."

Mary Ann, again following her boss's orders, told Margo that she had to have a female investigator, so Margo said she would call her in a couple of days to give her a name and phone number. Margo got the sense that Mary Ann would've said anything to get Margo to help her.

What she didn't know was that Mary Ann had been following Gene's orders for three months now, using her personal credit card to buy a pager and a phone for herself and one each for the man she knew as Edwin Adams, the costs of which he promised to reimburse; that Mary Ann had also taken out the four accidental death policies and was just about to complete a sixty-hour private investigator's training course that Gene had paid for her to take at the community college where Margo worked as a lieutenant; or that Gene had had her visit Kathy Farrell to talk about her own divorce, for which Gene said he'd pay, claiming that Kathy was involved in the scam too.

In late May, Margo took her first formal training class on how to use pepper spray, a requirement of her Virginia peace officer certification. At the time, she had no clue what a lifesaver that class would turn out to be.

At 10 AM on June 4, Margo and Kathy arrived at the office of Doug Bergere, Gene's new attorney, where Margo would give her deposition. At long last, they were set to go to trial on the divorce on July 15.

The four of them sat around a large table that could seat eight, with Margo and Gene facing each other.

Margo averted her eyes from Gene's, but even his presence was unnerving.

"How long were you married when you separated, twelve years?" Doug asked.

Gene laughed and muttered under his breath, "No, but it feels like it."

Margo had been prepped to give simple answers and not volunteer any information, so she ignored him. "Eight years," she said.

As Doug asked about the kidnapping in 1993, Margo cried as she began to recount the details, getting so emotional that she needed to take a ten-minute break partway through. She hated that her attacker was sitting across the table, probably enjoying how victimized and terrorized she still felt by what he had done.

The deposition lasted four hours, including a lunch break. Afterward, Kathy praised her for holding up so well.

"Every time I hear you tell that story, it's consistently the same information," she said. "I believe you because the story never changes."

They went back to Kathy's office to prepare for the next day, when Gene would give his deposition, then Margo went home, feeling drained. Although she dreaded being in the same room with Gene for another day, she felt satisfied with her performance so far.

The next day was gruelingly long and torturous, but at least Margo didn't have to sit facing Gene. She sat off to one side, scribbling notes, while Gene spent a full day giving nonresponsive answers to most of Kathy's questions. He was so uncooperative that they had to schedule a second session a week later.

Many of his answers would provide telling contrasts to Margo's account of why their marriage had failed, and would also show interesting conflicts with claims he and his attorneys would make in criminal court seven months later.

Perhaps most important, Gene said he had no mental or physical condition that would impair his long- or short-term memory, had never been treated for any psychiatric problem, and did not suffer from any chronic condition. He also did not recall having any stress indicators while working undercover in the FBI other than the death of his mother and his marital discord.

At one point, he produced a property and custody settlement agreement with Margo's signature, whose contents were exactly opposite to those in the document they'd had notarized during the 1993 abduction. Margo realized that he had taken her signature page and tacked it onto a new document that gave him all their marital assets and sole custody of the girls.

Among his other responses, Gene claimed he had never seen or owned a taser. He said he had learned about forensics and had worked four or five homicides while he was in the Army's Criminal Investigation Division. His taste in porno movies was "a white male and a white female making love together, period." He'd started following Margo and Patsy after going to a party at Patsy's house in summer 1992. That September he'd uncovered physical evidence of their lesbian affair in the inscriptions Patsy had written in Margo's books, which he photocopied in Margo's office, where he also confiscated the photo of Patsy and Margo from her desk.

His intent, he said, was to win sole custody of his children.

"I didn't want my two daughters raised by a lesbian," he said.

Just as he did in the first session, Gene evaded most of Kathy's questions all day long, so they had to schedule a third session for July 1.

On Saturday, June 22, the weather was nice and not too muggy when Margo and her neighbor Beth picked up the girls in the Food Lion parking lot. As usual, Gene stood with his arms crossed, leaning against his Dodge Dynasty, as he watched the girls walk toward Margo's Prizm.

Margo purposely didn't schedule anything, so that the girls could spend a relaxing weekend playing with the neighborhood kids, while she watched them and talked to Beth. The only thing out of the ordinary was that Gene called Saturday to say goodnight to the girls and told them he missed them. This seemed a little odd, considering that he'd only just seen them. He'd never done that before on a day that Margo had the kids.

In the back of her mind, she was thinking about the training course she would attend later that week and how it wouldn't be too long before she and Gene would finally resolve their divorce and custody dispute in court. It was about time.

Margo was right about one thing. Gene always had a reason for doing what he did. Only she never would have guessed what he was up to this time.

Chapter Ten

The Main Event

On Saturday, June 22, after dropping off the girls with Margo, Gene met up with his assistant, Mary Ann Khalifeh, who was expecting to do a weekend of surveillance with her boss, Edwin Adams, on the insurance fraud case.

Gene told Mary Ann to rent a room at the Holiday Inn on Dumfries Road in Manassas in the early afternoon, then told her to drive her Acura to a soccer field near the hotel, where he picked her up and took her to Dulles Airport. From there, she took a shuttle bus to the Budget rental car lot, where she picked up a tan Ford Windstar van and drove back to the hotel. She stayed the night alone.

The next day, while Margo and the girls went to church, hung around the house, ate dinner, and watched TV, Gene kept Mary Ann busy with an elaborate series of tasks, swapping vehicles numerous times across two states.

At 7:30 AM, he told her to follow him in his Dodge Dynasty to a mall in Martinsburg, West Virginia, where he dropped off an old Plymouth Voyager van that he said his associates needed for the surveillance. They drove back together in his Dynasty to Manassas, where he transferred two gym bags into the Windstar van, saying they contained investigative equipment they might need.

Gene kept Mary Ann occupied running errands that afternoon while he drove to Richmond and rented a hotel room. He also leased a car and left it at the hotel, but said nothing of this trip to Mary Ann.

As Gene instructed, Mary Ann took the rental van to Potomac Sports on Minnieville Road, where she put a $175 Taurus revolver and several rounds of ammunition on her credit card.

"I kept telling him 'I don't want a gun,'" Mary Ann later recalled, saying that Gene replied, "You don't necessarily have to use it, but it's good to have."

Next, she drove to a nearby shooting range to practice using her new weapon, another task she didn't particularly enjoy, so she was somewhat relieved to find that the range was closing when she got there at 4:30 PM. Gene told her to go back to the Holiday Inn and wait for further instructions.

Mary Ann had been suspicious of her boss's true intentions for months. She even had her boyfriend try to follow him, but Gene immediately caught on, lost his tail, and called Mary Ann, furious.

"What are you doing? You've got somebody following me," he snapped.

Many of the instructions he'd been giving her seemed to conflict with what she'd learned in the training course at NOVA. But she stuck with the job because she'd already invested hundreds of dollars in the phones, pagers, gun, and various other items he'd told her to buy.

"I wanted to make sure I got my money back," she later said.

Around 7:30 PM, Gene called and told her to drive her own car to meet him at a 7-11. From there, he had her follow him in her own car to a number of different locations he said were important in their investigation, talking to her by cell phone as he gave her the tour. They ended up at the house of a minister he said was involved in the scam. He told her to park and keep watch, then took off in the rental van around nine.

The Reverend Edwin Clever and his sons spent the day together, stopping at McDonald's, Dairy Queen, and the Giant grocery store before heading home for the evening.

At 9:45 PM, Edwin got a call from Gene, posing as a food representative who had called a week earlier and said he wanted to see the food bank at the Prince of Peace in Manassas the following Sunday; his organization was considering making an anonymous donation to Edwin's church. At that time, Gene had suggested they meet up on Sunday afternoon, when no one else would be there, but Edwin had said it would be better to wait until the youth choir had finished, around 8:30 PM.

When Gene called the night of June 23, he said he was close to the church with his female partner and asked if Edwin could meet them there. That way, his partner could go on to a motel while he and Edwin talked. The pastor didn't really feel like going out that late at night on a Sunday, but he reluctantly agreed.

Edwin unlocked the front doors of the church around ten. He picked a magazine off the floor and went to put it in the wooden rack at the other end of the room, when a man in a ski mask jumped out of the stairwell, holding a gun.

"Do you want to live?" Gene asked, pointing the gun at Edwin's chest.

"Yes, everybody does," Edwin said.

Initially, Edwin thought the armed man was a friend with whom he'd recently had a discussion about guns, and who was now playing a joke to make his point. But Edwin soon realized that this was no joke.

Gene turned him around, jabbed the gun into his back, and told him to lie on the floor. He put his knee in Edwin's spine, cuffed his hands behind him, and shackled his ankles together.

"Are you by yourself?" Gene asked.

"Yes, I'm supposed to be meeting someone else, two other people."

Gene put a porous cloth bag with a drawstring over Edwin's head and pulled it closed. The bag was somewhat transparent, so Edwin could see shapes moving against the light.

"Well, there isn't going to be anyone else coming. My boss made the call to you to set this up."

Gene sat Edwin in a chair in the hallway, then started asking him about the church bank accounts. When Edwin said there were some accounts he didn't know anything about, Gene struck him in the back of the head.

Gene said someone had been embezzling money from his boss and laundering it through Edwin's church. He wanted to know if Edwin was part of the scam.

"You're going to help me," Gene said. "Do you know why?"

"No."

"Because I have someone watching your children," he said, adding that he could've "taken" Edwin and his kids at the Giant or Dairy Queen earlier that day.

"Do you know a Marguerite Bennett, a.k.a. Elizabeth Akers?" he asked.

"Yes, I know a Margo Bennett."

"Did you know that she is an embezzler and a lesbian?"

"No, I didn't know that."

By this point, Edwin realized that the masked man must be Gene Bennett, Margo's crazy estranged husband who had kidnapped her in 1993 and then went to prison. He'd run into Gene briefly three times before, once in the early 1990s, then twice only two months earlier at the hospital when Lindsey was having heart surgery. After praying with Margo, her friends, and family in the waiting area, Edwin went to check on Gene, who was sitting by himself in another room. Gene seemed to appreciate the gesture and was very friendly. Edwin felt that Gene's mood was kind of "blank," though, so it was hard to tell if he was hiding his emotions or didn't have any.

Gene moved Edwin into an office, then back into the hallway, where he strapped a fanny pack around the minister's waist. After establishing that Edwin had not been in the military and knew nothing about plastic explosives, Gene said he'd loaded up the pack with C-4.

"I'm putting enough explosives around your waist to blow up this church and flatten all the trees around it," he said.

Edwin heard Gene talking to someone on a cell phone several times in an adjoining room, so he figured Gene had associates who were watching Edwin's kids at the house. He was right. Sort of.

One of those calls, around 10:15, was to answer a page from Mary Ann, who was still parked outside Edwin's. She told Gene she was nervous because one of the elderly neighbors was looking suspiciously at her and her car. Gene told her to wait while he called the minister, then called back and instructed her to drive to the Catholic church across the street from Prince of Peace and to park next to the rental van.

She stayed at the church lot for about an hour until Gene called again. This time, he told her to go to the Giant parking lot and look for a Jeep Cherokee, another car involved in the surveillance.

Gene disappeared for a while, leaving Edwin to sit in fear, wondering about the pack strapped to his belly. He was sure Gene planned to kill him and Margo and harm his children.

Next, Gene told Edwin to call Margo and lure her to the church with the ruse that he needed her help dealing with an abused wife. But he told Edwin to pick the name of someone who was no longer a church member, someone Margo didn't know. Edwin wracked his brain to think of a family whose names Margo would recognize so that he could tip her off covertly.

Gene had Edwin practice what he was going to say and struck him in the back of the head again when he fumbled. Finally, after Gene was satisfied, Edwin made the call to Margo around 11 PM.

Margo had just drifted off to sleep when the phone rang. She reached over her seven-year-old daughter, Lindsey, to pick up the receiver, but heard only dead air.

Lindsey had trouble falling asleep, so she would often curl up in bed with Margo at night, resting her head on her mother's shoulder.

The phone rang a second time. Margo still heard nothing on the other end.

The third time, she heard her pastor's voice.

"Hi, Edwin," she said. It was hard enough to get Lindsey to fall asleep without all this disruption.

"I've gotten a call about domestic abuse—Tammy and Clarence Johnson, one of the families in our church," Edwin said flatly. "Do you remember them?"

Edwin sounded tired. His voice was not as animated as usual. But he always talked a little fast, so Margo had no way of knowing that something was wrong.

"Yes, I know Tammy," she said.

Margo didn't know the family well enough to understand that Edwin was trying to warn her by using a different last name for Tammy and Clarence Batchelett and by calling Clarence by his full name rather than C.E., his usual nickname.

"They've been fighting," Edwin said.

"Fighting?" Margo asked, thinking that the police would be better equipped to handle a domestic violence case.

"They've been yelling and arguing," he said. "The children were scared, so they've gone to Tammy's mother's. I thought it would be a good idea to take a woman along. Can you help me?"

Margo had been studying to be a peer counselor at the church, which was about fifteen minutes from her townhouse in Wood-bridge. It was a little inconvenient to be running out in the middle of the night when she had to be at work early the next morning, but this was all part of the volunteer counseling job.

"Of course I'll help you," she said. "Do you want me to meet you at their house?"

"No, I'm at the church. I'll wait for you here."

Margo moved carefully away from Lindsey and out of her bed, then went to tell her sister Letta, who was staying in the basement apartment, where she was going. The kids were asleep, Margo said, and she'd call in a little while to tell her how long she'd be.

"Okay, be careful," Letta replied.

Margo got her purse and packed her .38 revolver, fully loaded with six bullets. Only now that she was in a hurry, she couldn't seem to find her can of pepper spray on the bookshelf in the living room where she usually left it, out of the girls' reach. At first, she decided to go without it. But by the time she got out to the car, an inner voice told her to go back and search again. This time she found it, right where she'd tried looking the first time.

That's when she saw Allison standing on the stairs, holding her favorite green blanket. She couldn't sleep either.

Margo hugged Allison, kissed her goodnight, and told her to go back to bed.

"I love you," she said. "I'm going to the church. I'll be back in a little bit."

Allison was afraid. She felt something was wrong.

Margo had quit smoking in college, but she'd secretly picked up the habit again after Gene's release from prison a little more than a year ago, when she'd seen him following her—stalking her, really—making sure she saw him watching her.

Margo grabbed a pack of Winston 100s from her purse and lit one, stopping at a red light near a 7-11 to throw out the butt. It was a comfortable night, warm enough to wear a short-sleeved T-shirt and jeans.

As she sped through the night, Margo went over in her head what she was going to say to the couple. This peer counseling program was one of the few activities that provided her with some relief from her nagging paranoia and fear of Gene. It also felt good to practice some of the hostage negotiation and counseling skills she'd learned over the years.

When she pulled up to the church around 11:25 PM, she recognized Edwin's Isuzu SUV parked near the entrance, but the building was dark. She pulled around the truck and parked in front, noticing that the door was propped open with a half-dead potted fern.

As she stepped through the first set of double doors into the foyer, where parishioners would leave their wet umbrellas, she started feeling a heaviness, a sense that something wasn't right. She gripped her pepper spray tightly in her left hand, her thumb on the button as she'd just been trained, apprehensive about what might be waiting for her inside.

"Margo," Edwin called out.

"Edwin, are you there?"

"Yes," he said, his voice muffled through a wall to her left.

"Where are you?"

"I'm in the secretary's office," he said, referring to the room connected to his office, which was off the lobby ahead. His voice sounded off. Unusually serious.

"Are you all right?"

"No, not really."

She opened the second set of double doors into the dark lobby area, which was steeped in the faint pink glow of the Exit sign at the far end of the room. A low light was coming through an open door a few feet ahead and to the left, which led to Edwin's office and then dog-legged into his secretary's office.

Suddenly, a door to the sanctuary burst open about ten feet ahead and to the right of her. A man in a ski mask jumped out with a gun and started coming toward her.

"Margo, don't fight me on this," he ordered.

Margo knew that voice almost as well as her own, and she recognized the bulky frame. It was Gene.

Margo immediately raised her hand and pushed the button on the pepper spray, aiming for his face. It was too dark to see much, but she saw him take a few steps quickly back, trying to get out of her range. Her survival instinct kicked in and she was airborne, plunging into Edwin's office, where she dove for cover behind the desk in the corner.

"Gene, no!" she yelled. "You're not going to do this!"

Margo dug around in her purse for her gun with her right hand, spraying Gene with her other hand every time he poked his head around the doorjamb.

"Margo, do you want to die?"

"You're not going to kill me, Gene. I am not going to let this happen. I am not going to let you do this."

"I don't want to kill you," Gene said. "I just want to talk to you. If I'd wanted to kill you, I could have had you any time."

"If you wanted to talk to me, you could've called me on the phone," Margo said. "I'm not coming out. You are not going to do this."

By her fifth spray, her can was out of power and barely spurted a few inches out. But by that point, she'd found her gun and had her trigger finger right where it needed to be. Margo knocked a stack of letter trays off the desk so that she had an unobstructed view of the doorway she'd just dived through. She balanced the gun on the corner of the desk, where Gene could plainly see it, aimed at his head.

"What do you want to do, get into a shootout right now, right here?" he taunted. "Let's just end it all right now. We can get in a shootout and see who's the best shot."

"I don't care, Gene; I am not coming out there."

"Edwin has got explosives around his waist. I'll kill us all. Come on, let's talk, or we'll all die. Do you want to die?"

"I don't care. You want to blow us up, blow us up, but I'm not coming out there."

Although it hadn't during the kidnapping, Margo's training had kicked in by now, and Gene could do nothing to override it. This time, she intuitively reacted with a game right out of Gene's own playbook, knowing that as long as she could keep the chaos going, he would not have the chance to come up with Plan B. Or so she thought.

Margo could see Edwin in the darkened secretary's office, with a bag over his head and hands cuffed behind him, up against the copy machine.

"Edwin, are you all right?" she asked.

"I think so," he said.

"Do you have explosives around you?"

"There's something around my waist."

"Why didn't you tell Edwin that you're a lesbian?" Gene interrupted. "Did you tell him about the money you stole?"

"I'm not going to let you do this," Margo said. "Just leave. Get out."

At this point, Edwin felt he should try to help.

"Gene, you don't have to do this," he said.

But Margo didn't want Edwin diverting Gene's attention and giving him an opportunity to calm down. She needed to keep the chaos going, but she was also angry, and her adrenaline was running high.

"Edwin, just shut up," she yelled. "This is all your fault. How could you do this to me? How could you call me and bring me into this?"

"Margo, I didn't know what to do. He told me somebody was with my kids. I'm sorry."

"God dammit, Edwin, if Gene doesn't kill you, I will."

"Don't you know I'm going to take the children and leave the country tonight?" Gene said.

"Gene, just do what you have to do. Get out of here. Just leave."

"You know I'm going to leave here and go and get the kids. You know I'm going to have to go through Letta. Is that what you want?"

Margo figured he meant that he would kill Letta if necessary to take the kids, but Margo was willing to call his bluff. "Gene, just do what you have to do. Get out of here. Just leave. I'm not coming out."

Margo didn't understand why he wasn't trying to shoot at her. All she could think was that he wanted to take her somewhere, to torture her, to make her suffer more than just a quick shot to the head.

She'd backed herself into a corner, literally, with no way out of the room except to get past Gene and the doorway he was guarding, and she knew that was highly unlikely, if not impossible.

"Edwin, are you ready to die? 'Cause I don't know how we're going to get out of this."

Edwin sighed and said, "I was afraid of that."

"Are you praying?"

"I've been praying."

"Pray for me too," she said. "I'm a little busy right now."

She made the decision then and there that she would have to shoot Gene and, with any luck, take him down.

She took careful aim at the spot where his head had appeared, but as she began easing back on the trigger, she could feel it slip. The trigger didn't catch. She also heard a click, which meant that the cylinder hadn't rotated inside the gun, so it wouldn't fire. She started to panic.

Please don't tell me my gun is malfunctioning, she thought.

She decided she would have to "single fire" the gun, so she pulled the hammer back with her thumb, cocking it, and took aim again at the doorway.

The next time Gene poked his head around, she fired. The bullet slammed into the doorjamb and the plaster next to it. Just a quarter-inch more to the right and she would have caught him in chest.

Dammit! she thought before snapping back into police action mode. *Don't panic. Get ready. Take the next shot.*

"You'll have to do better than that," Gene said.

Margo crawled around the edge of the desk and tried to reach up and grab the telephone. She had five bullets left, and she was going to use them wisely.

"I wouldn't do that if I were you," Gene said, tauntingly.

Margo withdrew back behind the desk.

Gene started throwing books and handfuls of papers into the office, apparently to draw her fire until she ran out of bullets, but he was careful not to put his head or body into her firing range again.

"Does he have a vest on, or doesn't he?" Gene asked in the same taunting voice.

Margo knew that Gene had been issued a bullet-proof vest by the FBI and that he could very well be wearing it. That meant she'd have to aim for his head, a much smaller target than his chest. But she also knew that Gene might be toying with her.

"Gene, just leave. Get out of here."

"I'm not going to leave," he said. "If I leave, you'll shoot me in the back."

"I'm not going to shoot you in the back. Just leave."

"You're going to follow me and shoot me. Give me your car keys."

"No, I'm not giving you anything. Just get out of here."

"What's it going to take to get you out of there, Margo, a gas canister?"

Margo hoped that this, too, was a ruse and kept yelling at him until he stopped responding.

It got very quiet in the church, but Margo couldn't be sure.

"Gene, just go. Just leave," she said.

When there was still no response, Margo reached up and pulled the phone by its cord off the desk and onto the floor. She didn't know if Gene was still lurking around, but if he was going to run into the room, she didn't want to be up and walking around. What she wanted was to call 911.

But as she started pressing buttons on the phone, she realized that Gene had disabled the lines: there was dead air on one of them, music on the other, and she couldn't get a dial tone. She figured Gene had used one line to call the other and then put it on hold.

"Edwin, the phones are dead. I don't know what we're going to do."

Finally, after pressing one button and then the other five or six times, she was able to free up one of the lines and call 911. It was 11:38 PM.

She laid the receiver down and shouted so that she could keep her hands free and her finger on the trigger, aiming at the doorway, in case Gene appeared again.

Margo continued to yell at Gene. She was afraid that he might come charging back in if he heard her talking to the 911 operator;

she also wanted the dispatcher to know what was going on at the church.

"Gene, just take your gun and get out. Edwin, do you have explosives around your waist?"

Once she figured Gene was probably gone, she picked up the receiver and talked directly to the dispatcher.

"This is Margo Bennett; I'm at the Prince of Peace United Methodist Church. My husband has been here with a gun and tried to kill me. I think he's on the way to getting my children; I need someone to check on my kids. I need police out here."

"Officers are already on the way," the dispatcher said. "I need you to calm down."

"I am calm."

"Is anyone there with you?"

As the dispatcher asked her a series of questions, Margo told Edwin to stand up so she could describe the explosives around his waist. She was not going to come out from behind that desk until she was absolutely sure it was safe. She told him to check the lock on the secretary's door to make sure that Gene couldn't come in that way, then she asked if he could remove the fanny pack. Edwin maneuvered his cuffed hands down his back to unclasp the pack, and laid it carefully on the floor.

Margo asked the dispatcher to call her house and tell Letta to take the kids next door to Beth's in case Gene showed up and tried to nab them.

A few minutes later, the dispatcher told her that the police had arrived at the church.

"The officers are ready to come in," she said. "Put your gun down."

"Tell them I'm not going to the door," Margo said. "They can break the windows to come in as far as I care, but tell them to please hurry."

She didn't know if Gene was still hiding somewhere, so she told Edwin to get down on the ground. "There may be shooting," she said.

The dispatcher tried again to get Margo to put her gun down, but she wouldn't until the dispatcher had listed the names of the officers who were going to come through the door.

Margo heard a group of officers come into the lobby and yell, "Police!" but she still refused to drop her weapon. Only after she had confirmed the officers' identities would she lay her gun on the carpet, stand up, and put her hands in the air.

"Edwin is in there on the ground," she said, pointing to the secretary's office.

The police led Margo and Edwin, whose ankles were still shackled, out of the church and across the driveway as quickly as possible, fearful that Gene was still around and would blow up the church, taking all of them with it.

Once they were thirty feet from the building, the police took off Edwin's handcuffs, and Margo asked if she could remove his leg irons. Margo used her universal key, which unlocked any set of cuffs, to free Edwin.

Detective Ron McClelland had worked the 3 PM to 11 PM shift that day and was en route to his home in Woodbridge when Margo's 911 call came in. All he heard over the police radio was something to do with a bomb at a church and that patrol officers were responding. He was only a few minutes away, so he headed over to see if he could help.

When he got there at 11:55, the patrol officers had already secured the scene and had separated Margo and Edwin. Ron, a redhead in his late thirties, interviewed them separately, Edwin in one police car and Margo in his vehicle.

As Ron questioned Margo, he could see she was shaken, but she was still able to give good details about what had occurred.

Around 12:15, Margo asked if she could use Ron's cell phone to call Letta at Beth's house to make sure the girls were safe. Carly, the daughter of Margo's sister Jackie, was staying with them too.

Letta had brought Margo's cordless phone to Beth's, and it rang while she was talking to Margo on Beth's phone. Margo could hear

Beth in the background, saying that Gene had just called to talk to the girls, but she told him they were asleep.

Letta was crying and her voice was quivering as Margo told her what had just happened, but Margo had to cut the conversation short so that she could get back to the interview with Ron.

A little while later, she called Dianna.

"Sorry to wake you up, but Gene's done it again," Margo said.

"You're shitting me," Dianna said.

"Gene tried to kill me tonight. Do you remember where Prince of Peace Church is? Can you come out here? I need somebody with me."

"Margo, I'll be there as soon as I can."

Dianna grabbed her gun and threw a few things into a bag, not knowing how long Margo might need her to stay, but suspecting it could be up to a week. She sped up I-95 from her house in Fredericksburg and arrived about an hour later.

Dianna parked her Lexus down the street from the church. As she went looking for Margo, the red flashing lights of law enforcement vehicles, including the state police bomb unit, lit up the black night.

As Ron interviewed Margo, he got in and out of his car periodically to talk to the other officers, coming back with new questions and updates on the case.

After returning from one of these breaks, he said, "We got a 911 call from Gene."

Ron turned up his police radio, so they could listen to the chatter. By then, the dispatchers had been handling a series of calls into the taped 911 line from Gene, who was at his house about three miles from the church. His first call came in at 12:40 AM.

"He hung up," the dispatcher kept saying. And then, "He's called back."

Margo was having a hard time focusing on what Gene was doing, but she tried to stay engaged so that she could help police respond to the ongoing situation.

Ron told Margo that police had evacuated some of the houses around Gene's because they were worried he had explosives there, too. He had refused to come outside, so a hostage negotiator had been called in to talk to him.

This was not only an unusual event for Prince William County, but it also caused a great deal of alarm about the potential public safety danger, so the police had alerted Paul Ebert, the county's chief prosecutor, an elected official known as the commonwealth's attorney, similar to a district attorney in other states.

"We were very concerned about what bombs were out there," Paul later said.

Ron waited until Dianna arrived, then headed for Gene's house.

"Sit tight," he told Margo.

Margo was trembling, partly from the adrenaline that was still raging through her body and partly from the cool temperature of a Virginia night, so Dianna led her back to her Lexus and wrapped a blanket around Margo. Dianna didn't really know what to say at a time like this, but she did her best to comfort her friend.

Gene called Mary Ann at 11:44 PM and told her to meet him at the nearby 7-11. She got lost on the way, so she paged him and he called her back around midnight to give her directions. When she pulled in next to him at the 7-11, he was sitting in the van she'd rented, which he'd backed into one of the parking spots out front.

He rolled down his window and told her to transfer all her belongings into the van and get in. She'd only handed him the bag with her new gun and ammunition when he blurted out, "Hurry up! We have to get out and follow them! We're going to lose them!"

Gene took off before Mary Ann even knew what was going on. She tried to get in her car fast enough to follow him, but he was long gone, so she drove back to the Holiday Inn to wait for him to call.

From there, Gene sped home and called 911, reporting that he was hearing voices and that his estranged wife was trying to kill him.

"She's got my kids. She stole my money. She put me in jail. She ruined me and now she shoots at me and tries to blow me up," he said. ". . . She's been in my house. . . . Both of my vehicles are gone. I had to get a vehicle from a friend of mine and they probably thought I stole it."

Then Gene started talking about someone named Ed, who was in the house with him.

"Ed says we've got to go now," Gene said, then hung up.

When Janice Hetzel, the police department's hostage negotiator, called him back, Gene said, "Ed says I can't talk to you anymore. This has gone far enough."

"Who is Ed?" she asked. "Please, Gene, tell me, who is Ed?"

"Ed, Ed just comes and it is terrible," Gene said, adding that he couldn't come out of the house because Ed wouldn't let him.

"Why?"

"'Cause we're afraid."

Gene demanded to talk to the police negotiator's counterpart at Quantico and then, before he hung up, he said cryptically, "I grabbed a gun from some asshole, threw it down on the way out."

When he called back, he was speaking in a very different voice, with an aggressive, angry tone.

"This is Ed. Give me that hostage negotiation bitch," he said, then hung up again.

The negotiator called him back, this time with Gene's attorney Reid Weingarten on the line.

"Gene?" Janice asked.

"This is Ed," Gene said. "That punk motherfucker ain't doin' nothin' no more."

"OK."

"I'm in charge. You got that?"

"Ed?" Janice asked.

Reid jumped in. "Gene, I'm on the line, it's Reid. Now what's going on?"

"What?" Gene said.

"Can you hear us, Gene?" Janice asked.

Gene answered in a soft, confused voice, as if he were in a dream. "What?"

"Reid, do we know somebody named Ed?" Gene asked.

"Huh? How does Ed fit in?"

"I don't know."

After Reid hung up, Gene told Janice he wanted help from his pastor.

"Bill has to come and get rid of the evil," he said. ". . . He'll make the Ed stuff go away. . . . I think Ed's—I hope—I think I locked Ed in the garage."

"You did?" Janice said. "That's a good idea."

"What if Ed gets out of the garage?"

"Gene, you know that is not going to happen."

Janice put the Reverend Bill Higgins on the line, who said he would meet Gene at Prince William Hospital, where Janice promised a doctor would check out Gene's complaints of burning eyes, problems breathing, and chest pains.

"I'm not going to hurt anybody and Ed's not going to hurt anybody else," Gene said. "Ed, Ed, Ed said it was OK to open the door. . . . Will you help make the evil go away?"

"Yes," the pastor replied.

Ron McClelland, who was standing with the other officers outside Gene's house during the long series of calls, said later that none of them believed Gene's act. In fact, they were all laughing at it.

"It was just so obvious that he was playing this role as Ed," he said. "The role he was trying to come up with was pretty clever; it was the only chance he had, but he didn't pull it off. . . . It was just ridiculous."

Gene surrendered at 4:13 AM. He was taken to the hospital by ambulance, then to jail.

Meanwhile, Gene had left a number of items in his wake in and around the church, including a pair of leg shackles in the hallway, some handcuffs in the grass down the street, and a large black gym bag in Edwin's office.

Each of the bag's four compartments was packed with a collection of obscure items, many of which were enclosed in their own plastic zipper-lock bags. Among the items was a bullet-proof vest labeled "E. A. Bennett," a manual for a BB or pellet gun that looked like a semiautomatic pistol, and some pellets. The bag also contained a stethoscope, several syringes, four small bottles of saline solution, three costume eye masks with elastic straps, nine bandannas, two pairs of gloves, some ladies' underwear, four drop cloths, baby wipes, a bottle of nail polish remover, a tube of Krazy Glue, two rolls of Ace bandages, some phone jacks, earplugs, a pair of handcuff keys, and a power converter cord that plugged into a car's cigarette lighter.

Packaged separately was a collection of matches, match heads, fish hooks, a razor blade, and detonator caps used in explosive devices. They also found keys they later learned would open a locker at the Woodbridge NOVA campus, where Margo worked, as well as lockers at the Alexandria, Manassas, and Annandale campuses.

Outside the church, police found a backpack marked with three vertical slashes that looked like the Roman numeral III. (This was the first of five similar packs they would find in different locations. Each pack was labeled with its own set of vertical slashes from I to IIIII, and contained its own set of particular items—swatches of tan carpet, of green-and-white striped dish towel, and of green towel. Each swatch was packaged separately in a plastic bag with strands of hair loosely attached.)

Also in this particular pack were two pairs of latex gloves; some mail addressed to Eugene Bennett and Elizabeth Akers (Margo's middle and maiden names); a quart-size plastic bag of a black mixture that turned out to contain ammonia-based fertilizer, fuel oil, and pyrodex, a black powder often used to make illegal pipe bombs; a set of keys marked "Reston"; and a note typed in capital letters that read, "Evidence—Evidence—Evidence. Do not disturb these items. Contact Lt. M. Bennett, NVCC Campus Police, 878-5744. Evidence—Evidence—Evidence."

Next to the backpack, police found a gray gym bag, which contained an on-off power switch, still in its original packaging; a pair of men's black rain rubbers; an alarm clock; a paintbrush; and a bottle of ibuprofen.

Over the next few weeks, as Margo heard more about the vast array of items that Gene had planted around the region, she could not help but draw on her FBI training to conjure up all kinds of theories about the horrors Gene had had in store for her, including a scenario reminiscent of a serial rapist she'd heard at Quantico that involved Krazy Glue-ing the victim's eyelids shut. But she wouldn't fully understand his scheme until the prosecutors pulled all the pieces together in their closing arguments at his trial seven months later.

Around 3 AM, Margo called Kathy Farrell from Dianna's car.

"This is Margo; are you awake?"

"Give me a minute," Kathy said groggily, roused out of a deep sleep. "Yes?"

"Gene tried to kill me tonight."

"Oh, my God."

Once Kathy got her bearings, she told Margo to try to get some sleep and come to her office in the morning. By then, Kathy said she would have figured out what they should do to get a jump on the divorce and custody case.

Ron returned briefly to tell Margo that he had gotten a search warrant for Gene's house and to stay put for the time being. Margo climbed into the backseat and caught some light sleep for about forty-five minutes.

Dianna was parked too far away for them to hear the loud enthusiasm of the bomb technicians and police officers who had gathered at the bottom of the hill in the church parking lot. After taking a sample of the black mixture from Gene's bag for testing, they rendered the remaining two pounds safe by destroying it. They laid down a concrete strip, poured out the powder, lit a fuse, then whooped as they watched it go up in flames. The white doughy material in Edwin's fanny pack turned out to be harmless Play-Doh.

The two women had watched the sun come up before a police officer told them they were free to go.

Back at the townhouse, Margo took a thirty-minute catnap and a shower, then called her boss to tell him she needed some time off to help the police with their investigation. He told her to take whatever time she needed.

As Margo and Dianna were leaving for Kathy's office, Carly and Letta came home with the girls after spending much of the night hidden away in the basement at Beth's sister-in-law's. Beth had taken them there so that no one, including Margo, would know where to find them.

Lindsey was too young to understand what was going on, but Allison, who was very much aware of the danger Margo had been in, ran into her mother's arms.

Margo hugged each of her daughters tightly.

"Your dad tried to hurt me last night, and now he's in jail," she told them.

Allison would always remember how a female officer had come down the basement stairs in the middle of the night, silhouetted by the hallway light above, and asked if Gene had any guns in his house.

"I know this is a big night for you," the officer said. "I just want you to know everybody is safe, your mom is okay, and I don't want you to worry because we've got more guns than he does."

Kathy had decided to petition the court for an emergency hearing to get temporary sole custody and a restraining order that would prevent Gene from contacting Margo or the girls until permanent custody arrangements could be made. Margo didn't want Gene calling the house collect from jail.

Kathy said she'd been wondering all these months why Gene had been dragging out the divorce proceedings. "I was waiting for the other shoe to drop," she said.

"Well," Margo replied, "it just dropped."

It was finally clear what Gene had been up to. His scheme would have negated the need for the three-day divorce nonjury trial, scheduled for July 15. Margo's death would have made it irrelevant.

Ron went to the hospital around 5 AM, where Gene kept making nonsensical statements, including a mumbled reference to room 116.

"Don't go there," Gene said.

"Why? Who's there?" Ron asked.

"Suzanne; it's really bad."

"Where's the room?"

"Near I-95."

Ron went directly to the Holiday Inn near I-95 on Dumfries Road to see if the person registered in room 116 was okay. The front desk called the room and got Mary Ann on the phone. She'd finally fallen asleep, and now the phone had woken her up again.

Mary Ann had called the police in the wee hours to report that her boss was missing, along with a gun she'd just purchased, which was now in his possession.

At 8:15 that morning, when the dispatcher told Ron and his partner, Sam Walker, that Mary Ann had called, the detectives looked at each other, intrigued and yet puzzled by the new development.

They immediately returned to the Holiday Inn and met with Mary Ann in her room. She told them her version of what had happened on Sunday, culminating with the strange meeting at 7-11 with her boss, Edwin Adams.

Ron and Sam figured that the man she described was Gene Bennett, so they took her to the station and showed her a lineup of six male suspects' booking photos. She pointed to Gene without hesitation.

From there, Mary Ann took Ron to where she'd last seen Gene's Dodge Dynasty, on Commerce Court in Manassas. After it had been impounded, investigators searched the trunk and found another blue backpack, this one labeled IIIIII.

Ron was amazed at how easily Gene had manipulated Mary Ann into buying life insurance policies, cell phones, and a gun. She didn't even seem shaken up. Initially, Ron thought that she was in on the scheme.

"I really thought she was putting on an act, but it turned out not to be an act," he later said.

Ron soon realized that Mary Ann had no idea what she had gotten herself into. Gene had found the perfect person to help pull off his wild plan.

Later that afternoon, Bob DelCore, the unofficial head of NOVA's five campus police departments, called Margo to say that she was being placed on an open-ended, paid administrative leave, while campus officials investigated her use of deadly force—by shooting at Gene—the night before. He told her that no one was saying she'd done anything wrong, but they had to look into it. He sounded sympathetic and asked if it would be all right if a peer counselor from the Fairfax County Police Department came and talked to her about the incident.

Margo wasn't concerned about the investigation because she knew the bureaucratic process had to run its course. She was confident that they would find the shooting justified.

She took the girls to their scheduled therapy appointment with Molly Ellsworth that evening, then spoke to the peer counselor around nine. She insisted that they talk in his car outside the townhouse because she didn't want the girls to hear their conversation.

"How do you feel about having shot at someone?" he asked.

"I feel fine with what I did," she said. "I feel I did the right thing."

Margo didn't read any of the newspaper articles that had come out that day, but she did watch the TV news that evening. The church incident was featured at the top of the hour on all the local news shows, so she was able to see only one of them.

Gene had been charged with abduction with intent to extort money, burglary while armed, making bomb threats, using a firearm while committing a felony, and possession of a firearm by a convicted felon. He was being held without bond pending a psychological evaluation. Margo wondered why there was no attempted murder charge.

It was very strange to watch her own story unfolding on television for the world to see, but all she felt was numb, as if she were watching something that had happened to someone else.

She'd sent the kids upstairs, worried that they might be scared to see their father's booking photo, which featured a man with tired eyes and unkempt hair and kept flashing across the screen. Thankfully, none of the news outlets had gotten a photo of her, only of her car parked outside the church, so she felt she still had some privacy and protection from the media. She had no idea how fleeting that feeling would be.

Margo went to bed around 11 PM, comforted to have Lindsey beside her again. Margo fell asleep all right, but then she started what would become a routine—waking up and lying awake for two and half hours, trying to connect the dots of Gene's scheme, then drifting off for maybe an hour before having to get up for work.

On Tuesday morning, Margo got a call from Detective Sam Walker, asking if she could come down to the station to answer some questions. She certainly was not expecting to hear what he had to say in that tiny interview room.

"Do you know a woman named Mary Ann Khalifeh?" Sam asked.

"No," Margo said, not remembering their meeting at the Polo Grill the month before.

"We don't have all the information on this yet," Sam said, "but it looks like your husband planned to kill you for some insurance money."

Margo was not surprised to hear that Gene had planned to kill her, but she was puzzled by the alleged motivation.

What insurance money? she wondered.

"It looks like Gene hired someone to help him kill you and the reverend. We don't know if he was acting alone. I'm telling you this now so you can be careful, but don't tell anyone. We don't have all the information yet."

Don't tell anyone? she thought.

Margo knew how much Gene hated her and wanted her dead, but she couldn't believe that he would be so greedy, that he would endanger other people's lives to get to her. She was also shocked to hear how much effort he had put into his plan.

Dianna was waiting for her outside, but Margo told her she wanted to wait until they got to Kathy's office to talk about her meeting with the detective.

Once they got to Kathy's, Margo relayed Sam's theory and words of caution.

"So why are you telling me about this?" Kathy asked.

"I have to tell somebody. You're my attorney," Margo said, meaning that Kathy was obligated to keep her secret under attorney-client privilege.

From there, they all headed over to the emergency custody hearing.

As they were walking into the courtroom, Kathy couldn't help but make a sarcastic comment to Gene's divorce attorney, Doug Bergere.

"Now do you believe her story?" she asked, referring to the kidnapping.

Doug simply nodded and looked down at the floor.

The judge granted Margo's request for a "no contact" order, prohibiting Gene from calling the girls, but that didn't stop him. He tried calling Allison collect a couple of days later, so Kathy notified the jail and asked them to stop Gene from calling the house.

Later that day, the police found the Windstar rental van. It was parked on Briarmont Lane, at the end of a long driveway of an occupied house that was up for sale, about a fifty-yard walk through the woods from Gene's house. Inside, they found a long-sleeved navy-blue work shirt, which, after undergoing forensic testing, proved to be spattered with pepper spray.

During the search, officers brought over a note pad, which Edwin had found in his office after the police left. Two pages in Gene's handwriting were each titled "Items To Check On."

The first page listed directions to the Pittsburgh airport as well as phone numbers for American Airlines and US Air, with a specific number and time for a flight from Pittsburgh to San Diego, followed by the notation "Call 911." It also listed phone numbers for two hotels in Martinsburg, West Virginia, where Gene and Mary Ann had left the Plymouth Voyager van on Sunday morning. Pittsburgh was the closest airport to Martinsburg.

The second page, under the initials "MAB," appeared to be a list of places he planned to leave various items tied to Margo, including "literature in car/purse," "keys in car/purse," and "keys on key ring."

Edwin's secretary had also found some male homosexual pornographic materials in his office safe, which was kept unlocked. These too were turned over to police.

News reporters started calling and showing up at Margo's townhouse that Tuesday. Letta had been handling the calls, but when she and Carly left in the late afternoon to pick up Jackie from the airport, Margo had to answer the doorbell herself. It was a young woman from the *Washington Post*.

The woman apologized for having to ask for a quote, but asked nonetheless.

Margo gave her the only comment she would make to the media until after Gene's trial: "Time will put everything in its proper perspective."

Margo and Letta went to Prince of Peace that night for a service to reclaim the church after the violence that had tainted its sacred space. Margo had learned of the service when she'd tried to reach Edwin by phone in the afternoon. A message on the church answering machine announced the service and said that Edwin was doing fine, but made no mention of Margo.

"That's when I really started to feel left out," she said later.

When they first arrived, no one would look at Margo or sit in the same pew. There seemed to be an unspoken barrier of blame or some emotion that she did not understand. Only one woman came over and squeezed her hand before the associate pastor began speaking.

"How are you doing?" the woman asked.

"Right now I'm feeling very alone," Margo said.

The associate pastor spoke for half an hour about the terrible experience that Edwin had suffered, then he asked church members to give comments of thanks.

Several people stood up and thanked God for saving Edwin before another woman pointed out that Margo had suffered and deserved their praise, too.

"I just want to give thanks that Margo brought her gun into this church, because if she hadn't done that, I can only imagine what could have happened," she said.

After that, others started looking Margo in the eye and including her in their remarks. The barrier had been broken.

"I was relieved that somebody was realizing that it was a horrible evening for me, my children, my sister, my family," Margo said later.

At the end of the service, Margo and Edwin stood in the middle of the center aisle, where church members lined up to give each of them a hug and offer their support.

This would be the last service Margo would attend at Prince of Peace. Being there was just too emotionally difficult, not to mention that she'd been outed by the media. Instead, she attended services at Diane Lytle's Presbyterian church, which was more accepting of her sexuality and where she was surrounded by strangers.

"I wanted anonymity for a while," she said.

Margo felt a sense of satisfaction that she'd struggled against Gene and done what she'd needed to survive. She was alive, he was in jail, and she and her children were safe once again. The storm, she felt, had passed.

She didn't realize that this was actually the calm before another type of storm moved in.

Chapter Eleven

The Investigation

Gene's Plot Unfolds

On the morning of Wednesday, June 26, Margo went to the store to buy every newspaper with a headline about her and Gene so that she could see what was being reported and also so that her daughters could read an objective account later if they so chose.

There were three—one in the *Potomac News*, one in the *Prince William Journal*, and one in the *Washington Post*.

"Ex-FBI Agent in Custody," read the *Journal* headline. Margo felt her stomach drop when she got to the sixth paragraph, which said, "A copy of the divorce papers obtained Monday by *The Journal* include allegations by Mr. Bennett that his wife had more than one lesbian sexual relationship. Among the affairs Mr. Bennett alleged was one with a prominent author."

The story quoted from the interrogatory response in which Gene alleged that Margo had met Patsy for romantic candlelit dinners and that he'd seen them kissing and hugging.

Oh, God, here it comes, she thought.

Although the article didn't name Patsy, Margo predicted that a media frenzy was about to begin.

She was right. The next article was even worse.

"Ex-Agent Alleges Wife Had Affair with Author," read the *Potomac News* headline.

Seeing Patsy named as her lover in the third paragraph sent Margo's anxiety skyrocketing.

Oh, my God, oh, my God, she thought. *This is going to be in every newspaper and on every news channel. How am I going to protect my kids? What's this going to mean at work?*

Things didn't get any better from there. The *Post* story, which had the headline "Psychiatric Evaluation Ordered for Abduction Suspect," named Patsy as well. It also gave Margo her first clue to what Gene's defense was going to be, quoting one of his attorneys, Jeffrey Gans, saying that his client was disoriented, said he was hearing voices, and believed he had "an alter ego named Ed that was bad." Gans told the *Post* that Gene "did not know what day it was" and also "could not account for his whereabouts during his time of the confrontation" at the church.

Margo didn't know that reporters had been calling Kathy since Monday. Kathy later told her she'd sealed the divorce records at the emergency custody hearing the day before, but it was too late to stop the media train. All they could do was try to slow it down.

Patsy had just gotten a three-book contract with Putnam, worth a reported $24 million to $27 million, and was set to release her seventh book in the Kay Scarpetta series, *Cause of Death,* in July. Patsy's celebrity had catapulted her ties to Margo and Gene's criminal case into an international news story with the kind of juicy hook that the media loved.

Margo was never able to determine how the first reporter got hold of the records, but she figured Gene must have given his criminal attorneys permission to release them. His divorce attorney, Doug Bergere, told the media that he and Kathy had requested that the documents be sealed.

That same day, Gene gave a thirty-minute interview to the *Potomac News* reporter for a story that appeared the next morning.

The article described Gene as tired and unshaven, wearing a short-sleeved orange jumpsuit and handcuffs as he spoke to the reporter by telephone in the visiting room.

"I've been without sleep for a long, long time," Gene said. "What day is today? . . . I don't know what's going on. Right now, I would just like to get some sleep."

Gene claimed he didn't recall abducting Edwin Clever or putting explosives in the church, only running out of the church after Margo took a shot at him.

"I would have shot back but I don't have a gun," he said.

Gene said he'd expected to have been granted full custody of his daughters at the July 15 divorce trial.

"I didn't want my children raised in a lesbian household. I don't think she's a proper mother for them," he said.

About a week later, movie producers started calling Kathy about doing a film on the case. But Margo wasn't interested. She felt the best thing for her was to lay low and be quiet.

Growing up, Margo was like her mother in that she kept her emotions inside. Afflicted with the typical middle-child syndrome, Margo felt invisible much of the time. She didn't try to speak up all that often, because even when she did, no one seemed to listen.

One night in Athens, Georgia, when Margo was fourteen, her family was sitting around the dinner table, talking about the activities they'd done that day, which included picking vegetables at a private garden they shared with several families.

"My favorite part was digging the potatoes," Margo said, her soft voice drowned out by the family's conversation.

"My favorite part was digging the potatoes," Margo repeated a little louder.

Still, everyone kept talking.

"My favorite part was digging the potatoes," Margo said even louder, prompting her mother to break out laughing.

But Margo was satisfied. Finally someone had acknowledged her.

Although she liked this type of positive affirmation, Margo didn't much care for being the central focus. In fact, she often liked being invisible because it meant less attention and, as a result, less discord. Shying away from confrontation, she often served as the family peacemaker and facilitator. Looking back later, she realized that she had probably cheated herself out of some much-needed nurturing and confidence building.

Now that the media was exposing her most intimate secrets and highlighting her questionable choices—first marrying Gene and then having an affair with a woman who became an internationally known author—Margo had to learn a whole new way of coping with unwanted attention. This was one choice she couldn't afford *not* to make.

Margo had to accept that her life would never be the same. She was embarrassed that her private life was media fodder for public consumption, but she finally decided she wasn't going to be embarrassed about who she was anymore.

"There were no secrets to be kept, and there's a great deal of relief that goes with that," she later recalled. "I also believed that I had done nothing wrong. I was the one wronged. People who knew me would stand by me—they knew what kind of person I was—and the people who didn't know me didn't matter."

Bob DelCore, NOVA's police chief, called Margo at home on Thursday afternoon to tell her that the investigation into the shooting was over. He said she was cleared to come back to work, but she could take all the time she needed.

Margo said she would be in the next morning. The sooner she got back to work, the sooner she hoped her life could return to some level of normality.

That same afternoon, Prince William County police officers Debra Twomey and Tom Leo went with the state police bomb squad to the Woodbridge NOVA campus—a four-story, cream-colored building surrounded by maple trees and a picturesque man-made lake. There they located the two lockers that corresponded to the numbers—4 and 28—on the keys marked "Woodbridge" that police had found in Gene's black gym bag.

With the help of a bomb-sniffing dog, they did a sweep of the campus and found that the keys unlocked padlocks hanging on lockers in the southwest corner of the building, down the hall from the student lunch area and about fifty feet from Margo's office.

But before they could go through the lockers, they had to obtain search warrants, which they finally executed just before 10 PM.

Locker 28 held another typed "Evidence—Evidence—Evidence" note, and locker 4 held another blue backpack, marked with a single vertical slash, or I.

After x-raying the pack, the police found that it contained not only more of the same carpet and towel swatches and black explosive mixture they'd seen before but also something much more ominous: a strange, foot-long contraption wrapped with shiny black electrical tape, with an on-off power switch that looked like the one from the gray bag Gene had left outside the church. They determined that it was a homemade pipe bomb, which seemed all the more peculiar because a black vibrator was attached to it. Why in the world would someone attach a sex toy to a pipe bomb?

Ron and his team of investigators would later discover that the swatches from the backpacks matched carpet and towels they'd found in Gene's house and, when put together like a puzzle, fit into one contiguous piece of each respective material. It was curious to them that these items, which would generally be gathered as evidence to catch a criminal, were turning up in nice, neat packages at each crime scene. It looked as if Gene had purposely planted these items so that investigators would follow a road map of sorts and come to a particular conclusion. But now that they'd found this pipe bomb, the investigators scratched their heads, trying to see the big picture. If Gene's plan had not been foiled, how would all this have ended?

It seemed from the evidence notes that Gene was trying to frame Margo for planting the bomb. The motive, they were guessing, was revenge.

"He had it bad for her," Debra Twomey said later. "He was one pissed off ex-husband."

Around 10 PM, Ron called Margo and told her about the backpacks and bomb. Given what appeared to be the sequential numbering of the packs, he said they were concerned that Gene had planted more explosives on other campuses, in other vehicles, and who knows where else.

Ron said they wanted to bring a bomb-sniffing dog to her house, but they didn't have enough available at the moment, so he told her to take the girls to sleep somewhere else, and they would come over the next day. Ron agreed with Margo's suggestion to stay the night at Beth's.

Margo grabbed the girls and some clothes and knocked on her neighbor's door with Letta.

"What is it now?" Beth's husband, Greg, asked when he saw the four of them standing on his doorstep.

"What makes them think if there's a bomb in your house and it explodes, it won't hurt us, too?" Beth asked after Margo relayed the news.

The four of them spent the night in Beth's basement.

Meanwhile, back at the college, the state bomb technicians tied a rope around the black device and dragged it down ten feet of hallway, through a set of double glass doors, and into an alcove just outside the building. Around 11 PM, they attempted to disable the bomb safely by shooting the cap off one end. Instead, they inadvertently detonated the device, which sent metal fishhooks and nails everywhere, shattered the glass doors and scorched the concrete walls, which were pierced with the sharp fragments. The explosion was forceful enough to shoot shrapnel through the walls and into the art classroom.

The next morning, Margo checked under the hood of her Geo Prizm to make sure it wasn't rigged to explode before she drove to work for her first day back.

Not long after she got to the office, she went to see David Karstens, the business manager for the Woodbridge campus and her direct supervisor. He warned her that if all the publicity surrounding the church incident caused students to feel she was unapproachable, the college might have to let her go.

Later, when Brenda Floyd, NOVA's vice president, learned what Karstens had said, she apologized to Margo. "We're 100 percent behind you," Brenda said. "That was an inappropriate thing to say."

Once the police and bomb squad determined that the keys in Gene's black gym bag opened lockers at the Woodbridge NOVA building, they wasted no time in searching for corresponding padlocks at the Manassas, Loudoun, Annandale, and Alexandria campuses during the early morning hours of Friday, June 28.

In the two Annandale lockers, 313 and 350, they found a maroon backpack labeled IIIII, with a toothbrush that later proved to have Gene's DNA on it, along with the usual swatches and black powder. Locker 350 contained a five-page typed note that outlined a series of business transactions and was peppered with the initials "MAK."

In the Alexandria locker, police found a backpack labeled IIII, which contained two books, titled *The 1995 National Directory of Bereavement Support Groups and Services* and *A History of Witchcraft*. In the bereavement chapter titled "It's Not Uncommon: Normal Grieving Responses After the Murder of a Loved One," the page describing how people often act after someone they love has been murdered was marked.

They found nothing at the Manassas or Loudoun campuses, so they checked the Northern Virginia Criminal Justice Academy in Ashburn, where Margo had been an instructor, then went to Dulles Airport to burn off the black powder they'd found in the vehicles and lockers.

The investigators tried contacting Patsy and her security people about the missing backpack II, but Patsy was out of the country, and her people did not want to cooperate.

Around noon on Friday, Ron went to the county jail to talk to Gene. Ron didn't expect to get much in the way of incriminating statements—his primary intention was to see if Gene would reveal where he'd planted backpack II or any other explosive devices they hadn't found yet.

Ron told Gene about the bomb-making materials they'd found in his car and the pipe bomb that had exploded at the Woodbridge campus.

"If you know where any of these other ones are, we need to know it."

But Gene played dumb. "I didn't hear about any explosive devices," he said.

Ron told him there was at least one the police couldn't find. "If it goes off and somebody gets killed, you're going to be held responsible," he said.

"I didn't have nothing to do with any bombs," Gene said. Then, in a confused voice, he said. "I, I, is my car blown up, too?"

Gene said he'd never made a bomb or had any training in explosives.

"I know you're looking at me for a lot of things, but I hope you open your eyes in those other areas that you're looking at, too," Gene said. "I'm talking about Mrs. Bennett."

"What about her?"

"I, I just hope you're not so blind sighted—focused on whatever you think I am or whatever I've done—that you are missing Mrs. Bennett."

"I'm not, you know, closing my eyes to anything," Ron said.

"Well, most people do."

"Do you think she may know where these bombs are at or where they've been placed?"

"Well, that's what she was screaming at me, that's all I know. That she was going to blow my ass up."

"Does she have experience with explosives?"

"She has it more than I do."

Ron assured Gene that the police would check into his allegations. "Well, I mean, believe me, we're looking at her," he said.

"There's nothing that this woman is not capable of," Gene said. ". . . She's so fucked up over this lesbian shit, and anybody finding out about it. . . . She is so intelligent and so devious and can get people to do things like I've never seen in my life before. She can control people. She can manipulate situations. . . . She likes to be the victim. She likes to be the hero. She likes to be in the limelight. She wants to be the little princess of everybody's eye. She feels that she was wronged by the FBI and you know she was forced to resign and the only reason she wasn't prosecuted was because I wouldn't testify against her. If you've done your research, you've read, you've seen my plea agreement. . . . They kept coming back, wanting me to testify against her and prosecute her and I said what good would that do? I'm sitting in jail for a year and she's sitting in jail for how many years for falsifying testimony and documents, and where does that leave my kids?"

Gene said he was unarmed at the church, yet the police kept asking where his gun was.

"I said, if somebody shoots at me and I got a gun in my hand, I'm going to shoot back, at least until I can find cover and get the hell out of danger. I didn't have no God damn gun, okay?"

After that, Gene refused to say anything more without his attorney present, although he kept trying to persuade Ron to disclose more about what police had found so far.

Because of the church incident, Margo had missed some of the classes she needed to complete her state police certification and graduate from the Rappahannock Regional Criminal Justice

Academy. Nonetheless, she went to the ceremony that Friday afternoon with her boss, Bob DelCore, because one of her officers was graduating.

Margo was wearing her navy-blue NOVA uniform, but the Prince William County sheriff clearly didn't know whom he was talking to when he made a flip comment to her afterward.

"The press is giving you guys a rough time," he said, laughing. "It's crazy, isn't it?"

Five minutes later, he came back over with an apologetic expression. "I'm sorry; are you doing okay?"

"Yeah, I'm doing fine," she said.

But it was the next comment, which Margo received from a female deputy in her forties—too old, she thought, to be gushing about celebrities like a teenager—that almost put her over the edge.

"I've always admired Patricia Cornwell," the deputy said. "Do you think you could help me meet her?"

Margo, appalled at the woman's lack of tact, could not believe what she'd just heard. "I haven't talked to Patsy in years," she said and walked away.

When she got home around three o'clock, the bomb squad was there with a dog, sweeping the townhouse. One of her elderly neighbors was outside talking to Beth, saying he was sure the police were looking for drugs. Beth set him straight.

The dog sniffed around and alerted in Margo's bedroom closet, where she used to keep a shotgun. It also alerted when it sniffed the driver's seat of her car, where she wore her uniform and gun. But the dog found no bombs.

After the police left, Margo felt the numbness from the last five days starting to slip away and reality setting in. The strong emotional front she had worked so hard to keep up for her children was starting to crack. She didn't want her daughters to see her that way, so she called Dianna, who invited her to stay over.

As Margo lay awake in Dianna's spare room, she started thinking about what could've happened to her at the church. Gene could have killed her, and her children could have been orphaned. The horror of what might have been, of how much Gene hated her and how trapped she felt, sent her into a vortex of fear from which she thought she'd never be able to escape.

She started to cry, just a little at first. But then the tears came faster and harder, her body heaving as she sobbed and couldn't stop. She got out of bed and went into her friend's room.

"Dianna, I can't stay in there by myself," she said, still sobbing.

"That's okay," Dianna said. "Do you want to sleep with me?"

Dianna held up the covers and Margo crawled in next to her. Dianna patted Margo on the back until she finally stopped crying and fell asleep. This was the second time in a week that Margo had woken her friend in the middle of the night.

When Margo went home the next day, she learned that a *People* magazine reporter had been driving around the neighborhood, looking for her house. Luckily, her neighbors said they didn't know where she lived. Margo was relieved because Allison had been playing outside, wearing the *All That Remains* T-shirt Patsy had given Margo at the book party in July 1992.

After that narrow escape, she and Jackie decided it would be best if Jackie took Carly and the girls back to Tuscaloosa for a couple of weeks. Margo wanted to be strong for her daughters, but knew she couldn't be until she had a chance to pull herself together. She also wanted to shield the girls from the media onslaught until the situation had calmed down. She had no idea that the publicity would increase even more in the coming weeks.

Margo called to talk to the girls each evening, but Jackie never told her that Lindsey cried every night as she slept with her head on her aunt's shoulder. Years later, when Margo learned how traumatized her daughters had been, she wondered if she'd done the wrong thing by sending them away.

"If I'd known what they were going through, I would've gone down to get them or had Jackie bring them back," she later said.

During the two searches of Gene's house on June 24 and 28, police found the Taurus revolver that Mary Ann had purchased, along with some loose .38-caliber cartridges and a gas mask, in his garage.

The house was extremely clean and well organized. In the bathroom, he had carefully rolled up his tube of toothpaste, using the same type of black binder clip that police had found on the bag of explosive mixture he'd left at the church, and his towels were neatly folded. Throughout the house, he had grouped similar items, such as batteries of varying sizes, in their own separate zipper-lock plastic bags, even within the same drawer. Investigators found numerous boxes of these bags in all different sizes.

In the pantry, they found some Play-Doh and two cloth bags similar to the one he'd placed on Edwin's head. They found two keys on the counter, one for the Plymouth Voyager van in West Virginia and one that said "Budget Rent-A-Car," which they later learned was for the car Gene had rented and left in Richmond. They also found an envelope of three-by-five cards that listed book titles about murder, extremist groups, and death in general, including *Cause of Death: A Writer's Guide to Death, Murder and Forensic Medicine*, *The Perfect Husband*, and *The Insider: The FBI's Undercover Wiseguy Goes Public*.

Upstairs, they found a derringer in his briefcase and a Soldier of Fortune book called *A True Story of Obsessive Love and Murder for Hire*, which told the story of a murder staged as a car accident. All the books they collected during the investigation came from the county library system and were overdue by months or even years.

They also found the missing photo of Margo and Patsy from the Globe & Laurel book party, along with several vibrators and a porno movie featuring two women having sex, with a note in Gene's handwriting on the back saying, "from MAB's van."

On July 2, Margo and Edwin met at the church with Ron and the two prosecutors who would be handling Gene's case—Paul

Ebert, who was elected the commonwealth's attorney for Prince William County in 1968, and Jim Willett, who had been a prosecutor for about thirteen years and would handle the Beltway sniper case seven years later.

After doing a walk-through to go over what had happened where, Margo sat in Ron's car, where he showed her photos of the massive quantity of evidence investigators had gathered so far. Ron discussed his various theories and asked for her help and insight into what leads to pursue from there.

Ron said he suspected that Gene was going to make it look as if Margo and Mary Ann Khalifeh were lesbian lovers by planting Allison's and Lindsey's hair in Mary Ann's house, as if Margo had brought them to visit.

A few days earlier, Ron had asked Margo if she had a P.O. box, because they had found one in the same strip mall where the Polo Grill was located, registered under the names of Edwin Adams and Elizabeth Akers. The five-page note found in the Annandale campus locker stated that Mary Ann was to call Margo by the name Edwin Adams and that Mary Ann should tell other people she was working for someone by that name.

Ron didn't go into great detail about everything in Gene's black bag, which the media had dubbed his "death kit" or "murder kit," but he told her enough to fuel her nightmares for years.

She wondered if, for example, he was planning to mix some nasty substance with the saline solution and inject her with it. Based on what she'd learned in her FBI training, she knew that when offenders take their victims away from the initial crime scene, abuse and torture generally follow.

"If all he'd brought was a gun, he'd have killed me," she said later. "If I'd left that church alive, it would have been a horrible night."

Margo was taken aback when Ron said he had to investigate the allegations Gene had made against her during the jailhouse interview. He said he didn't believe them, but the best way to discount such accusations was to disprove them.

"Look all you want; you're not going to find anything that supports that," Margo said.

Once she'd seen all the evidence photos, she started to get a clearer picture of what Gene had been planning to do.

"It was very sobering to see how obsessed Gene was by creating such an intricate, elaborate plot," she said later. "The end result that I think he strove for was vindication—that I was the terrible part of his downfall—and the secret vengeance he would have exacted on me. My reputation would have been destroyed and he would have been the sympathetic figure."

Still looking for backpack II, the police sent out a teletype to alert other agencies statewide about the missing Budget car Gene had rented. On July 4, Ron was notified by the Richmond Police Department that the car had been located at the local Fairfield Inn. So Ron hopped in the car with Debra Twomey and made the ninety-minute drive to Richmond to check it out.

When they arrived, the hotel was swarming with police and local and state bomb squad technicians. The hotel staff told them that Gene had checked into room 157 on Sunday, June 23, after paying for four days with his credit card. He'd never checked out.

After the fiasco at the Woodbridge campus, the bomb techs used a robot to search the room before anyone went inside.

Inside, police found a dress shirt, tie, and jacket hung up in the closet and a pair of navy-blue work pants lying on the bed, still in their original packaging. The pants matched Gene's long-sleeved, navy-blue shirt that was covered with pepper spray. Cologne and hairspray for men were sitting on the bathroom counter.

In the red Ford Contour that Gene had parked outside the room, police found a map book of metropolitan Richmond, with a letter tucked in between pages 23 and 24—pages that detailed Patsy's Windsor Farms neighborhood, which was a mere five-mile drive from the hotel. The trunk contained a hamper holding items similar to those found in the other bags and backpacks.

Margo learned about the Richmond search on the TV news that night. If Gene had been successful in killing her and Mary Ann, she figured he would already have established an alibi and claim that he'd never left the hotel.

The next day, Margo came home from work to an empty house and started to panic. It was still light outside, yet she stood paralyzed, too scared to climb the stairs to her bedroom to change clothes. She knew she was being irrational. Gene was behind bars, but she still feared that someone working for Gene was upstairs, waiting to jump her.

"My brain was saying this guy is not all-powerful, yet at the same time, he had this power over me," she said later.

Dianna had given her the name of a counselor who specialized in posttraumatic stress disorder. Margo and the therapist, Nancy Davis, had exchanged messages but had yet to connect. Margo tried her again, and this time she reached her.

"Margo, you know he's in jail," Nancy said.

"I know that, but I'm still scared. I'm too afraid to go upstairs in my own house."

"He's not there. He's not going to hurt you. We will deal with your fears, but you are safe in your own house right now."

Margo's panic eased after they agreed to meet the following Tuesday morning for two hours. She trusted Nancy as a professional and was relieved that she didn't have to cope with this by herself any longer.

On the morning of her appointment, Patsy's latest novel, *Cause of Death*, had just hit the stands. Margo faxed a copy of a *New York Daily News* story about the whole mess to Kathy Farrell with a wry note: "It's a sensation-seeking rag article. Nonetheless, it's fun to read over a cup of coffee. The only way I can get over this is to plow straight ahead. I see the shrink this morning from 9 AM to 11 AM. If she keeps me/commits me, I'll have them call you."

The story was mostly about Patsy and how "getting to be famous and very rich did her no favors," according to Dot Jackson, an old friend of Patsy's from the *Charlotte Observer*. Dot was quoted as saying, "I remember seeing Margo Bennett once in Patsy's company, and Margo seemed to be a plain, quiet person, not the sort that you would associate with scandal."

Margo vaguely remembered the name Dot Jackson and linked it to the woman who dreamed about the blood in Patsy's bed. She didn't appreciate being described that way, but she shrugged it off, thinking, "This woman doesn't know me."

Nancy quickly determined that Gene's assault on Margo in 1993 had left her with more emotional damage than his most recent attack.

As Margo described the first incident, she could still see the taser in his hand and remember kicking at the strip on the garage door, fighting for her life while he held her down. But Nancy helped her realize the important difference between the two events.

"The first time, he had me A to Z. I had no control," Margo said later. "He used everything he knew about me against me, totally violated any sense of trust I had in him. The second time, I was able to fight back and I won. I lived through it. I was able to protect myself. I was able to protect Edwin. I saved us. I was strong enough to come out of it. He didn't get me in '96."

After the *People* magazine reporter showed up in the neighborhood, Margo called her parents to give them an idea of what to expect from the national media.

"You're going to hear a lot of stuff," she told her father. "Gene is making accusations that I was with another woman and, Dad, it's true. It happened."

Ed's response surprised her: "Well, things happen in our lives," he said. A decade earlier, he would have been shocked and appalled, but Margo figured that at sixty-nine, he'd gained a new perspective.

That said, after the tabloids got hold of the story a couple of weeks later, Ed wouldn't let his wife, Dean, talk to anyone outside the family about the situation. In fact, Dean told Margo that he wouldn't even let her talk about it to Dean's youngest sister, Martha, who had read about the whole thing in the *Star*. After talking to her mother, Margo became worried that Dean wasn't handling all the publicity well, so she called Martha to get her assessment.

Martha said that when she saw Gene's booking photo, she thought, "My lord, he looks like a crazy man."

Then Martha started choking up. "I don't care who you sleep with, and you don't have to tell me," she said. "I am your aunt, you are my niece, and I love you and I will support you in anything that you want to do."

"It means a lot to me to hear you say that," Margo replied. After they hung up, she called her mother back and urged her to confide in Martha, regardless of what Ed had said.

Margo went to pick up the girls in Tuscaloosa on July 12 and stayed a few days. The *People* magazine story came out midway through her trip, so Margo bought a copy at the grocery store to show her parents. Referring to the love triangle with Patsy, the headline read, "Stranger Than Fiction."

While her mother was getting her hair done on Saturday morning, July 13, Margo sat talking with her father in his truck outside the beauty shop.

"I don't know how you have survived through this," he told her.

"I guess I came from sturdy stock," she said, which made her father chuckle.

That same week, an article came out in *Newsweek* about Patsy, noting that her new book was debuting at number one on the *New York Times* best-seller list. The second paragraph included the inevitable mention of their affair, saying Patsy was "in the middle of a made-for-tabloid scandal."

Patsy told *Newsweek* she didn't want to talk about the "alleged relationship with Marguerite," saying, "My personal life is not anybody else's business. . . . I don't believe people should be defined by their sexuality. People can think what they want. There's nothing I can do."

The article said *Newsweek* "could not locate Marguerite," which amused Margo. However, that fleeting comfort lasted only until she saw the huge story splashed across the Style section front of the *Washington Post* on July 28, with a headline that read, "The Ex Files: Here's What Can Happen When Two Heavily Armed People Fall Out of Love. A Story of Sex, Guns and a Crime Novelist's Nightmare."

"Margo pulled out a gat and squeezed off a round. Damn near winged the sumbitch, too," the article said to describe her actions in the church. "The story is all tabloid. In fact, for a respectable national newspaper like this one to dignify it with a big feature story containing mugshots and everything—well, for that to happen, the story would have to have a sophisticated theme featuring timeless universal truths and, ideally, Greek or Latin phrases. Here, then is the theme: Sometimes, homo sapiens behave very, very badly."

Margo thought that the writer, Karl Vick, made light of the trauma she'd been through, as if she were a character in a theatrical farce. But she was most hurt by the way he'd made her look like such a terrible mother. "It made me seem very careless, uncaring, and crazy on my own," she later said. The only redeeming thing she could say about the article was that it didn't portray her as a victim.

Margo was never tempted to call the newspapers to tell her side of the story. "I felt that truly, in time, the information would get out, and I believed I'd be vindicated," she said.

Gene's preliminary hearing was scheduled for August 13. Margo met with Jim Willett and his boss, Paul Ebert, for the first time about two weeks before the hearing.

Paul had the corner office, which was much larger than all the other prosecutors', and was strewn with piles of papers and books. Margo had to fight back laughter when she saw a joke sign on his desk, featuring a phony classified ad that read, "Woman that can cook and clean fish, tie flies, and owns boat and motor. Please send picture of boat and motor."

At first she thought he was a sexist old Southern redneck, but she soon learned that he was just a boating enthusiast with a playful sense of humor. Jim was far more straitlaced, but they both took their jobs very seriously.

The two prosecutors reassured Margo that they believed her story. They thought Gene was very dangerous, and they were going to do their best to put him away for a long time. It seemed important to them that she trust them to handle this case, because they obviously needed her to be a strong prosecution witness. As they asked her a series of questions, they gained her trust in short order.

"How would you answer if we asked you, 'Have you ever committed perjury?'" Paul asked.

"I would tell you no."

Jim and Paul both looked surprised.

"I would tell you no because by law I never have. My testimony was coerced, and that's not perjury."

After the two prosecutors exchanged glances, Margo could perceive their heightened sense of respect for her. Yes, she did know her stuff.

"What would you say if I asked you, 'Have you ever lied under oath?'" Paul asked.

"I would say yes, I have."

"Why?"

"Because I thought my children's lives depended on it."

"What would you say if we asked you if you'd ever had a homosexual relationship?"

"I would tell you no, I haven't had a relationship, but I have had two intimate encounters with Patricia Cornwell."

"You're prepared to admit that?" Paul asked.

"Yes, I am."

Paul and Jim started talking as if Margo weren't there, saying they didn't want to divert the judge's attention with the divorce and the emotionally charged nature of her homosexual affair because they felt it would be a diversion from the central issue—the crimes Gene had just committed. For that reason, they thought Margo shouldn't testify at the preliminary hearing, only at the trial.

"I think you're right," she interjected.

After that, the three of them discussed how best to bring out the homosexuality issue in court at trial.

"Let us be the ones to bring this issue out, take the wind out of their sails, and make sure the jury understands that we're not trying to hide anything," Jim said.

When the meeting was over, Margo felt relieved that she didn't have to testify at the hearing and would be able to put off being grilled by Gene's attorneys. She also felt reassured to have such competent and dedicated lawyers on her side.

During the ninety-minute preliminary hearing before Judge Thomas Gallagher, the prosecutors called Edwin to testify and laid out the skeleton of their abduction and explosives case, which was enough to certify the five felony charges against Gene and send the case to the grand jury for a possible indictment.

Gene's attorney Reid Weingarten spoke to reporters after the hearing. "The center of this case is Gene Bennett's effort to protect his children," Reid said. "Twenty years in the FBI did not prepare him for his wife's alternative lifestyle, a lifestyle he believed to be abnormal and presented a danger to his little girls."

On September 3, the grand jury indicted Gene on six charges, after adding a new one—that he had obtained more than $200 under "false pretenses" from Mary Ann.

Despite this good news, Margo's financial house imploded in October, when a creditor sent an order to NOVA to garnishee her wages. She immediately met with an attorney and filed for

Chapter 7 personal bankruptcy in Alexandria. Her total debt was approaching $500,000, including more than $150,000 in attorneys' fees. Despite the bankruptcy filing, she continued to make small payments to Brian Gettings, Frank Dunham, and Kathy Farrell, and before she was done paying them, she'd spent all her retirement money.

That fall, Margo met about a dozen times with Jim Willett, often together with Paul, as they built their case for trial in January.

In the beginning, Margo talked to Jim with her arms crossed, her body language self-protective and her voice timid. Jim saw before him a very frightened woman who was trying to be brave and do what she could to help them.

"Her life was on the edge, and she was holding on as best she could. She wasn't going to give up, but it was an extremely precarious position," Jim later said. "She had to put her faith in the system, in me, and in the jury, and the system isn't perfect."

Paul and Jim both came to respect and admire her courage and self-discipline as she tried to hold her family together amid the media onslaught.

"She was really, really alone at that place in her life at that time," Jim said. "I've told her on more than one occasion how great she did, how courageous she was, and how valuable her contribution to the success of the prosecution was."

Paul, who had tried the John and Lorena Bobbitt penis-severing case in the same courthouse three years earlier, felt that the Bennett case was more complex than any other he'd prosecuted. One of the biggest challenges was to decide which of the several hundred pieces of physical evidence should be presented to the jury, and in what order, so as not to cause confusion.

"It was so convoluted, I was concerned whether the jury was going to be able to grasp the whole picture," Paul later said.

Their other concern was the judge they'd been assigned. After serving in the ROTC in college, Richard Potter went to law school and was promoted to second lieutenant, working briefly in Army intelligence during the Vietnam War before practicing law for sixteen years, including twelve representing criminal defendants. As a judge, however, he had a reputation for being unpredictable.

Margo was officially awarded full custody of the girls at the final custody hearing on November 18, when she also arranged for a social worker to review Gene's letters to the girls before sending them on. Margo didn't want to be accused again of blocking communication, but she also didn't want Gene to have their address. The property portion of the divorce had been severed from the custody case because Margo was still going through bankruptcy.

Afterward, Allison wrote a pithy letter demanding accountability from her father for what he'd done to her mother. Margo read the letter and suggested that Allison wait until after the trial to send it.

"If he's found not guilty, he gets to come home," Margo said.

"Good point, Mom," Allison replied.

Margo shook her head and chuckled at her precocious ten-year-old.

Later that month, Margo was still wondering why police had not filed any attempted murder charges, so she called Detective Ron McClelland.

"I realize that Gene kidnapped Edwin, but there's nothing in this about what he intended to do to me. Is that going to be addressed?" she asked.

"We're looking into that," Ron said. "We're going to do something. I just don't know what."

On December 2, Ron told Margo that the grand jury had indicted Gene on three new charges: the attempted murder of Margo, possession of explosive materials, and possession and/or manufacture of a bomb.

Not long after the grand jury issued its final indictment, Paul said he'd been unofficially contacted by Gene's defense attorneys, who were feeling him out about a plea bargain. Paul asked Margo how she felt in case they made an official offer.

Margo wasn't opposed to a plea, but she thought that the last agreement let Gene off far too easily. Margo was also convinced that Gene would come after her again if he could, so she wanted to make sure he was a very old man once he was released from prison.

"The only way I'd be comfortable with a plea would be if he was gone for a long time," she said.

"I was thinking thirty years," Paul said.

"Thirty years would be okay."

Margo was interviewed twice by the prosecution's psychological expert, Stanton Samenow, for a total of three hours.

"How have you been?" he asked.

"I guess I'm paranoid, because it bothers me that I can't go in a room without worrying if someone is on the other side of the door."

"Paranoia isn't really paranoia if it's based in reality."

"Well, I guess I'm doing okay then."

Margo had received a similar psychological evaluation during the custody battle, shortly before the church incident.

Clinical psychologist Gail Nelson said Margo's paranoia registered at a level that occurred in only 10.4 percent of women. "In the context of this custody litigation, and considering Mrs. Bennett's description of her abduction and threat by Mr. Bennett, it is my opinion that affirmative responses on this scale reflect reality-based concerns, and not any psychopathology on Mrs. Bennett's part," she wrote.

"Mrs. Bennett's liability as a primary caretaker is primarily her tendency towards submissiveness and dependency. These tendencies prevent her from making appropriate decisions and inhibit her ability to be confrontive towards others who may attempt to influence her actions and feelings. It is probable that because her mother was in a passive role in the family, Mrs. Bennett learned these traits early in life. They have affected her intimate relationships and her self-esteem in a negative way."

Margo continued to work with therapist Nancy Davis to prepare herself to testify at the trial. Following Nancy's advice to wear a new outfit that would make her feel strong and powerful, Margo bought a bright red silk blouse and a navy-blue skirt suit.

Nancy also told her to form a picture of Gene in her mind, then make him smaller and smaller. Margo visualized a tiny Gene Bennett, jumping up and down and stamping his feet, throwing a temper tantrum because he was so small.

Then Nancy told her to put him away somewhere so he couldn't get out. Margo pictured putting a bell jar over little Gene at the defense table, where he would be contained and couldn't bother her.

Next Nancy said, "Think about someone who is always there for you. Picture that person."

Margo saw Jesus in her mind's eye.

"Picture him giving you something, what you need to get through this."

Margo visualized Jesus holding a cardboard box the size of a laptop computer. He carried it over and held it out to her with both hands. The flaps were open and the box was empty.

"You already have everything you need to get through this," Jesus said.

And with that, Margo knew she was ready.

Chapter Twelve

Prosecution

Crazy Like a Fox

In the week before the trial started, Margo met with her daughters' teachers, principal, and school counselor to discuss what they could do to shield the girls from publicity and taunting by their classmates. Margo told the officials quite candidly that she was prepared to testify that she'd had two intimate encounters with Patricia Cornwell. She also said she expected media scrutiny to be intense.

"Please watch out for my children," she said.

The school officials listened to her intently and agreed to keep the newspapers out of the library during the trial. The day it started, Allison's fourth-grade teacher promptly shut off the classroom television as soon as she saw a story about Patsy and the Bennett case featured on *Good Morning America*.

Kathy Farrell told Margo not to read the newspaper or watch the TV news during the trial so as not to compromise her testimony, but Margo asked Letta to collect the papers every day in case she and the girls wanted to read them later. Margo stored them in her bedroom closet, out of the girls' reach, and made sure to turn off the downstairs TV at night, although Lindsey later told her that she'd secretly sneak upstairs and turn on the TV in Margo's bedroom. Letta videotaped all the TV news clips, but Margo couldn't bring herself to watch any of them until 2006, during an interview for this book.

In the midst of all the stressful trial preparation, Margo crossed two other important legal milestones: her divorce decree was finalized, and her bankruptcy petition was granted.

On Monday, January 27, 1997, Judge Richard Potter held a hearing on the defense's eleven pretrial motions at the Prince William County Judicial Center in Manassas, a city of about thirty-five thousand people and the site of the Civil War battle of Bull Run, thirty-five miles southwest of Washington DC.

Gene sat at the defense table, flanked by his four attorneys: Reid Weingarten, Mark Hulkower, Jeffrey Gans, and Raymond Patricco, all of whom worked for the high-powered law firm of Steptoe & Johnson in Washington DC.

The prosecutors told Margo that she didn't have to show up until Tuesday, when the trial officially started with jury selection, so she did not attend.

The defense motions included a request to sever the trial into three proceedings so that charges relating to the events at the church, to the explosive materials, and to the allegations related to defrauding Mary Ann Khalifeh could be heard separately.

Reid, Gene's lead attorney, argued that these charges were unrelated and prejudiced each other. But prosecutor Jim Willett maintained that they were tied into Gene's overall plan.

The defense also requested to move the trial to another venue because of the overwhelming volume of negative publicity about Gene and, short of that, to sequester the jury.

"We've seen the Commonwealth proclaiming Mr. Bennett's sane, that he's a scam artist. We've seen internationally recognized author, Patricia Cornwell, saying that he's a dangerous man, he should be locked up," Reid said.

Of the eleven motions, the judge granted only two, including a request to cover the cost of fees for bringing in out-of-town witnesses. Reid had argued that Gene was too poor to pay for the services of his four attorneys, let alone the cost of witnesses. Apparently, Reid and his colleagues were representing Gene pro bono.

Judge Potter, noting that the news reports submitted by the defense came from such national publications as the *Wall Street Journal*, *Newsweek*, and *Time*, remarked, "One has to wonder where exactly the defendant would have the court transfer venue to?"

He decided the trial would proceed as scheduled the next day, Tuesday, starting with jury selection and opening statements.

Even though Margo wasn't scheduled to testify until Wednesday, she had butterflies Monday night. Feeling apprehensive about the impending cross-examination, she slept poorly, plagued with anxiety dreams. In one of them, she was in the kitchen, where everything, including her clothes, were white. As she was going into the pantry, Gene, who was also dressed in white, popped his head out from behind the door and said, "Did you think I was going away?"

When she woke up, she followed her therapist's advice and went back into her thought process to give the dream a good ending: she grabbed a knife and cut Gene's throat.

Because she was a witness at the trial, Margo wasn't allowed to sit in the courtroom until closing arguments, in case the prosecutors recalled her to the stand.

Nonetheless, Margo wanted—and felt she needed—to be in the courthouse so that she would be available to answer any questions Paul or Jim might have.

"If this man didn't go to jail, I was going to die. Really quick," Margo later said. "So it was important that I give them my total support. I really felt like they had put together a good case. The only thing I couldn't predict was how the whole homosexual thing was going to impact the jury. You just never know when you make an emotional argument like that."

For the duration of the trial, Margo and Dianna holed up in the commonwealth's attorney's lobby, one floor below the courtroom. They passed the time by talking and reading magazines, stretching their legs occasionally by walking around the courthouse.

On that first day, Margo and Dianna got to chatting with the first prosecution witness, David Corley, who'd found Gene's handcuffs and mask in some grass near the church.

At one point, David came back from a walk, smiling.

"You owe me," he said to Margo.

"Why?" she asked.

"None of those people out there knows what you look like, and they kept asking me if I'd seen you," he said, referring to the reporters. "I said nope."

He was right. As she and Dianna wandered around, Margo was amused that no one recognized her. She no longer looked like the gaunt, dehydrated woman whom the *Washington Post* had photographed outside the federal courthouse the day of her aborted testimony in 1993. Her weight was back to normal, and her hair was shorter and much blonder.

Judge Potter's honey-colored, wood-paneled courtroom was rather intimate, seating as many people as could squeeze into the gallery's three rows of pewlike benches.

Despite Gene's later attempt to claim that he was confused throughout the proceedings, the prosecutors saw Gene attentively taking notes and whispering to his attorneys, looking coherent and very much involved in his own defense.

Before the judge started jury selection, he acknowledged that one of the defense witnesses, the Reverend Bill Higgins, was his pastor at the Manassas Baptist Church. No one objected. He never mentioned whether he'd ever met Gene there, although years later, he said he had not.

The judge read all nine charges to the jury pool, then announced that a panel of thirteen, including one alternate, would be chosen. He estimated that the trial would take six days.

Justice moves fast in Manassas, Virginia. Unlike in California, where choosing a jury can take days, the attorneys picked a panel—with twice as many women as men—in just two hours.

Nonetheless, Reid took the opportunity to mention Patricia Cornwell's name several times, underscoring that her "lesbian relationship" with Margo had horrified his client.

After the lunch break, attorneys for both sides gave their opening statements, which took an hour and fifteen minutes.

Prosecutor Jim Willett started off by describing Gene as a master of his art, who was "trained in deception" by the FBI and used "wicked instruments of terrorism" for his own purposes.

"It is that training, along with his motive, that makes him one of the most dangerous individuals that you'll ever see," he said.

Jim said that this case was not about whether Gene was insane or had mental problems. "This is a case about hatred and revenge, pure and simple."

He quickly summarized the events leading up to the church incident, characterizing Mary Ann as the "unwitting dupe" Gene had chosen to help carry out his scheme.

Going back over the history of the Bennetts' marriage, the fraud case, and Margo's affair with Patsy, Jim said, "He had in his own mind great reason to hate Marguerite Bennett. She left him. She broke up their marriage. She went into the bed of another woman, humiliated him, devastated him. . . . When he got out of prison, you bet he had a motive . . . to commit that crime."

Jim outlined the kidnapping and subsequent trial, admitting up front that Margo had given false testimony and had had sex with Gene in a hotel, but only because she thought her children's lives were in danger.

Jim cast doubt on the qualifications of the defense's primary psychological expert, Dr. Bishop, saying that although he was "very, very qualified as a therapist," he was not a forensic expert. Because there was no way to test whether Gene was telling the truth, he said, Dr. Bishop had to take Gene's word about not remembering Mary Ann or that he'd been hearing voices "from somebody named Ed."

"He has to take the word of a man who stole from the FBI, a man who abducted his wife once, tried to abduct her again, abducted a minister, planted a bomb in a college campus, and a man whose job for twelve years with the FBI was to lie, was to convince people he was something he was not, to convince criminals that he wasn't a law enforcement agent, but a criminal like themselves. I will ask you if you do not think that a man of such capability could fake mental illness."

In contrast, Jim told the jury, the prosecution's psychological expert, Stanton Samenow, had examined hundreds of people, including those who were insane and those who were faking insanity. "He will tell you he saw no evidence whatsoever that the defendant was insane at the time he committed these crimes. In fact, he will tell you that he was a man who was always in control, whose ideal in life was to control people. . . . [He] might need therapy, but [he] is not criminally insane."

Reid Weingarten's oratory style was far more theatrical than Jim's.

"By the opening statements of Mr. Willett, you would think this could be a movie. But if you went to the movie theater and you saw this, you'd say it couldn't happen like that. Nobody acts like this."

Reid said that the defense would spend most of the trial trying to make sense of Gene's actions, contending that he was not guilty by reason of insanity.

"We will not prove that Gene Bennett is a drooling lunatic and we don't have to under the law," he said. "What we will prove is that Gene Bennett . . . suffers from a mental illness that prevented him from understanding his acts and controlling his acts."

Reid didn't differ with the prosecution's characterization of his client's success as an undercover agent; however, he used that fact to bolster his argument that slipping back and forth between undercover personalities was the ultimate cause of Gene's mental breakdown.

Reid said there would be no "gay bashing" or criticism of Margo for being a lesbian. Nonetheless, Reid proceeded to paint her as an evil wife who secretly plotted to steal Gene's children and then turned him into the FBI for fraud so that she could get an upper hand in the custody battle, because in Virginia, he said, courts frowned on a lesbian lifestyle.

"If she was going to keep custody of her little girls, she had to destroy him and for all intents and purposes she was successful."

Reid claimed that the Justice Department had not believed Margo's kidnapping story back in 1993.

"Judge, I'll object to that, because first of all I don't think that's factually accurate," Jim said.

"We can prove that, Your Honor," Reid retorted. ". . . They accepted a plea agreement with Gene whereby he was sentenced to twelve months. To be sure, if the Justice Department had concluded at that time that Margo Bennett had been kidnapped, they would not have accepted the deal that they did."

Reid said Gene started losing time and hearing voices in prison, "when he never slept a wink," and his insomnia only worsened after he got out.

"He was mistreated by the system. He was separated from his kids. It was a horrible year for Gene Bennett. And when he was released . . . [he] was a shell of his former self."

Reid said Gene's mental health steadily deteriorated as he lost "his career, his friends, his freedom and his wife." His so-called scheme, Reid said, was a "caricature or a cartoon of undercover activity. . . . Overall, this is a disorganized, patternless, pointless, irrational scheme of events that had absolutely no chance of success," which only guaranteed that "he would lose the only thing he cared about, his little girls."

Reid said Gene suffered from a mental condition called disassociation, whereby his personality split and he involuntarily assumed a different state of consciousness. The events leading up to the night in the church did not constitute a sophisticated plot, as the prosecution argued, but rather "a cry of desperation by a very sick man."

"We will prove that essentially what happened was Gene was out of his mind in the church and when Margo peppered him in the face, he was shocked back into reality. . . . When he realized he had been shot, he took off," leaving his paraphernalia behind and calling 911.

Reid told the jury that when they listened to the 911 tape, "You will hear Gene Bennett in his own voice and you will hear a man who is painfully exhausted . . . painfully mixed up, painfully disorganized, a man who slips in and out of reality. You will hear Ed . . . the alternative personality who gives Gene his directions, and you will hear Gene dealing with it."

In summation, he said, this case is "basically about a man who simply couldn't face the prospect of his little girls being raised by lesbians. This is a case about acts that are so bizarre they could not have been committed by a sane man."

Reid asked the jury to "return a fair and just verdict that reflects this fact, and allows his poor, tortured soul to begin to heal."

After the judge excused the jury for the day, Jim and Paul returned to their office, looking pleased.

"How'd it go?" Margo asked.

"It's early, but we're off to a good start," Paul said.

That night, Margo's minister, Diane Lytle, called after watching the TV news and expressed concern about Jim's statement that Margo "went into the bed of another woman."

"They're making you look to be a tainted woman," Diane said.

Margo called Jim to relay the concerns, but he said the news media had taken the comment totally out of context.

"I'm making you out to be a survivor in this because that's what you are, so you have to trust me," he said.

Margo was relieved. She spent the rest of the evening mentally preparing for her testimony.

The next morning, Margo felt strong, powerful, and ready for battle as she put on her new trial outfit.

Because the media had already exposed the intimate details of her personal life, Margo felt less scared and vulnerable about exposing them to the jury.

"It made it easier to go into court, to testify wide open, showing them my emotions, my fear, the terror I went through, exposing everything, ripping open the curtains covering my emotions and my heart," she said later.

Finally, it was time to go. As Margo walked to the courtroom upstairs, she could feel her heart pounding against her chest.

Margo strode into the packed courtroom, confident and assured, her head high, just before 10:30 AM. She intended to kick ass, and nothing and no one was going to stop her.

"I knew that I had to give good testimony in order for them to see that what Gene did to me was wrong, that this was not my fault," she later said.

It helped Margo to see Dianna and Kathy sitting in the gallery for moral support.

For the four hours that Margo was on the witness stand, less than ten feet away from the judge and directly in front of the defense table, she did not look at Gene once. Just as she'd practiced visualizing with her therapist, she'd put him in the bell jar. The only time she even looked over in his direction was when Paul Ebert, who led her through her testimony, asked her to identify the defendant.

As Margo gave a blow-by-blow description of the church incident, she relived those moments of terror and her fight for survival all over again. Paul had her walk over to a large diagram, which illustrated the layout of the building, so she could point to where Gene had jumped out at her and where she'd dived behind the desk for cover.

"He was holding a gun in his hands and he was saying, 'Margo, don't fight me on this.' He ran toward me—I was standing in this area right here—and I immediately raised my left hand with pepper spray and started spraying toward him," she said, extending her arm to illustrate.

The TV cameras picked up this unscripted, dramatic moment and showed it on the local news that night.

As she recalled asking Edwin to pray for them, Margo's voice cracked, and she almost started crying. This was the only time she let the story get to her. But she was able to quickly regain her composure and move on.

Paul led her through her marriage to Gene, outlining how the fraud case came about and how she'd met Patsy. Then, acknowledging that she'd had intimate contact twice with the author, Margo described her separation from Gene, his indictment, then how he'd kidnapped her.

After Margo explained that Gene had left her in the van to meet with his attorney, Reid objected to the suggestion that he was somehow complicit in Gene's actions. This was ironic considering that he'd indicated during his opening statement that the kidnapping had never occurred.

"Could you bring up that I had nothing to do with this? I mean, this is serious," Reid asked the judge in a bench conference. ". . . I think there's the potential that we have to move for mistrial."

Judge Potter denied the motion and Margo returned to her story, acknowledging that she'd had sexual relations twice with Gene that week—before the defense could bring it up on cross-examination.

"Why did you do that?" Paul asked.

"Because he wanted to."

Similarly, she explained why she'd testified falsely during Gene's fraud trial, and pointed out that she met with federal agents immediately afterward.

"Did your attorneys have you run under a polygraph?" Paul asked.

"Yes," Margo replied.

This exchange triggered an objection from Reid, which was sustained by the judge. Nonetheless, Reid again moved for a mistrial. The judge denied the motion, but did not direct the jury to ignore Margo's response.

After lunch, Mark Hulkower made the same motion again, claiming that mention of the polygraph had "irreparably tainted these proceedings" because evidence that a defendant or a witness has taken a polygraph test was not admissible in Virginia courts. The judge denied the motion again. This issue would later become part of Gene's appeal.

Finally, the cross-examination Margo had been dreading began.

After establishing that Margo had told Paul on direct that her relationship with Patsy had nothing to do with her divorce, Reid asked, "Yet you admitted to Mr. Ebert that you had an adulterous lesbian affair with Patricia Cornwell while living in that house with Mr. Bennett?"

Margo had been analyzing each of his questions, weighing her words carefully.

"No, I didn't admit that to Mr. Ebert. I said I had two encounters with Ms. Cornwell."

This time it was Paul who asked for a bench conference. He told the judge that he didn't believe that the details of Margo's interaction with Patsy were material.

"To start with, I don't believe that a homosexual relationship is legally seen as adulterous," Paul said. "In any event, to go into all this detail, I don't think is appropriate. . . . She's admitted she had some intimate contact with Ms. Cornwell."

Reid continued, asking, "Didn't Gene complain to you that your office looked like a shrine to Patricia Cornwell?"

Margo denied that Gene had made such a complaint and also that she'd replaced pictures of him and the children with photos of Patsy.

"Is it your testimony that you had no idea that Gene was upset about your relationship with Patricia Cornwell?"

"As far as I know, Gene was not aware of the contact I had with Patricia Cornwell until the criminal trial in June of 1993," she said.

From there, Reid attacked her motivation for reporting the home relocation scam to Tony Daniels the day after Gene served her with divorce papers.

"Did you tell Tony Daniels that the reason you had waited so long to surface these allegations was because you were trying to 'hold the marriage together'?"

"Yes, I believe I told him that."

"And were you trying to hold the marriage together while you were having intimate contact with Patricia Cornwell?"

The judge sustained Paul's objection to the argumentative question.

At this point, Reid switched his line of questioning to the kidnapping and the inevitable topic of the two nights Margo spent with Gene in the hotel, pointing out that they both drank wine, as if to imply these were romantic evenings.

"And you prepared to make love with your husband?" he asked.

Margo felt her blood pressure rising, but did her best to maintain her composure in front of the jury.

"No, I did not make love with my husband," she said, emphasizing the words "make love."

"Did you have intimate sexual relationship?"

"I already testified that we had intimate contact."

On redirect, Paul asked Margo when Gene suggested that they have a threesome with another woman.

"Earlier in our marriage he had indicated to me that it would be exciting for him if he watched me have sex with another woman."

"What was your reply to that suggestion?"

"No way."

At the end of the day, the judge instructed the jury not to watch or read any news stories about the case.

The prosecutors were grinning as Margo walked into Paul's office.

"You did a great job," he said.

Margo was all over the TV news that night, and although she didn't watch it, a couple of her friends called to tell her how well she'd done.

"I heard your voice crack and it sent chills up my spine," her neighbor Beth said. "I started crying."

The next morning, the *Washington Post* article repeated Margo's careful wording about her affair with Patsy, describing it as "two intimate encounters." Unlike the previous feature story, which Margo had thought made her look silly, this one described her as "poised and confident" and speaking "in measured tones." Margo was pleased when she eventually read it.

Patsy's agent, Esther Newberg, said only this about Margo's testimony: "I find the whole thing typical of what's going on in the American press today. I certainly hope this sells more books for Ms. Cornwell."

An editorial in the *Potomac News* underscored the feelings Margo experienced while she was under cross-examination. "Far too often, courts allow victims to be put on trial along with the accused. That's what happened to Ms. Bennett when she was grilled about her intimate contact with Ms. Cornwell. . . . Criminals— not their victims—are the ones who should be on trial."

On day three of the trial, Monday, February 3, the *Richmond Times-Dispatch* put Gene and Margo into the same league "in the annals of troubled marriages" as John and Lorena Bobbitt.

And on day four, the last seven prosecution witnesses testified before lunch.

Among them was Jay Mason Jr., a firearms forensic scientist, whom Paul showed the same type of BB gun pictured in the manual police found in Gene's black bag at the church. (Police never recovered the actual gun he had that night.)

"Sir, in your expert opinion, is that weapon capable of inflicting serious bodily harm?" Paul asked.

"Yes, it is," the scientist said, adding that until recently the handgun, also known as an air gun, was used by the military and could fire BBs, .177-caliber pellets, or darts. "It's designed to have the appearance of a government-model .45 pistol."

By the time the prosecution rested, it had successfully laid out enough evidence, tying it into Gene's intricate and elaborate scheme, to show there was a method to his madness. The question was whether Gene's attorneys could convince the jury that the madness was real enough—or in this case, irrational enough—to prove their insanity defense.

At the end of the day, Margo asked Paul and Jim how they thought the prosecution's case had gone.

"It went as well as it possibly could have," Jim replied. "We hit the ball, and it's just a question of whether the jury is going to do the right thing."

Chapter Thirteen

Defense

Incompetent Evil Ed

Despite strenuous objections by the prosecution, which wanted to keep the defense from playing tapes of Gene's three-plus hours of 911 calls the night of the church incident, Judge Potter decided that the jury could hear the recordings.

Because it was already 4:30 PM, the jury heard only the first half hour of calls, finishing up the next morning. The judge cautioned that the tapes' contents should be used only to consider Gene's state of mind and his ability to form intent to commit the offenses for which he was on trial, not to prove the truth of his words.

On the tapes, Gene repeatedly alternated between two conflicting personas: a confused, tired, and helpless victim and a sharp-tongued negotiator.

Gene started off by reporting to the dispatcher, and then to Sergeant Reese, that his wife had sprayed him with Mace, shot at him, and was trying to blow him up and steal his kids.

He volunteered to the sergeant that he was a former FBI agent who had gone to prison "for signing a false statement."

"You went to prison for that?"

"Yeah, how 'bout that? They're a little hard on FBI agents if you step on their dick, but that's the way it goes. I fucked up so I had to pay the price. I just didn't appreciate [my wife] rattin' me out eight years after the fact."

As they were talking, one or more police cars pulled into Gene's driveway, and he complained that someone was shining bright lights at his house.

"Who's here?" he asked.

"I don't know. I'm checking it. . . . Did you attach a bomb to the minister?"

"No."

"Did you handcuff the minister to the bench?"

"Look, I want to know who these people are in my front yard or we're going to have a real serious problem. . . . Tell them to shut the lights off. I don't need it."

Minutes later, the confused Gene was back on the line. "I can't remember anything," he said. ". . . I got permission to go to Richmond and I'm supposed to be there in the morning to talk to my lawyer. What the hell am I doing here? . . . I want the voices to stop. I want some clarity. I want to talk to my babies."

Not long into the call, Sergeant Reese handed the phone over to the hostage negotiator, Janice Hetzel, who asked Gene what it would take to get him to come out.

Back in negotiator mode, Gene told Janice to get a hold of his Army buddy, Donald Albracht, from the FBI's Kansas City office and Steve Spruill from the Washington field office, "a voice I know." Later, he said he didn't trust that the local police weren't amateurs or under the control of his wife, so he also demanded to talk to Dale Pruner, another Army buddy, who happened to be working as Quantico's duty agent that night.

When Janice said she wanted to work with Gene and get him medical attention for his respiratory problems, chest pain, and eye irritation, he snapped at her.

"Save the bullshit, okay? I've been through the whole hostage negotiation thing, I've been through the SWAT thing. . . . If I was going to hurt somebody, I would've done it then, okay? . . . I'm not violent. I don't want to hurt nobody. I don't want to bother nobody. We just want to be left alone."

After Janice got Steve Spruill on the line, Steve tried to talk Gene into giving himself up, but Gene seemed more interested in complaining about Margo and her lesbian lifestyle.

"Sounds like you're in a jam, bud," Steve said.

"Nobody believed me before and nobody is going to believe me now. . . . I'm fighting, man. I'm fighting it."

"Who are you fighting?"

"I'm fightin' the demons, man. . . . She won last time, hands down, and now here we are again."

"You know what you're doing right now, you're helping her win . . . by holing yourself up in that house," Steve said. ". . . You have caused everything that is happening to you . . . and it's not going to go away."

"All right," Gene said. "You tell your family I'm sorry we bothered you. . . . Ed says we've got to go now."

Reid talked to Gene on and off the recorded line, but the jury heard only what was on the tape.

"Gene, I had a long talk with them," Reid said. "They understand the background. . . . They understand the lesbian allegations and then how she's gone berserk. They understand how manipulative she is."

Reid tried to defend his client to the negotiator: "Let me just say this. Ever since I have known him, and I have known him for years . . . there's never been any indication whatsoever through this whole turmoil of him threatening anybody. This is really a function of his relationship with his wife. An unbelievably nasty dispute, but he is of no risk to anybody."

After Gene had hung up for the umpteenth time, Janice called back with Reid on the line. Gene's voice was barely audible.

"I'm tired," he said.

"Gene, I think you've been drugged," Reid said. "I think someone gave you something. . . . The guy who's talking on the other end of the line is not the guy I know is you. . . . I have no idea about what happened tonight. I have no idea whether or not this is going to lead to a new legal predicament."

After putting on Gene's former colleagues to testify what a methodical and impressive undercover agent he'd been in his prime, the defense then called its first expert, Michel Girodo, a professor from Ottawa, Canada, who had worked as a psychologist for more than twenty-five years. With a PhD in social personality psychology, he had done postdoctoral work in clinical psychology and forensic psychiatry, studied the psychological effects of undercover work on law enforcement officers, and served as a consultant for Canadian and U.S. agencies, including the FBI, where he'd worked in the same unit at Quantico with Margo for a time.

Michel noted that undercover agents misrepresent themselves to suspects by using their personality as an "instrument" or "tool" to create a separate identity, clinically known as depersonalization or dissociation.

"Dissociation is where you forcibly, through an act of will, decide to suppress who it is that you are for the moment and suddenly superimpose upon your sense of self a brand new identity. It occurs quickly, dramatically, and rapidly."

In some agents, he said, this false identity could be reactivated involuntarily, and in stressful situations, they could slip back and forth into different roles without conscious control, even more dramatically when the operation was stressful or potentially life threatening. Sometimes this could happen years after an operation was over.

He said he would have psychiatric concerns about an agent who devoted much of a ten-year career to deep undercover work and also about a highly successful operative who constantly sought out such work.

"Why is that?" Mark Hulkower asked.

"Because, after a period of time, we have the impression that people need undercover work as much as sometimes drug users need a good shot. It stimulates them. They get excited. . . . Indeed, a personality disorder associated with long undercover work called narcissistic personality disorder, one in which people are self-indulgent, feed their personality, their egos, has arisen."

That, he added, is why undercover agents need to be very closely supervised, and because the level of supervision varies among agencies, he recommends that agents' time spent undercover be limited.

In the past fifteen years of his research, Michel said, he'd seen reactions to undercover work, including anxiety, depression, aches and pains, stomach problems, paranoia, phobias, and "psychotic thinking disturbances." His research showed that these conditions occurred in an average of 20 percent of the agents he studied, compared with 12 percent of the general population.

"In the same way that undercover work is unique, there's a tremendous paradox about it all, so absurd, that the people who are really good at this work should be prevented from doing it."

On cross-examination, Jim asked Michel to estimate the percentage of agents he'd treated or evaluated who had later committed criminal or violent felony acts.

"A very small percentage."

After explaining the legal standard in Virginia, Jim asked what percentage of this small group would be considered to be criminally insane.

"Given your description and given the people that I have seen, not one of them would meet those conditions," Michel said.

Asked if these agents also engaged in a type of gamesmanship, by predicting how people would react, Michel said, "They have to be smarter than the criminals and anticipate two steps ahead of the criminal."

"So they always try to have a backup plan?"

"I'm not sure what you mean by 'backup plan,' but they think of contingencies."

The next expert witness was psychiatrist Robert Bishop, whose diagnosis of Gene provided the backbone of the defense's case.

Dr. Bishop said that he worked at a psychiatric hospital in Falls Church, consulted for the FBI, and had conducted sanity hearings for criminal defendants when he was a Navy psychiatrist. He said he was asked to evaluate Gene in August 1996, a process that took ten to twelve hours, including more than three hours of interviews with Gene.

Gene told him he'd had chronic, long-term insomnia since childhood and had suffered a number of closed head injuries with some periods of memory loss. Gene said he had reported these conditions to a girlfriend.

(The doctor's written evaluation of Gene said he was "physically disciplined" by his father, "often with a closed fist and frequently in the head. There were unprovoked beatings. He remembered fearing his father particularly when he was drinking." However, Gene never mentioned any head injuries or abuse by his father to Margo, nor did he complain of insomnia.)

Dr. Bishop said Gene had been referred to his partner, Dr. Alen Salerian, by the FBI's Employee Assistance Program for chronic insomnia and stress in 1993. When Gene told him about the blackouts, Dr. Salerian recommended a sleep study.

Gene told Dr. Bishop that he sometimes felt as though he could see himself from a distance, as though he were not real. He reported experiencing déjà vu and also jamais vu, whereby a person in a familiar situation suddenly can't recall where he is. The latter, Dr. Bishop explained, is usually associated with serious psychopathology.

Gene told him that in late 1995 he started hearing a voice that identified itself as "Ed," which the doctor described as "a dark, menacing voice that would at times command him to do things that he did not want to do, or do things that were inconsistent with his behavior." Gene also said that since 1992 or 1993, he had occasionally heard his own thoughts out loud, "as if they were coming from outside his head."

"What kind of things did the voice tell him?" Mark asked.

"The voice might tell him to shoplift something, . . . to keep detailed records of what he was doing and his behavior, . . . [or] not to go to church."

"Did the voice tell him to do things that Mr. Bennett didn't do?"

"At times, he was able to resist it, other times not. In fact, very consistent with people with dissociative disorders, which is the diagnosis that Mr. Bennett has, there are times when, under stress . . . he would be more prone or more apt to either lose time or to hear the voice."

He said Gene reported losing his memory for hours, sometimes for an entire day. During the weekend of the church incident, for example, he said Gene recalled little after dropping off his daughters with Margo until Allison called him Saturday at 10 PM, crying, saying she'd overheard her mother talking about moving, when he "came to." Recalling only fragments of the next day, Gene said he remembered nothing after leaving the University of Richmond campus until he "came to" in a dark hallway, where he felt a burning sensation and his heart racing, and recognized his wife.

At the end of the day, Jim talked to Margo about Gene's claims.

"Do you know anything about Gene talking to Allison and Allison crying, upset about moving?" he asked.

"We were planning on moving, but it was to the townhouse next door," Margo said. "I was standing right there while Allison was talking to her father, and she wasn't crying."

Margo checked with Allison as soon as she got home.

"Did you think I was taking you away from him?" she asked.

"No, he's lying," Allison said. "I did not say that."

"Okay."

But Allison wouldn't let it go. "I want to go and testify and tell them he's lying."

Margo said she would think about it. She called Allison's teacher and therapist, both of whom said Allison was a strong-willed girl and that if she needed to do this, Margo should let her.

Still, Margo was worried that Gene might retaliate against Allison. She was also concerned about the impact of Allison's knowing she'd contributed to the possible conviction of her father.

But she ultimately decided that Allison should have the closure she sought.

"So much of Allison's life had been out of her control, and this was her choice," Margo later said.

She called Jim and filled him in.

"I don't know if I want to use her, but can you have her at the courthouse tomorrow morning?" he asked.

The next morning, Allison got dressed in her blue denim dress, a purple turtleneck, and tennis shoes. She was a little nervous about seeing her father, but she wasn't scared about taking the stand.

Jim introduced her to forensic psychologist Stanton Samenow, a rebuttal witness for the prosecution who would testify later that day, and the three of them chatted a bit.

Margo sat with Allison, who spent the day drawing and coloring, waiting to be called.

"You don't have to do this," Margo kept saying.

"I know," Allison replied.

Dr. Bishop continued his testimony for another hour and forty minutes, during which some jury members made audible "ha" noises of disbelief.

In addition to dissociative disorder NOS (short for "not otherwise specified," meaning it was atypical or unusual), he said he had diagnosed Gene with obsessive-compulsive personality disorder with features of antisocial personality and narcissistic personality, and also with dysthymia, a chronic, smoldering depression.

He explained that people with dissociative disorder could lose consciousness as if in a trance or a fugue, be rendered unable to say who they are, or form new identities.

Using the 911 tape to illustrate, he said Gene displayed fear and confusion, used the term "we," and spoke in a different voice when Ed was in charge.

He said Gene's years of working undercover for long periods with little supervision, compounded with all the recent stressors in his life, primed Gene for the triggering event of his dissociative state that final weekend—Allison's call.

Dr. Bishop stated that the evidence that clearly linked Gene to the various crime scenes was also representative of his irrational state, describing the vibrator pipe bomb as "at the very least a cry for help."

In conclusion, he said, "Mr. Bennett did not appreciate the nature and character of his acts at the time of the offense" or their consequences, nor could he tell right from wrong.

Under cross-examination by Jim, Dr. Bishop acknowledged that a person who was dissociating was not necessarily criminally insane.

Asked if he had verified whether Allison's phone call took place, Dr. Bishop said, "I am aware that that phone call took place through Mr. Bennett's report to me."

"Did you verify it independently?"

"No."

"Did you talk to Allison?"

"No."

"Dr. Bishop," Jim said, "I have. Would you like to now—she's in my office—before you render a final opinion in this case?"

Mark Hulkower objected, but the judge wanted to hear the answer as much as everyone else in the courtroom.

"No," Dr. Bishop said.

Moving on, Jim noted that Gene had told psychologist Stanton Samenow that "at one point in time, he had everything; now he's got nothing, and [Margo] was the cause. Did he express a similar sentiment to you?"

"Yes."

"Is it fair to say that he is obsessed with his hatred for his wife?"

"It's frequently on his mind. . . . He has been obsessed about that, yes."

As Jim led the doctor through some of Gene's actions, Dr. Bishop contended that Gene was in a dissociative state when he told Mary Ann to rent cars and obtain the insurance policies, cell phones, and pagers, and also when he answered each of her calls or pages as Edwin Adams. However, he said, Gene was probably coming out of it when Margo called him "Gene" in the church and he responded.

Jim handed the doctor Gene's notepad, with the scribbled directions to the Pittsburgh airport and the notation "call 911."

"It's possible, is it not, doctor, that as a contingency plan, if caught, the defendant decided that he would feign insanity so that he wouldn't go to prison?"

"That's always possible," Dr. Bishop said.

Reid's next witness was Gene's minister, the Reverend Bill Higgins, who said he first met Gene in fall 1993 after a service at the Manassas Baptist Church.

On the Thursday before the church incident, the pastor said, he saw Gene at church, looking worse than he'd ever seen him. "His face was strained. His eyes were bloodshot. He was like a man who was caught under a tremendous, tremendous burden."

The pastor said he arranged with police to meet Gene at the hospital that Sunday in hopes of getting him to surrender. He said Gene's body looked like a rag doll as he was wheeled in on a gurney, his hand was cold to the touch, and he was mumbling under his breath.

"He talked about Ed some more. He talked about Mary. But none of it was put together in sentences that made any sense."

With that, the defense rested its case, and prosecution began putting on its four rebuttal witnesses.

The second witness was psychologist Stanton Samenow, whose specialty was antisocial behavior. He'd spent eight and a half years at St. Elizabeth's Hospital in Washington DC, doing clinical research into criminal behavior; opened a private practice; and wrote the books, *The Criminal Personality* and *Inside the Criminal Mind*. Just as Dr. Bishop had for the defense, Stanton had interviewed and evaluated Gene for the prosecution.

Stanton testified that he spent eight and a half hours interviewing Gene—two or three times longer than the defense's expert. He also conducted interviews with Margo and Allison, listened to Gene's 911 tape, and reviewed a voluminous number of documents pertaining to Gene's fraud case, including Margo's interviews with federal investigators about the kidnapping.

"Now, sir, did you in fact reach a conclusion as to whether or not the defendant was insane in your opinion on the day of the alleged crime?" Paul asked.

"I did reach such a conclusion."

"And what was that conclusion?"

"That Eugene Bennett was not legally insane at the time of the crime."

The psychologist explained that during their interviews, Gene was "lucid, straightforward, very clear and very organized in telling me about his life. . . . There was a lot of pressure, and this is a man that rose to pressure and welcomed it."

He noted that, in many cases, Margo and Gene gave completely different versions of events. But given the allegations of abusive treatment made by Margo and her former nanny, Stanton concluded, "This is a man who was going to get things the way he wanted them, whatever the means were, whatever it took. This is a person who always had a plan. . . . This is a person who was deliberate, who was calculating, and who was rational."

Gene told Stanton that Allison's call the night before the church incident "got him tremendously upset." However, Stanton told the jury that he'd talked to Allison himself and heard a very different story.

"Allison told me this morning that she never told her father on the phone that she was going to move, . . . that she did tell her father several weeks before that they might move to, I think it was a town house next door, and that his reaction was, 'Well, I don't understand why you're going to move from one house to another,' but that he wasn't particularly upset."

Stanton found it curious that Gene said he'd lost all this time and forgot placing the ad in the *Washington Post*.

"This is a man who had a very good memory," he said. "This is a man who, for many hours, went into tremendous detail with me about the things he did remember about so many aspects of his life, and he was extremely clear. And he said to me that I knew more about the crimes that occurred on June 23 than he did."

But Stanton said the events of that night required "a very organized mind, a very ingenious mind, a creative mind, a mind that can plot, plan, and deliberate. . . . Once you understand it, you see that a person who's insane is not going to be able to do this."

He noted that it was very convenient for someone who committed a crime to try to avoid the consequences by claiming memory loss. "But there was nothing I could find in the eight and a half hours that I spent with [Gene], or the collateral interviews, or the documents I read, that said to me that this man was insane other than that he said, 'I don't remember.'"

He noted that Gene issued a number of conditions to police during the 911 call, clearly illustrating that he was "a man who is in control and he knows what he's doing." He demanded to know that his children were safe and to talk to people he knew from the FBI, to his lawyer, and to his minister. "At the very end, he even wants to be sure that his house is locked up after he leaves it."

Asked if he thought that Gene had been malingering—another term for faking—during the interviews, Stanton said, "I think the whole thing is malingering."

Dismantling Dr. Bishop's diagnoses one at a time, he said that if someone were truly disassociating, it was not probable that he would snap into another personality when the phone rang.

He said he also did not agree with the doctor that Gene had obsessive-compulsive personality disorder, although he did concur that Gene had antisocial and narcissistic personality features.

"In your professional opinion, did he understand the difference between right and wrong?"

"I think so."

"Was he able to understand the nature and consequences of his act?"

"Yes."

During the lunch recess, Jim asked Margo and Allison to hang around a while longer. Once Stanton Samenow finished testifying, Jim said he would know whether he would call Allison to the stand.

Judge Potter called a short recess after Reid was done cross-examining Stanton, during which Jim ran up to Paul's office to talk to Margo and Allison.

"Stanton's testimony went well," he said. "I'm not going to need Allison. Take her home."

Jim had two kids himself, including a daughter around Allison's age. Looking down at Margo's daughter, he said, "Allison, you're a brave girl."

Last up was Evan Stuart Nelson, a forensic psychologist who specialized in assessing whether criminal defendants were malingering. He had treated and assessed people with dissociative disorder, specifically multiple personality disorder, at the Indiana School of Medicine and was now in private practice.

"Why is it important to be—have expertise in malingering in making an assessment for the courts in a criminal proceeding?" Paul asked.

"When somebody is charged with a crime or when they're interested in receiving financial damages in exchange for mental illness that they incurred because of some traumatic incident, there are strong motivations to be seen as mentally ill and . . . to fake symptoms or exaggerate symptoms."

In his experience, Evan said, it was rare that someone with this disorder could stay lucid, focused, and organized for a two- to three-hour interview.

"This hearing voices, being psychotic—the whole realm of 'I feel out of my mind, my mind is controlled, I'm hearing voices,' are the most frequent malingering symptoms in a criminal forensic context in every study that I have ever looked at."

Paul asked for Evan's opinion on the likelihood that a hypothetical person who had committed the crimes of which Gene was accused would meet Virginia's test for legal insanity.

"It sounds really unlikely," Evan said. "You're talking about a sequence of rather unusual but highly organized behaviors toward a specific goal. . . . Unless there is some indication of a delusional understanding of what that goal is, it doesn't sound at all like somebody who is out of control or doesn't understand what they're doing or that it's wrong to them."

"When you assess for this disorder, are there any other diagnoses you consider?" Paul asked.

Evan said he would consider schizophrenia, but said malingering was "really high on the list," because people had heard a lot about this particular disorder in the media. But for him, behaviors such as committing illegal acts and lying, then claiming to have no memory and showing no remorse, more aptly fit the description of a psychopath.

By the time Evan was finished, he and Stanton had successfully poked holes through Dr. Bishop's diagnoses, methods, and testimony. But Jim and Paul knew no case was won until a jury delivered a guilty verdict.

When Margo later learned about testimony from defense witnesses that Gene had claimed that he'd had insomnia and blackouts back in 1993, she figured he'd been planning for years to use this insanity defense—probably even prior to kidnapping her.

Margo remembered how Gene had planned the Nickelride raid at Tony's down to the minute and figured he had done the same thing with this murder plan of his. Unlike Nickelride, however, this one turned out to have a fatal flaw.

"This one would've been foolproof if I hadn't had the pepper spray," she said. "I was the unpredictable factor."

Chapter Fourteen

Vindication

Monday, February 10, was day seven of the trial, which was starting its third and final week.

Judge Potter had given the prosecution an hour and the defense ninety minutes for their closing arguments, and thirty minutes to the prosecution for its rebuttal.

In their closings, Jim and Reid summed up their cases, highlighting their best witness testimony and trying to undermine that of the other side.

Paul got to have the last word in his rebuttal argument before the jury began deliberating.

Paul said he took no pleasure in asking the jury to convict a former law enforcement officer who had done so much good for his country. He contended that Gene didn't kill Edwin Clever before Margo arrived or knife her in the church parking lot, because he knew he would go down for murder. So instead he came up with a plan "that defies imagination."

"I asked you folks on voir dire if any of you couldn't accept that there are times when the truth is crazier than fiction and all of you said you could accept that premise. Well, folks, this is a case where the truth, perhaps, is stranger than fiction."

Paul had been saving one piece of evidence for this very moment, as the pièce de résistance of the prosecution's case, when the defense could no longer offer some crazy explanation.

"I think it tied everything together. It told its own story," Paul said later. "I thought it was going to kill the defense. They kind of skimmed over it and they thought we were going to overlook it. . . . When the jury got the full flavor of it, I think that was the end of the case."

Paul began to read aloud part of the five-page typed note that Gene had planted in the Annandale campus locker, explaining that it was a business plan Gene had drafted to read as if Margo had written it.

" 'I will control the finances, clients, and business money concerns as required. . . . She will obtain life insurance in the amount equal to four times the amount of financing that I provide or arrange.' This is ostensibly Margo's notes about her business arrangements with Mary Ann, prepared by that man," Paul said, pointing at Gene.

" 'I will hold the policies and she will name the beneficiaries that I direct,' " he said, pointing again, "prepared by that man. 'I will use my alias/DBA name of Elizabeth Akers with no questions asked by MAK.' "

Then, turning to the jury, Paul said, "almost like Ed Adams, isn't it?

" 'Convince MAK to take a job at McDonald's. Convince her to work a demeaning job when not in class and convince her that it is an assignment for a client.'

"This, I should say, takes it all: 'MAK, Mary Ann Khalifeh, will always refer to me as Edwin Adams to friends, family, etcetera as her boss, partner, associate, etcetera. . . . It's much safer this way now. I can work several [angles] all at once with little risk of exposure. [I will win at all levels.]'

" 'Have MAK rent van and room for dry run on 6/22, 23. Run through all phases. Use this time to teach her some surveillance work. . . . Get her weapon[s training and certification] in order.'

"That will answer for you, I believe," Paul said, "and I can't speak for you folks, some of the questions you might have as to why in the name of God would somebody do what he did."

If Gene had pulled off his scheme, Paul said, he would have been a hero, "the person who was wrongfully convicted in the first instance, and Margo would have been the crazy, dingbat lesbian who put pornographic material in her lockers along with all of this other evidence." Mary Ann, a "blind little lamb," he said, would have ended up dead as well.

Paul told the jury that Gene had already manipulated Margo, the family's nanny, Edwin, Mary Ann, even Dr. Bishop, his own attorney, and the police.

"Don't let him manipulate you," he said. "Don't let him manipulate the system. Hold him to the burden that the law holds him to."

Jim and Paul had successfully tied all the evidence together so that for the first time in Margo's mind—and, she hoped, the jury's as well—she could see how the dots in Gene's cunning scheme were connected. Finally, she understood.

By this point, Margo felt pretty confident. Juries were always unpredictable, but she believed that the prosecutors had done a remarkable job.

At 1:07 PM, Judge Potter announced the identity of the thirteenth, alternate juror, and told the other twelve members to begin deliberations after lunch.

He called court back into session three times that afternoon, first to announce that the jury had requested the exhibit list, next that the jury wanted to see a transcript of Gene's 911 tape, and then that the jury wanted a legal definition of "to defraud." Margo and Dianna trekked up to the courtroom each time, as did Gene and his attorneys.

Margo was in the second row behind the prosecution's table for the last session that day, when, for the first and only time during the trial, she met eyes with Gene as he walked into the courtroom. He glared at her with an expression that said, "You piece of dirt, I'm not done with you yet."

Afterward, as she was walking with the prosecutors back to their office, Jim said, "If they're getting hung up on the little things, it means they've already decided on the big things."

"And that's a good thing, right?" Margo asked.

"Quick decisions on the big charges are usually good decisions."

Judge Potter excused the jury at 6:10 PM.

The next morning, the jury began deliberating again at 9:10.

Everyone was back in court at 4:35 PM, when the judge said he needed to correct some jury instructions. He excused the panel once more, and about half an hour later, the moment of truth finally arrived.

"The verdict's in," Jim said as he walked purposefully into the lobby, where Margo was pacing. "Let's go."

She couldn't help but fear that the jury might let Gene off.

"What if they let him go?" she asked Dianna. "I'm dead."

"That's not going to happen," Dianna replied.

Paul asked Margo if she was willing to speak to the media after the verdict. She consulted with Kathy Farrell, who said it was okay, but cautioned, "Don't say anything that's going to jeopardize the property hearing. I'll signal you if I think it's going too far."

They met Edwin in the hallway and walked into the courtroom together. Edwin sat on the aisle, with Margo to his left and Dianna next to her, each of them hoping the jury would recommend a harsh punishment for Gene.

The media took their usual spot in the back, and Letta made it just in time to squeeze into the row behind Margo.

Margo had a clear view of the jury box, which was only a few feet away. She intentionally did not look at Gene as he walked in with his legal team, but focused rather on the members of the jury as they filed in and took their seats at 5:34 PM. All told, they had deliberated for twelve hours.

"I wanted that jury to be looking at me as the verdict was coming out," she later said. "Whether I lived or died was in the hands of those people."

The courtroom was quiet as the judge began to read the verdict on each charge.

Gene stood at the defense table, looking down as the judge read the jury's findings. As the announcements continued, he whispered to his attorneys, but showed no emotion.

"In case number 39955, we, the jury, find the accused, Eugene Allen Bennett, guilty of abduction with the intent to deprive Albert [Edwin] Clever of his personal liberty, as charged in the indictment and affix his punishment at ten years. Signed, foreperson."

Margo heard her sister whisper a loud, "Yes!" and immediately started feeling a sense of relief.

"We, the jury, find the accused, Eugene Allen Bennett, guilty of use and display of a firearm in the commission of a felony, as charged in the indictment, and affix his punishment at three years imprisonment.

"We, the jury, find the accused, Eugene Allen Bennett, guilty of statutory burglary with a deadly weapon, as charged in the indictment, and affix his punishment at twenty years imprisonment."

As the guilty charges began to pile up, Margo felt her tension ease, as if air were slowly seeping out of a balloon. She didn't have to be so strong or fight any longer. It was over. Finally, over.

When the judge came to the attempted murder charge, one of the male jurors, who appeared to be in his early fifties, stared directly at Margo. As the judge said, "Guilty," Margo mouthed "Thank you" to the juror, who simply nodded and looked away.

This was the vindication she'd been waiting for all those months before they finally charged Gene with trying to kill her.

After Judge Potter finished reading all nine charges, he announced that the sentencing would take place on May 15 at 9 AM, then dismissed the jury.

Margo was so overcome with gratitude that she'd lost count of how many years the jury had recommended that Gene spend in prison, but she knew it was enough time that she felt safe again. She hugged Jim in an embrace that was featured on the front page of the next morning's paper.

"Thank you," she said.

"You're welcome," he said.

Detective Ron McClelland, who'd been adding up the sentences as the judge read off each charge, told Margo he'd counted sixty-one years.

"We'll have to wait and see what the judge does at sentencing," he said.

As the media started setting up their cameras for the press conference, Dianna hugged Margo, saying, "He's not going to hurt you. He's going to be gone for a long time."

Margo and Paul put their arms around each other's shoulders in a half-hug. "It was a good verdict," he said.

Margo smiled and nodded.

After dozens of news stories had been written about her, Margo was ready to say a few words to the media.

The reporters started firing questions at her, repeatedly telling her to look into the camera.

"It's a good start. We can relax for a while," Margo told them. "I'm just happy to have this process over with. Obviously, I'm very relieved. I think that we can, we meaning the children and I, can relax for a while. I do feel there's a future now."

When the questions started moving toward Margo's future, Kathy shook her head no.

"Folks, I need to go," Margo said.

Margo, Letta, Dianna, and Kathy walked over to a pub near the courthouse for a celebratory drink.

"I wouldn't let just any of my clients be interviewed by the TV reporters, but then you're not just any of my clients," Kathy said.

Margo laughed.

After Dianna drove her home, Margo realized that she was out of milk, so she went to 7–11 to get some. In the newsstand, she saw a photo of herself with her chin in her hand, and a blurry Dianna on the front page of the *Potomac News*. She bought a copy and took it home to show the girls.

That night, she fell into a deep, uninterrupted sleep.

Margo started reading the local paper again the next morning, although she waited a couple more weeks before she delved into the stories from earlier in the trial. She was surprised to see that Dr. Bishop had diagnosed Gene with an antisocial narcissistic personality.

Wow, that guy was right on, she thought. *I can't believe Gene's own witness testified to that. Gene is mean, and he doesn't care about it.*

Two weeks after the verdict, Allison mailed the letter she'd written to her father back in November.

> Dear Dad,
>
> While you're in jail, I want you to think about something: if you had killed mom, don't you think we would feel the same way you did when you're [*sic*] mom died? And also, how do you think I would feel if you had killed mom? Dad, obviously you didn't think about that. Well I want you to think about it now. I am getting my hair cut up to my ears this Saturday. And now I am 5′2″ tall. Dad, I really do want you to think about those things. And when you can come up with an answer, write it on a separate sheet of paper and use the backs so you don't wast [*sic*] paper.
>
> Your Daughter, Allison Akers Bennett

Gene wrote back promptly, addressing his comments to her and Lindsey. He said he was very happy to get Allison's letter, complimenting her spelling and writing.

"You asked several complex and difficult questions. I cannot adequately address those questions in a letter," he wrote. "I promise you both that when I see you, and you are old enough to understand the entire situation, I will answer all of your questions completely. Until then I want you both to live full and healthy lives and to enjoy each and every day to its fullest."

In an apparent attempt to distract them from the questions he didn't want to answer, he put forth his own set of questions—about school and their favorite movies, TV shows, books, recreational activities, and foods. He asked them to send some recent photos as well as their latest report cards. He also expressed concern that they might succumb to peer pressure to use drugs and alcohol. In what would become his usual closing, he told them how much he loved them and asked them to write when they could.

He also enclosed a letter he'd sent earlier, in which he asked a number of other questions. "You are both wonderful young ladies and I have always been very proud of you," he wrote. "I know that you are very confused over how things are, and have been since summer time. By the time you both get old enough to understand everything, I hope to have everything sorted out."

Shortly after the trial, one of Gene's neighbors came up to Margo in a bookstore, where she was flipping through Frank Sinatra CDs.

"Are you Margo, Allison and Lindsey's mom? I can't tell you how much I've been worried about you."

The woman said she'd never really trusted Gene and had always felt something wasn't quite right about him.

"Are the girls okay?" she asked.

"They're doing very well," Margo said.

"Is it okay if I hug you?"

"Sure."

"I'm glad you're okay."

Margo found the exchange a little strange, but nice. She didn't even know the woman's name.

Dianna called in early April with a message from Patsy, who used this indirect form of communication because Margo had suggested that they have no contact after the kidnapping in 1993. There was a story just out in *Vanity Fair*, featuring an interview with Patsy that talked in some depth about their affair, and Patsy wanted to warn Margo that the article included some comments the writer had taken out of context. Patsy hadn't meant for them to sound offensive.

On April 9, newspapers across the country ran wire stories with highlights from the article, which was published in the magazine's May issue.

Margo went out and bought a copy of *Vanity Fair* the day after Dianna's call. The article left her feeling sad and disappointed. She felt particularly hurt by a comment that was excerpted in other publications, including *The Advocate*, a national gay magazine: "It wasn't even two trips over the rug, as we say here. . . . It was very brief in every way you can imagine."

Margo was surprised to see such a callous comment coming from Patsy. It sounded as if their interactions were nothing more to Patsy than casual sex, that they meant nothing to her. The Patsy she'd known was never that crass.

"It was so stupid of me! So reckless," Patsy said of their affair. "I mean, here she was, a married woman! With two children! This whole thing with Margo—Margo and I just didn't know each other that well.

"If I broke up their marriage, it was only because at one point I told her if she didn't get away from him he would probably kill her," Patsy said, a comment that Margo remembered making herself the day they'd talked down by the reservoir at Quantico.

Looking back later, Margo said, "I was a bit stunned, and did it hurt my feelings? Yes. Did I spend time dwelling on it? No."

Margo had been praying since the verdict that the judge would do the right thing at the sentencing hearing.

"My prayer was that Gene would be in jail for a long, long time and that I wouldn't have to go through this again. Ever," she said.

The night before the hearing, Margo was exhausted, yet she woke up around 4:30 AM and couldn't get back to sleep.

She spoke to God out loud as she drove to the courthouse, saying she didn't want to be afraid anymore. She didn't want to die at Gene's hand in a third attack. And she didn't want her children to live with the horror and the torment that their father had killed their mother. She prayed that the judge had kept an open mind and would confirm the jury's recommended sixty-one-year sentence, but she knew that this was ultimately in God's hands.

"If it was God's will that Gene would get out of jail, then he'd get out of jail," she later said.

The thirty-minute hearing started off with testimony from probation officer Elnora Cunanan, who said that Gene claimed he had not understood the trial process. She said he complained that he'd endured long days sitting in a freezing holding cell and was weak from not eating the rancid sandwiches he'd been served. He also claimed that he'd been denied showers for more than three weeks. But in fact, Elnora said, Gene had showered eleven times and refused to shower nine others.

Asked if she'd seen any indication that he was confused during their interview, Elnora said, "He appeared to understand what was going on."

Reid argued that the judge shouldn't fix a sentence that penalized Gene for committing a violent offense in 1993, when he'd been charged only with obstruction of justice.

He said he felt optimistic about Gene's future. "We know full well that Gene's going to have to pay the piper, but . . . this guy still has something to salvage. He made an enormous contribution to his country. . . . It doesn't serve society and it doesn't serve him well just to toss him away. We would respectfully request a reasonable sentence that gives him the opportunity to heal and come back one day, make a contribution and see his children."

Paul, however, reminded the judge that Gene was already on probation for another crime when he committed his most recent offenses, and that he'd already had the opportunity to redeem himself after going to prison the first time.

"No doubt this man had—did do some good for the nation. He was certainly very capable, but you can make the same argument about Hitler. Hitler did good things for Germany . . . but neverthe-less, he committed atrocious crimes, just as that defendant did."

Paul pointed out that Gene had four excellent attorneys, yet he still had the nerve to complain that he didn't understand what was going on. Furthermore, he said, Gene not only told the proba-tion officer that he still harbored ill feelings toward Margo but also had not accepted responsibility for his actions, an indicator that he couldn't be rehabilitated.

Paul asked the judge to impose the jury's recommended sentence. "I say that nine-tenths of the people that walk in this courtroom have some sort of mental disorder or they wouldn't be here. But the jury found he was not insane and that's the test. So I ask the court to do the only thing that you can do, and that is to keep him behind bars, where he can't harm his wife or any other innocent person."

Judge Potter gave Gene the opportunity to deliver a long speech, which he read from a legal pad. Even Margo thought he sounded sincere.

> I'd like to thank you for giving [me] this opportunity to address the court and to apologize. I sat in silence during my trial. I was horrified at the things that I was accused of doing to Margo, Mrs. Khalifeh, and Reverend Clever. I was in some semblance of a daze during portions of my trial. I'm not claiming to have any problem with the way I was represented . . . so if there's any confusion over that, I'd like to clear that up. . . . I'm really stunned to find what I have become, what I have always despised and that's—I've be-come a criminal liability to the community and to society. . . . I wanted my life to be dedicated to protecting my country, . . . and through my careers in the military and law enforcement, I tried to express those ideas and values, and I've fallen very, very short. . . .
>
> What's happened here will never go away. It will haunt me and these other people forever. When I look in the mirror, I'm forced to face the fact that I did this to myself. I don't blame any-body else. The harsh reality is that, and I've accepted it, my life

has been soured, not because of what Margo did to me and my children, but because of what I did. . . . Even though I've strayed a long way from my days in law enforcement, I moved even further away from my life as a father to Lindsey and Allison. Throughout their young lives, I've been a father who fought to love and protect my daughters, and now I've become the person who fathered them the greatest harm. . . .

I'm a reasonably educated man, but I don't possess the words or vocabulary to express the pain that I experienced because of this. Every day I'm housed in a small cell and have nothing to do all day but think about this. . . . I am sincerely sorry. Words are cheap, but that's all I have to offer. . . .

I would like to strongly encourage anyone . . . in law enforcement to stay as far away from undercover work as they can. Leave it alone. No matter how strong a person is or how great the assignment may appear, . . . the potential for harm is too great and the loss of one officer's mental health is not worth the results.

I don't think it's stretching the facts to say that I was one of the best, and now I'm a walking case history and study for the downside of that. . . . I hope to get the mental health treatment that I need while I'm serving my sentence. . . . I hope that someday in the future I can once again be an asset to our society and community and especially to my wonderful little girls.

As she listened to Gene's speech, Margo didn't feel angry at him. He was saying all the right things.

"Part of me was saying, 'I wish I could believe him,' and the other part of me was saying, 'It's just words; Gene is good at this, and I hope the judge is not believing him,'" she said later.

Paul noticed that Gene never actually apologized directly to Margo. Paul didn't expect that he ever would, especially if he thought he could win his freedom on appeal.

Judge Potter followed up with a few comments of his own, describing this as a "rather unusual case in many ways." He said that as he read the sentencing memo written by Gene's attorneys, he was struck by the similarity between the crimes Gene had investigated as an undercover agent and the offenses of which he'd been recently convicted.

He described Gene's actions as "bizarre," but also "meticulously planned and extremely dangerous." After reviewing the various sentencing guidelines, he said, he had decided to exceed the state's because of the jury's recommendation, but also because he wanted to deter Gene and others like him from committing similar crimes.

However, he told Gene that he was also suspending a "portion" of the sentence "to allow you the opportunity to rehabilitate yourself with the use of supervised probation."

The word "portion" proved to be quite an understatement. As Judge Potter went through each of the nine charges, he proceeded to lop large chunks of time off the corresponding sentences the jury had recommended, suspending some of them entirely.

With each reduction, Margo felt herself becoming increasingly nauseated.

"It was like new math," Margo later said. "I didn't know how he was coming up with his numbers."

By the time the judge had finished, he had suspended thirty-eight years, leaving Gene with a sentence of only twenty-three years—a huge disparity from the jury's recommended total of sixty-one. He also gave Gene ten years of probation.

Margo couldn't believe what she was hearing. She was so upset, she'd lost track of the tally partway through, only this time it was her anger and disbelief that were distracting her. She'd felt a weight lifted from her shoulders during the reading of the verdict, but now it was bearing down once again.

How dare you say that all of this that we went through is worth twenty-three years, she thought as she stared at Judge Potter. *What happens when he gets out?*

Gene would be eligible for parole in 2016, after serving 85 percent of his sentence, which would otherwise go into 2019. He would be only sixty-one when he got out, and Margo knew that after lifting weights and working out in prison as most inmates did, he would still be young and fit enough to finish the job he'd started—killing her.

The harsh reality was that she was not, in fact, done dealing with Gene Bennett.

Reid told the *Washington Post* that he was "disappointed and saddened" by the judge's decision, but not surprised. He planned to file an appeal on Gene's behalf.

Recently, the judge explained his reasoning. "Retribution is important to a sentence, but so is rehabilitation," he said. He added that he thought his sentence was fair "given other verdicts" for murder, and described the work by the defense attorneys as "probably the best attempt to prove insanity in a case that I've seen."

The media immediately assembled on the courthouse walkway for another press conference. By the time Margo got outside, the anger was boiling up inside her.

She had written a letter to the judge before the sentencing, explaining that she and her children had consistently been in therapy and that if Gene were released sooner than the sixty-one years the jury had recommended, she would live in constant fear that he was going to kill her. Yet the only thing the judge had asked her during the hearing was whether she had any expenses that needed to be reimbursed as part of Gene's restitution fee.

She vowed to write Judge Potter again just before Gene's release date, saying, "Watch the obituaries. If I'm dead, then it's on you."

Paul and Jim were shocked by what the judge had done; Ron McClelland was angry too. Ron told Margo that he'd been worried when Judge Potter got the case. Other judges, he said, would have accepted the jury's entire sentencing recommendation without question.

It was a sunny day, a little breezy, but the sky was clear. There were fewer reporters than after the verdict, but the drill was the same.

"What's your reaction to the sentence?" one of them asked Margo.

Shaken and pale, she did not try to hide her disappointment or fear. "Continuing to live is my biggest concern," she said. "Twenty-three years is a substantial amount of time for me to recover and get on with my life, but what do I do when that twenty-three years is over?"

As for Gene's speech, she said, "I heard the words he said, but I still have to go home and deal with two children who know their father tried to kill their mother."

"What do you plan to do when he gets out?" another reporter asked. "Will you move to another country?"

"There's no place where I can hide," Margo said flatly.

Looking back recently, Paul agreed. "If I had to bet on it, I'd say the chances are she's probably a likely candidate [to be a victim of] some future criminal act. I don't know, this guy could change, I guess. . . . He sat in a jail for a year, seething. . . . This was his effort to retaliate against her. . . . I thought the judge let him off pretty easy."

Later that month, former FBI agent Bob Ressler called Margo, looking for information about how Patsy had come up with the plot for *All That Remains*. He said he was helping a family that had filed a lawsuit against the author, accusing her of using private information from a family member's autopsy file.

Margo wouldn't have helped Bob even if she'd had any information, because she had no reason to want to hurt Patsy. "Sorry, Bob," she told him. "I have nothing that can help you."

The following month, Dianna called with another message from Patsy, that she wanted to talk to Margo.

"It's got something to do with the statute of limitations and this lawsuit. I don't know," Dianna said.

In light of Bob Ressler's query, things began to make sense. Margo wanted to let sleeping dogs lie with Patsy, but she returned the call as asked, feeling a little nervous as she dialed Patsy's number. It had been a long time since they'd talked, and much had happened in between.

They talked for about fifteen minutes, chatting a bit before getting down to business.

"You've been through a lot," Patsy said. "How have you been?"

"The girls are doing good," Margo said. "I'm doing fine. It's been tough, but we're doing okay."

Patsy wanted to know if Margo could remember the date of the early release party at the Globe & Laurel for *All That Remains.* Patsy and her attorney wanted to argue that it was too late for anyone to file a lawsuit because the statute of limitations clock had started that night, when she'd signed the first copies of her book.

Margo pulled out her copy and read Patsy the date of the inscription. She also mentioned Bob Ressler's call.

Before they hung up, Patsy told Margo that if she ever wanted to write a book about her story, she would help if she could.

This was the last time she and Patsy ever spoke.

Margo, John Hess, and I each tried independently to get Patsy to do an interview for this book, but her agent's assistants said Patsy wasn't interested.

Chapter Fifteen

Damage and Recovery

Now that the trial was over and the publicity had abated somewhat, Margo shifted again into healing mode, focusing on her daughters, her job, and her church activities.

In spring 1997, after going five years without a relationship while she worked through the confusion and denial about her sexuality, Margo found herself involved with a woman she'd met at a Christian weekend retreat.

"It was a convenient romance," she later said. "It was a good chance to see if I was ready to have a relationship of this type."

But it didn't last long. Margo was still short on time and emotional energy after everything she'd been through, and she didn't want to spread herself too thin. Her relationship with Joanne* lasted only a couple of months, but it threw a few challenges her way.

One day, Allison walked in on Margo and Joanne kissing. Even though Margo had discussed her sexuality with Allison soon after the church incident, it didn't really hit home until Allison saw it with her own eyes. She ran upstairs to her room, crying, and shut the door.

Margo knocked and asked if she could come in. She lay down on the bed next to Allison, who was facing the wall, away from her mother.

"You promised you would quit," Allison said, referring to a conversation they'd had almost a year ago. Margo remembered their talk, but she'd never said any such thing.

"Allison, I can't help but be who I am," she said, pausing. "Do you still love me?"

"Yes, of course I still love you."

With that, Margo went downstairs and told Joanne she needed to leave. Joanne was irked that Margo didn't want to show affection in front of the kids, but Margo said she had to put them first. When a similar incident occurred some weeks later, Margo ended the relationship.

At the time, Margo thought Lindsey was too young to understand so she waited another year to explain that she was gay. Her younger daughter was very supportive.

"I just want you to be happy," Lindsey said.

Later that summer, Margo started dating Susan*, a divorced woman who worked at her daughters' school and had two children of her own. Margo thought Susan would better understand her and her kids' needs.

Margo, her daughters, and her sister Letta moved into Susan's house within a few months, which, Margo realized later, was far too soon. But her lease on the townhouse was up, and she was having a tough time financially. She thought that cutting her household expenses in half would be a good thing.

"I just couldn't make ends meet," Margo said later. "Then I found that although I could make ends meet, I wasn't here for the kids, and Allison started making bad choices."

Life with Gene as a father had caused damage to her children, but Margo had no idea at the time how it would manifest itself. The bigger fallout was still to come.

On top of being teased about what had been written about her family in the papers, Allison was also given the nickname "Jolly Green Giant" for being the tallest, skinniest kid in school.

"Your mom's a lesbian and your dad makes bombs," the kids would say.

When she couldn't take it anymore, she got into a fight with a boy whose taunting was relentless.

"If you say it one more time, I'm going to hit you," Allison told him.

"Your mom is a lesbian," he said, which got him a punch in the face.

The year after Margo and the girls moved in with Susan, Allison progressed to middle school, so she didn't have to deal with as much teasing. Luckily, Lindsey, who was a far more emotionally sensitive child, never seemed to have that particular problem.

Around this same time, Allison started making cuts on the inside of her forearm with a razor blade. Her sixth-grade teacher had asked her to write an autobiography, and it had triggered some disturbing memories about her father's drinking and abusive behavior.

Allison said cutting herself provided a distraction and a release for her overwhelming frustration, "if I was real, real, real upset and didn't know what else to do."

She did it about ten times over a six-month period, until she scared herself with how much bleeding she'd caused. She finally broke down and confided in a teenage neighbor, crying as she poured out her woes. About a year later, she cut herself again when the stress got to be too much. Overall, however, she didn't seem to feel the need to do it anymore.

In fall 2000, Allison's school called Margo, asking if her absence that day was excused. Margo rattled off the names of Allison's friends, learning that they too were absent. So Margo, dressed in her campus police uniform, went looking and quickly found them at one of the girls' townhouses. She took them all back to class.

The summer after the trial, Margo had to take a second job at IKEA to make some extra cash. Although she'd been promoted from lieutenant to captain and was put in charge of all five NOVA campuses, the raise she received wasn't big enough. She was enjoying having the kids full-time, but that joy came with expenses.

The relationship with Susan went well until Susan and Allison began to argue. Margo also didn't like the way Susan tried to discipline Allison and Lindsey as if they were her own children. Letta, who was living in the basement apartment, tried to step in, but that only made things worse.

So in spring 1999, Letta returned to Alabama, and within a couple of months, Margo and the girls moved into a house she'd just bought.

In fall 1997, Margo was invited to guest lecture on stalking at Marymount College in Arlington and George Washington University in DC. As she discussed the different types of stalkers, she wove in her own story about Gene.

After each talk, students came up to express their appreciation. Some said they'd known stalking victims, but had not understood what their friends had gone through until they heard Margo's lecture.

"This experience gave me the opportunity to be some kind of motivation or inspiration for others," she later said. "Granted, we all live in our own little worlds, and I haven't had a chance to reach out and touch people beyond my little world, but the touching I've done has been worthwhile. And there's more that I can do."

It helped her feel as though her experiences had had a purpose, especially when someone would tell her, "I'm going through a tough time, and I've looked at you and thought, 'If she can do it, I can do it.'"

In late 1997, Allison was going through her mother's closet when she came across a shoe box containing the photos Margo and her attorneys had taken to document the injuries Gene had inflicted during the kidnapping.

"Mom, did Dad do this to you?" Allison asked.

"Yeah, you don't need to be looking at that," Margo said, trying to protect her daughter's memory of her father, or whatever was left of it.

It was only after Allison read about the kidnapping in a narrative written by Margo's friend John Hess, describing her troubled life with Gene, that Allison learned exactly how those injuries came about.

"Is there anything else you want to know?" Margo asked, after Allison had read John's account.

Allison said no. "I was pretty mad," she later said, but "there wasn't a whole lot I could do. . . . My opinion of him couldn't get much lower."

Lindsey never wanted to hear the details of the kidnapping or, for that matter, of the church incident either.

"I'm very happy not knowing that much," she said recently.

The entertainment industry tapped into Margo's story almost immediately after the trial. In 1997, Margo saw an episode of *Law and Order* that seemed to be loosely based on her love triangle with Patsy and Gene.

In 1999, Margo got a call from Jack Nasser, a TV and film producer, inquiring whether she would be interested in selling the rights to tell her story in a movie or TV series. She asked for $100,000, thinking no one would pay that much, and about a year later, they agreed on $65,000. Margo figured she'd use the money to pay for the girls' college education and maybe save some for a trip to Disney World.

In early 2001, a movie called *The Hostage Negotiator* aired on one of the cable networks, saying it was "inspired by a true story." However, the story line bore little resemblance to Margo's life. For one thing, the person with whom her FBI agent character was supposedly having an affair—or at least that's what her unstable, corrupt FBI agent husband suspected—was a man.

In May 2002, the Discovery Channel aired a fifty-minute documentary titled *The Prosecutors: A Question of Sanity*, which reenacted the church incident and included a segment from Gene's 911 tape, with him speaking as Ed. Because Margo had already sold the lifelong rights to her story to Nasser, who wouldn't allow her to be interviewed or have her name used without compensation, the producers had to use a pseudonym and an actress to play the victim's role.

Allison was flipping through the channels with a friend when they came across the documentary. It was creepy hearing her father's voice on TV like that, switching "personalities" on the 911 tape.

"I was like, if anybody can't see through that, then Jesus Christ," she later said. "He was crazy enough to think he could get away with all that, but at the same time he realized he could make himself look crazy to get away with it. There's a lot of stuff about him that doesn't add up, which I guess he was counting on."

Gene sent a steady stream of letters to Allison and Lindsey from prison, always speaking to them as if they were still the same young age as when he saw them last.

Typically the letters followed the same format. They reminisced about the girls' childhoods or his own. They described his exercise regimen, how dull his days were, how he was dealing with the diabetes he'd developed in prison, and how much he missed and loved them. He often offered parental advice, bolstered by an article he'd cut out of a magazine and enclosed, or referring to a program he'd seen on television. He asked questions about what they were doing in school and asked them to write back. He told them his love for them was unconditional and would never stop.

Allison eventually grew tired of reading Gene's letters because they so frequently listed numbered questions, but she still cashed the $25 money orders he sent for birthdays and Christmas.

In June 2001, Allison was fourteen when she decided she wanted to visit him. Margo couldn't bear to take her, so she asked a friend, a lieutenant who worked for her at NOVA, to accompany Allison.

Gene spent most of their three-hour visit giving his version of what had happened between him and Margo since they first met. He described the kidnapping in 1993 as a mutual attempt to get back together, and the church incident as one big blur during which he didn't know what he was doing and had no control over himself.

Gene immediately followed up the visit with a letter, telling Allison how proud he was of her, how beautiful she was, how "smart, mature, so very sweet and very articulate."

"I enjoyed hugging you and being able to touch your hands and hold hands with you once again," he wrote. "When you were young we held hands all the time, whether we were in the car, or at a store or in a restaurant. I am glad that we had such a strong father-daughter bond between us when you were younger and growing up. All these times are so precious to me and I was so happy to watch you grow up."

He said he was very pleased to learn that Allison had the trial transcripts at her house and suggested that she read and compare them to what they discussed during her visit. He also encouraged her to read the entire criminal and divorce files to answer any further questions she might have.

"I know you were and probably are still angry and frustrated with me. That may never go away or it may soften or lessen over time. My love for you is total and I will always be your father, even though it is hard for me to be a parent under these circumstances."

Four months later, Gene wrote her a fourteen-page letter, saying he was perplexed that he hadn't heard from her since her visit. He said he was going to contact his lawyer and ask him to arrange a court hearing to determine what the problem was. He said there was "an obvious choke point that needs to be addressed," implying that Margo was to blame.

Allison fired back a letter, addressed to "Gene," and blasted him for insinuating that Margo would try to keep his letters from her.

> How dare you accuse my mother of not giving me your letters. I've gotten every last one of them. . . . It's MY choice not to write you back. I don't write you because I don't want to. You talk about being my father—yeah, and what a great one you are. What kind

of "father" tries to kill the mother of his children, the one who gave them life! What kind of father rots in jail while his daughters grow up? . . . If you bring ANYTHING to court, I swear on everything I love that I will legally disown you. . . .

You no longer have the right to try to play head games, so cut the crap. You'll never be able to get in between this family. You can never break us; don't waste your time trying. So don't try to act like a father to me. You aren't one. . . . You got too bold, Gene. You finally snapped my last nerve of patience with you.

Gene wrote back a seventeen-page letter, waiting until the ninth page to address his daughter's anger.

"After I read and contemplated that letter, it occurred to me that perhaps you may not have prepared that document on your own," he wrote. "Sometimes, when a young person is as angry as you seem to be, others prey on that anger and can easily take advantage of that emotion, that vulnerability, and seize the opportunity to manipulate and plant negative ideas very easily."

Even though he was in prison, he wrote, he'd done many positive things with his life, which should not be negated by the incident in 1996. He said he once loved Margo "very deeply and completely," and that Allison and Lindsey "were born out of that intense period of love." When Allison reached her early twenties, he said, he believed that she would see the world in a totally different light, "possibly even me, too." But nothing could ever break the bonds they'd formed when she was growing up.

At that point, Allison quit writing him back.

Allison met her boyfriend Tom*, who was three years her senior, in late 2001. Allison asked Margo if Tom could move in with them for a month because his father had moved in with a girlfriend and Tom's mother lived a couple of hours away.

Initially, Margo wanted to help the young man, but she soon came to feel that he was taking advantage of the situation. One month had turned into three, and Allison, who had been earning

A's and B's and taking advanced placement courses, was skipping school, smoking pot, lying around in bed all day with Tom, and arguing more and more with Margo.

"I felt that she was under his spell," Margo said later. "She was not thinking about what she was doing and how it was impacting her future. She was escaping the reality of our lives through this guy."

One morning, Margo dropped Allison at the bus stop for school, then doubled back and caught her hiding behind some bushes so that the bus would go by and she could hang out with her boyfriend.

"That's when I said enough," Margo said, and kicked Tom out for good.

But that didn't stop Allison.

About a month later, Margo went out of town and left the girls in the care of a friend. Allison said she was going to stay with a girlfriend, but actually went to Virginia Beach with Tom, where they stayed in a hotel for four or five days.

After Margo returned from her trip, Allison left again for a couple of days, sleeping with Tom in his car or on friends' couches. Margo lay down the law when Allison came home.

"You live by my rules if you're going to be here," she said.

"So, I guess I won't be here then," Allison replied.

Allison wrote her mother a letter before taking off again with Tom in early July 2002, explaining that Margo's perception of her was all wrong.

"She thought I was in a downward spiral, doing a ton of drugs. She was worried about me smoking weed," Allison later said.

Margo reported Allison as a runaway to police and reported Tom for contributing to the delinquency of a minor, so a warrant was issued for his arrest. He was picked up on the delinquency warrant when he went to court on another offense and was taken to jail.

Meanwhile, Margo was so concerned about Allison's emotional state that she read her daughter's diary. It was worse than she'd suspected. Allison was expressing suicidal thoughts. She was severely allergic to ibuprofen, yet Margo found a new, unopened bottle of it in Allison's bedroom.

Margo immediately began researching drug rehab programs and made arrangements to take Allison to the Aspen Achievement Academy in Utah as soon as she could find her.

About a week later, Allison called Margo from a friend's house to let her know she was safe.

"Where are you?" Margo asked.

Within fifteen minutes, Margo showed up with two law enforcement officer friends, Cindy and Karen. Margo grabbed Allison by the elbow and put her in the backseat of the car between the off-duty officers. Allison was high on marijuana.

When they got back to the house, Margo went upstairs to make final arrangements with the Aspen program. Margo heard the phone ring and came downstairs, where she could hear Allison talking to Tom, who had called from jail.

Margo grabbed the receiver.

"Leave her alone," she said, and hung up.

Allison started screaming at Margo and ran for the front door, hitting Cindy when she tried to stop her. Karen grabbed Allison and put her in a headlock, while Cindy and Margo held her legs down and Lindsey stood, watching. They finally got Allison into a chair, where Karen pressed her shoulders down so that she couldn't hit anyone again.

On the way to the airport, Margo called the airport police to caution them that she was taking Allison to rehab in Utah and that Allison might cause a scene. When they got there, three officers were waiting to escort them to the gate.

Once they arrived in Utah, Margo and Cindy marched Allison into the hotel room, took the phone apart, put a mattress on the floor against the door, and slept on either side of her so that she couldn't escape in the middle of the night. As Margo lay on the mattress, she remembered how Gene had made her sleep in the closet back in 1993, while he slept on the other side of the door.

The next morning, on July 16, 2002, an elderly couple came to take Allison to the Aspen program, in the small town of Loa. When Allison burst into tears, crumbling into the little girl she once was, Margo wondered if she was doing the right thing. But by the time she got home, she was comfortable with her decision.

The insurance company announced that it wouldn't cover the Aspen program after all, suggesting that Margo bring Allison home and take her to a local outpatient clinic. But Margo refused.

"I told them that was not a choice," she later said, explaining that she used the Nasser movie money to pay for the program.

Margo learned about Allison's cutting in one of the weekly conference calls she had with the counselors, and mentioned it to Lindsey. But Margo didn't fully understand the extent of Allison's problems until she received her daughter's thirteen-page psychological evaluation, which came a month into the program.

Among its findings, the report said that Allison's verbal reasoning abilities were in the "superior range," but she suffered from depression and anxiety. She had reported drinking alcohol since the eighth grade, and at one point, was drinking before, during, and after school, twice to the point of alcohol poisoning. She also reported smoking marijuana regularly and that she'd used Ecstasy, mushrooms, and painkillers.

Margo thought back to her own troubles with her father and her subsequent self-destructive sexual promiscuity, and realized that the damage Allison must have suffered was far more significant.

Margo started looking to leave NOVA in June 2002. She was finally making ends meet, but working two jobs and picking up training courses here and there had left her exhausted.

"I was looking for a clean break, an opportunity to start a new life," she said recently.

After teaching some courses on the West Coast each year, Margo had set her sights on California. She applied for a captain's position in the campus police department at the University of California, Berkeley, and was thrilled when she got it.

In August, as she was packing her belongings, she tried to cull the unnecessary remnants of the past. She came across her stack of Patsy's novels and decided she didn't want them around as a reminder anymore. It seemed like a waste to toss them, but rather than give them away and take the chance that Patsy's personal inscriptions could end up on eBay, she sent the books to Dianna to hold for her.

Margo decided to keep the three silk ties that Patsy had given her. She later tried to give them to Allison, when she got a job at Safeway that required a tie. But Allison said they weren't her style and put them away with the stuffed animals in her closet.

Margo and Lindsey started heading west to California in early September, picking up Allison from rehab in Utah along the way and driving straight through to the Bay Area.

When Margo started her new job, there was a controversy among some of her new coworkers, who were upset that the chief had hired someone who had lied under oath. However, no one but a female sergeant asked Margo about it directly.

"What happened?" she asked.

"I thought my children were going to die," Margo said, explaining the situation.

"Well, what else could you do?"

That controversy has since died, and Margo is happy to continue to work in community policing, where she'd started back in college. Margo said that the UC Berkeley police department is considered to be among the best in the country because it got so much practice dealing with the riots in the 1960s.

She still shoots her gun every few months for quarterly qualifications, but, she said, "As a manager, my weapons of choice are now a pen and paper."

Within three weeks of moving to the Bay Area, Allison met a girl who introduced her to methamphetamine. She started snorting it, then switched to smoking it.

At a family gathering on her sixteenth birthday, Allison made an unexpected announcement.

"I need to leave," she declared. "I'm hurting you all too much by staying."

Margo was well aware of the post-rehab tension in the house, but she had no idea that this was addict talk from a teenager who had started doing drugs again.

Given Allison's past habit of running away, Margo reluctantly chose to let her go. It was the only way she thought she could keep the lines of communication open with her troubled daughter if something should go wrong.

A week or two later, Allison moved in with her friend, then into a former warehouse in Oakland that she called "a crack shack," where she had her own floor.

One day, Margo picked Allison up from the Sizzler restaurant, where she'd gotten a job on her recent birthday, and noticed she was covered with red sores that looked like bug bites. Margo also saw how skinny Allison was.

"I don't know what you're doing, if it's coke or heroin or meth, but look at you, it's killing you," she said.

"Yeah, I know," Allison replied.

Allison moved back in with Margo around Christmastime and stopped using meth shortly thereafter. She was tired of feeling as if she had the flu, only ten times worse, having no appetite, going for four days at a time with no sleep, and having the light hurt her eyes.

"It kills you," she later said. "It's poison."

Margo hadn't known exactly what drug Allison was taking, but she could clearly see that her daughter had stopped using it. Margo was pleased that the $18,000-plus she'd spent on the Aspen program had done some good after all.

She's never had to worry about Lindsey doing drugs or getting into trouble. If Margo ever questioned Lindsey's after-school activities, Lindsey would gently remind her mother, "Mom, I'm the good kid, remember?"

Margo's father died in December 2000, and her mother followed in February 2003.

Soon afterward, Margo dreamed that her mother was lying next to her on the pillow, smiling, happy, and peaceful. When Margo woke up, it occurred to her that her father was probably somewhere in between here and Heaven, unable to get to that peaceful place. She was certain that he was waiting for his children to forgive him for the way he'd treated them.

"He'd never asked for that forgiveness, but I felt we needed to give it," she said.

Margo talked to both of her sisters, separately, about her dream and the need to forgive their father for his abusive behavior toward them and their mother. Jackie, who shared with Margo that he had groped her in bed too, said she was probably on target. Letta just nodded and said, "You may be right."

Allison was alarmed to see some cuts on Lindsey's upper arm in 2003.

"What's that?" Allison asked. "Did you do this to yourself?"

"Yes," Lindsay said, then started crying.

Allison asked Lindsey what prompted the cutting, but Lindsey wouldn't elaborate. Lindsey didn't want to tell her sister that it was Allison herself. Allison, feeling protective, told her little sister that she had to stop, or it would only get worse. She continued to check Lindsey's arm periodically and was relieved that there were no more cuts.

"I knew I wasn't going to hurt myself, but with her, she's not unstable or anything, she's just very emotional," Allison said later. "And that made me worry a little more."

Lindsey later said that she'd cut herself after getting into a fight with Allison for inviting her friends over to smoke pot. This was the second and final time that she'd cut herself—on the left arm and leg—because she found that it helped only temporarily. She felt guilty and even worse afterward, so she stopped, worrying that this would become an addictive cycle.

In 2004, Lindsey asked Margo if she could see a therapist for some problems dealing with a close friend at school.

Margo was immediately concerned because Lindsey had expressed self-destructive thoughts shortly after they'd moved to the Bay Area.

"Are you having feelings like you want to hurt yourself?" Margo asked.

"No," Lindsey said.

"Have you ever cut yourself?" Margo asked, bracing for the answer.

Lindsey said yes, and explained that Allison had already talked to her about it.

Knowing that Allison had done the same thing, this shocking development made Margo feel even more guilty that she hadn't given her daughters enough care and support.

"They had been through a tremendous trauma, and I had obviously overlooked something," she said later. "I didn't do it right."

When Gene was first incarcerated, he sent letters to the girls through a social worker, who forwarded them to Margo via a private P.O. box she'd rented in Woodbridge. But when the social worker retired in early 2004, the courts didn't appoint another one because Allison and Lindsey were teenagers by then, so Gene had no way to reach them.

About a year went by before Gene started sending the letters to Margo's office at UC Berkeley. Then, several months later, he sent them directly to the house she'd purchased in July 2006, saying a friend had done some research to find out where they lived.

Seventeen-year-old Lindsey took particular umbrage at this, viewing it as an invasion of their privacy. Gene's move seemed like one big head game to her, so she began returning his letters to him, unopened.

"I just didn't want to deal with his crap anymore," she later said. "It's, like, he doesn't know me. What could he say that would interest me?"

Gene responded by leaving the return address off his letters.

The last letter Lindsey remembers reading was one addressed to her and Allison; Gene had enclosed an article contending that girls with absent fathers were statistically more likely to lose their virginity early and get pregnant.

"He still tries to, like, parent," Lindsey said.

Eventually Gene got the message and stopped writing letters to Lindsey for the most part, although he continued to send her Christmas and birthday cards with money orders enclosed.

At first, Margo always opened Gene's letters and read them before giving them to the girls, but when Allison and Lindsey stopped wanting to read them, Margo decided simply to leave them unopened, regardless of what money orders they might contain. Allison still reads some of her father's letters and cashes the money orders.

Although Gene kept talking about his diabetes, Lindsey said she didn't believe that he really had the disease.

"I want him to stop writing, but I don't want to communicate with him to tell him that. . . . He's lost the right to have any place in my life. He tried to kill my mom; he was emotionally abusive to me and my sister. . . . He was a jackass as a father. I don't have any real happy memories involving him."

Gene seems to be well aware of her anger. In November 2002, he wrote to her regarding the TV shows about his case that had been airing, saying he hoped that they didn't upset her and her sister too much, or cause them any further embarrassment or trouble at school.

"I know you were very, very angry, disappointed, mad etc. at me for causing you so much pain and complications in your young life," he wrote. "Anger and being mad are normal behavioral responses. What I want to tell you is that it is okay to be mad and angry with me. I also want to tell you I hope you vent this anger at me, towards me, and not others around you."

Saying he'd discussed this issue with counselors over the years, he suggested that Lindsey try writing letters to deal with her emotions. "It's not healthy to stay mad and angry for such a long time. . . . I've had a hard time letting go of my anger, frustration and disappointment over a lot of things also. It's not easy to do."

Lindsey grew up plagued with health problems, shyness, and social awkwardness. Big-boned like her father, she too has fought to keep her weight down.

She was diagnosed with dyslexia in the second grade after the teachers figured out that she was failing because she couldn't read.

"I still can't spell. I'm okay at math. But I'm really good at and do like English," she said recently.

Lindsey started coming out of her shell after she got involved in theater at school in 2003, when she worked on the stage crew for a production called *Yippie Skippy, There's a Monkey in My Pants*, becoming incensed when the teachers wanted to shut down the performance because it included profanity and content they thought was racist and otherwise inappropriate.

In spring 2004, she made the swim team; in 2005, she joined the *Cougar*, the high school newspaper, as a writer. The following year she became the arts and entertainment editor and worked as a lifeguard.

She was accepted by the Building with Books program, which entailed spending two weeks building a schoolhouse in Nicaragua in summer 2005. Although she'd grown up thinking she wanted to work with animals, after the Nicaragua trip she switched her focus to helping people and ultimately decided she wanted to work toward a nursing degree at Cal State University, Chico.

Lindsey, who has spent much of her life in therapy, was still seeing a counselor regularly in summer 2007, mostly to deal with stress. Allison, who has seen nearly a dozen therapists, said they haven't helped her a whole lot.

Unlike Allison, Lindsey hasn't dated much. As of summer 2007, she'd only gone out with two boys, one whom she liked quite a bit and the other who liked her quite a bit. Neither worked out.

She and Allison aren't all that close these days. Allison thinks that Lindsey is a "very 'good girl,'" and Lindsey thinks that Allison is not sensitive enough to other people's feelings.

Even so, Lindsey said, "I know she still cares about me." That is certainly true. Although the two sisters have very different personalities, interests, and lifestyles, Allison said, "I love her to death."

After she stopped using meth, Allison tried to get her life back on track, but her former high school turned her away, saying she would do better at an alternative high school. She took auto shop classes for several semesters at the College of Alameda while attending the alternative school, with an eye on a career as a mechanic. After graduating at seventeen, she went to Diablo Valley, a junior college, for one semester.

She has always liked to read. In fact, Patricia Cornwell is still one of her favorite authors.

Allison started dating Chris Sugg in December 2003 and found out she was pregnant in May 2006. She moved into an apartment with Chris in October. At the time, Allison was working at Trader Joe's grocery store, and was contemplating a visit to see Gene in prison with her new baby. "I'm just really curious to see his reaction," she said.

While Allison was still pregnant, Margo said, "I'm trying to step back and let her do what she needs to do. I told her I'll buy the crib, but I can't do it all, and I shouldn't. I don't think she has a clue how she's going to support this kid, but it'll happen."

Allison had her baby, Serena, on January 1, 2007. She was a healthy six pounds, eleven ounces. That summer, Allison was back working at Trader Joe's and happily raising her baby with Chris.

Asked if she had any interest in going into law enforcement, Allison replied, "Never." She has no interest in returning to college, but said she hoped to get into real estate someday.

She has also reconsidered and decided against taking Serena to visit her father in prison. "I don't want to put my daughter in that type of situation—to be used against me, my mother," she said.

People have repeated to Margo the old adage, that which doesn't kill you makes you stronger. She jokes that she wants to kill them for saying it, but she knows it's true.

"I know I can get through anything. I know that I have gone through a unique set of circumstances, to be at this position in my life for a reason. I feel powerful in the sense that I know nothing's going to break me. Yet, at the same time, I know that I'm capable of being hurt. It's one of the lessons we have being on this earth that you get to feel these things."

"When I pray, I thank God for the experiences that have made me who I am. Without them, I wouldn't be who I am, so the bad makes the good even sweeter."

These experiences have also helped her see what's really important in life: her kids, her freedom, and the opportunity to help other people.

Back in 2002, when Allison was so troubled, Margo didn't know if they'd ever be close again. But more recently, Allison has commented several times that she knows how bad her life would have been if Gene had killed Margo. In the birthday card that she gave Margo in 2006, she wrote, "You've sacrificed so much for us."

"To know that she's capable now of understanding some of what I went through makes me feel complete," Margo says today.

Sometimes Margo thinks the reason she lived through all that trauma with Gene was to save her children from being raised by him. "They now have the freedom to be who they want. Allison is still floating around, but I see her going in the right direction. Lindsey just needs to build her self-confidence."

Although her life as Gene's wife and as a mother has been challenging at times, Margo says she's done her best to protect and care for her children. She thinks that they've turned out pretty well.

"I raised my daughters to have a mind of their own and speak up. It's been painful, but I'm very, very proud of my kids."

It wasn't until 2002, when she was forty-eight, that Margo found a woman she sees as her other half, someone with whom she has a soulful bond and believes she'll be with for the rest of her life.

They shook hands when they first met, and both felt an immediate connection, a familiar, comfortable feeling as if they'd known each other for a long time.

"It was as if our lives came together for a reason," said Margo, who turned fifty-four in 2007.

Looking back, she now sees that her interactions with Gene forced her to come to grips with the fact that if she were not in a relationship with another woman, she would not be in a relationship at all. She also realizes that she wouldn't have "the maturity of soul" to have found such a strong connection without having progressed through the trials and tribulations that brought her to that point.

"I finally understand what it is to have a good healthy, loving relationship. It's just so nice. It's everything I've longed for in a relationship. The ability to love someone and be loved, care for her and trust her, makes my life full."

Gene's appeal was rejected by Virginia's Court of Appeals in March 1999. In February 2001, the Attorney General's office for Virginia informed Margo that the petition he filed for a writ of habeas corpus in 2000 had also been dismissed.

He is due to be released on July 9, 2016.

"I wish they could've given him a longer sentence so he wouldn't bother my mom, because our family is going to have to worry when he gets out," Allison said.

But Margo doesn't sit around and fret about the day Gene will get out of prison. She is simply determined to be ready if he attempts to come after her and take his final revenge.

"God didn't let me survive the first two attacks to have me fail if he tries again."

About the Authors

Caitlin Rother is the author of *Poisoned Love*, the true story of the Kristin Rossum murder case, and the thriller *Naked Addiction*. Rother, a Pulitzer Prize–nominated investigative journalist, worked for daily newspapers for nearly twenty years before she started writing books full-time. Covering topics ranging from criminal justice to government, politics, and human drama, she won many awards for her narrative stories, establishing a solid foundation for writing book-length nonfiction. She was a staff reporter for the *San Diego Union-Tribune* and the Los Angeles *Daily News*, and has written for *Cosmopolitan*, the *Los Angeles Times*, the *Washington Post*, the *Chicago Tribune*, and the *Boston Globe*. She also has made dozens of media appearances on TV news and crime shows, including E! Entertainment network's "Women Who Kill," Oxygen Network's *Snapped* series, and Greta Van Susteren's *On the Record*. Rother lives in San Diego, California. For more information, visit her Web site at http://caitlinrother.com.

John Hess, a retired FBI supervisory agent and Quantico instructor, is the author of *Interviewing and Interrogation for Law Enforcement*, a textbook dealing with the skills investigators need for obtaining the truth from both witnesses and suspects. He is also the coauthor of *Writing for Law Enforcement*, which addresses a serious shortcoming among many in law enforcement, and has written articles for various professional journals over the years. Since retiring from his twenty-seven-year career with the FBI, Hess has addressed numerous professional groups including the CIA, DEA, and United Nations inspectors prior to their departure for Iraq. He lives in Fredericksburg, Virginia.

Index